Staatsverständnisse

edited by

Rüdiger Voigt

Volume 102

Bart van der Steen | Marc de Kesel [eds.]

Party, State, Revolution

Critical Reflections on Žižek's Political Philosophy

 **Nomos**

The Deutsche Nationalbibliothek lists this publication in the Deutsche Nationalbibliografie; detailed bibliographic data are available on the Internet at http://dnb.d-nb.de

ISBN   978-3-8487-4044-4 (Print)
        978-3-8452-8343-2 (ePDF)

British Library Cataloguing-in-Publication Data
A catalogue record for this book is available from the British Library.

ISBN   978-3-8487-4044-4 (Print)
        978-3-8452-8343-2 (ePDF)

Library of Congress Cataloging-in-Publication Data
van der Steen, Bart / de Kesel, Marc
Party, State, Revolution
Critical Reflections on Žižek's Political Philosophy
Bart van der Steen / Marc de Kesel (eds.)
179 p.
Includes bibliographic references.

ISBN   978-3-8487-4044-4 (Print)
        978-3-8452-8343-2 (ePDF)

1. Edition 2017
© Nomos Verlagsgesellschaft, Baden-Baden, Germany 2017. Printed and bound in Germany.

Editorial

Throughout the course of history, our understanding of the state has fundamentally changed time and again. It appears as though we are witnessing a development which will culminate in the dissolution of the territorially defined nation state as we know it, for globalisation is not only leading to changes in the economy and technology, but also, and above all, affects statehood. It is doubtful, however, whether the erosion of borders worldwide will lead to a global state, but what is perhaps of greater interest are the ideas of state theorists, whose models, theories, and utopias offer us an insight into how different understandings of the state have emerged and changed, processes which neither began with globalisation, nor will end with it.

When researchers concentrate on reappropriating classical ideas about the state, it is inevitable that they will continuously return to those of Plato and Aristotle, upon which all reflections on the state are based. However, the works published in this series focus on more contemporary ideas about the state, whose spectrum ranges from those of the doyen *Niccolò Machiavelli*, who embodies the close connection between theory and practice of the state more than any other thinker, to those of *Thomas Hobbes*, the creator of Leviathan, to those of *Karl Marx*, who is without doubt the most influential modern state theorist, to those of the Weimar state theorists *Carl Schmitt*, *Hans Kelsen* and *Hermann Heller*, and finally to those of contemporary theorists.

Not only does the corruption of Marx's ideas into a Marxist ideology intended to justify a repressive state underline that state theory and practice cannot be permanently regarded as two separate entities, but so does Carl Schmitt's involvement in the manipulation conducted by the National Socialists, which today tarnishes his image as the leading state theorist of his era. Therefore, we cannot forego analysing modern state practice.

How does all this enable modern political science to develop a contemporary understanding of the state? This series of publications does not only address this question to (political) philosophers, but also, and above all, students of humanities and social sciences. The works it contains therefore acquaint the reader with the general debate, on the one hand, and present their research findings clearly and informatively, not to mention incisively and bluntly, on the other. In this way, the reader is ushered directly into the problem of understanding the state.

Prof. Dr. Rüdiger Voigt

Table of Contents

The Two Žižeks: The Performer and the Leninist

Bart van der Steen

Introduction: More questions than answers? Žižek and the State

Slavoj Žižek is one of the most prominent public intellectuals of the left.[1] His central claim holds that 'today, it is more crucial than ever to continue to question the very foundations of capitalism as a global system'.[2] To do so, Žižek proposes 'reloading' Lenin and updating Leninist notions of the proletariat, the political party and revolution. The precise contents of these updated notions, however, remain curiously underdeveloped. This volume therefore sets out to critically discuss Slavoj Žižek's conceptualization of politics, political organization, and especially the (past, present and future) state. It seeks to investigate Žižek's works in search of a coherent state theory, and to subsequently examine its internal consistency and critical potential.

In recent times, Žižek has become more controversial than ever, especially among the left.[3] Fierce criticisms notwithstanding, Žižek remains one of the most prominent contemporary radical thinkers. He has received unofficial titles such as the Elvis of Cultural Studies, the Rockstar Philosopher and the most controversial political thinker of our times. Indeed, his writings oscillate between cultural analysis, philo-

---

1 I would like to thank Marc de Kesel, Irina Pulyakhina, Lauren Lauret, Charlotte van Rooden and Jasper van der Steen for their comments and suggestions in writing this introduction.
2 Žižek 2008.
3 Although Žižek was heralded in the 1990s and after as the new promise of the radical left, his status has become more contested over the last few years. His response to the Occupy movement of 2011 was disappointing to many, since he dismissed the movement's strategies without positing a viable alternative. At least from this point onwards, many started to criticize Žižek's dual position of, on the one hand, emphasizing the need for identifying revolutionary actors and organization while, on the other hand, dismissing all contemporary forms of radical organization. Žižek subsequently had a public falling-out with Noam Chomsky, who accused Žižek first of all of misquoting him and subsequently of a deliberately obscure use of language. Finally, Žižek alienated large parts of the radical left with his comments on the refugee crisis of 2015-2016, in which he, among other things, emphasized the supposedly different culture of the refugees arriving in Europe.
    Although Žižek's attitude towards revolutionary organization, his style of writing or his claim that Europe's 'Christian legacy is worth fighting for' all have a longer history, it was mainly the changing setting of new mobilization in the US, a refugee crisis in Europe and a populist right-wing backlash in both regions that renewed the controversial nature of Žižek's claims and statements.
    For these controversies, see: The contributions to the present volume by Sina Talachian and Alex Del Duca. See also: Thompson 2013; Žižek 2015; Ibid. 2015a; Riemer 2015; Kriss 2015; Ibid. 2015a.

sophical investigation and political intervention. In his most successful works, the three overlap.[4]

Žižek's political project revolves around his plea to 'repeat Lenin'. He defines this project as follows:

> The idea is not to return to Lenin, but to *repeat* him in the Kierkegaardian sense: to retrieve the same impulse in today's constellation. The return to Lenin aims [...] at repeating, in the present world-wide conditions, the Leninist gesture of reinventing the revolutionary project in the conditions of imperialism and colonialism.[5]

In another text, Žižek explains that 'to repeat Lenin is to accept that "Lenin is dead", that his particular solution failed, even failed monstrously, but that there was a utopian spark in it worth saving'.[6] The question that really interests Žižek is 'how to redeem the emancipatory potential of these failures through avoiding the twin trap of nostalgic attachment to the past and of all-too slick accommodation to "new circumstances"'.[7] Žižek thus endeavors to recover the Communist Idea.[8]

Closely related to Žižek's explicit call to repeat Lenin is his supposed endorsement of revolutionary terror. A guillotine features on the cover of his *In Defense of Lost Causes*, while he has selected and introduced texts by Robespierre and Mao.[9] Unsurprisingly, Žižek has been dismissed by many as a reckless and/or ruthless Stalinist.[10] His appeal is, however, more nuanced. In his introduction to Mao's *On Practice and Contradiction*, Žižek does not shy away from pointing out the cruelty of his rule, calling Mao a 'Marxist master of misrule' and stating:

> [H]e caused the greatest famine in history by exporting food to Russia to buy nuclear and arms industries: 38 million people were starved and slave-driven to death in 1958-61. Mao knew exactly what was happening, saying: 'half of China may well have to die'. This is the instrumental attitude at its most radical: killing as part of a ruthless attempt to realize a goal.[11]

Žižek makes his stance more explicit by stating: '[W]here do I stand with regard to Lenin and Stalin? Not only did I extensively analyze Stalinism [...] I also explicitly pointed out how Stalinism was a consequence of Leninism.'[12] Žižek is thus acutely aware of the danger of revolution giving way to mass terror. However, it remains unclear where the line is to be drawn between the one and the other.

---

4   For introductions to the philosophy and politics of Žižek, see: Butler 2006; Dean 2006; Sharpe and Boucher 2010.
5   Ibid.
6   Žižek 2001.
7   Žižek 2008a, 3.
8   Žižek and Douzinas 2010; Ibid 2013; Taek-Gwang Lee and Žižek 2016.
9   Žižek 2007; Žižek 2007a.
10 Johnson 2009; Kirsch 2008.
11 Žižek 2007b, 10.
12 Žižek 2008.

Although the contours of Žižek's politics and political framework are sketched out above, there remain a remarkable number of dangling loose ends. These stem mainly from his writing style. Žižek has continuously produced an impressive stream of texts, which rarely dwell on one and the same topic for any great length of time. This prevents him from systematically working out the contents of reworked Leninist notions, such as the proletariat, the party and the state. Žižek's almost rhizomatic writing style, seemingly intuitively jumping from one topic to another, has added to the confusion. Sina Talachian sums up this critique in stating: 'It is not uncommon that an argument contained in one text is presented differently in another – or even in another section of the same text – in a contradictory fashion.'

The way in which Žižek reworks central Marxist notions such as the proletariat, the political party and the state is illustrated in his remarks on the slum dwellers of the new megacities. Žižek defines them as 'a necessary product of the innermost logic of global capitalism', whose characteristics 'fit the good old Marxist determination of the proletarian revolutionary subject'. He refers to Hugo Chavez in his outline of a revolutionary strategy:

> The course on which Chavez embarked from 2006 is the exact opposite of the postmodern Left's mantra [...] far from 'resisting state power', he grabbed power (first by an attempted coup, then democratically), ruthlessly using the state apparatuses and interventions to promote his goals; furthermore, he is militarizing the favelas, organizing the training of armed units. And [...] now that he is feeling the economic effects of the 'resistance' to his rule by capital [...], he has announced the constitution of his own political party![13]

In this scenario, the term proletariat is given new content. Still, it remains unclear if the slum dwellers have become the main embodiment of the proletariat, or if it consists of other groups as well. Even more unclear are the implications of this scenario for the political organization of the proletariat, the contents of their revolutionary politics and the character of the state power that they aim to 'grab'. Žižek has claimed that 'the goal of revolutionary violence is not to take over the State power, but to transform it'.[14] However, it remains unclear what this truly entails.

Despite this lack of clarity, a coherent political framework lies at the heart of Žižek's work. It allows him to interpret both past and contemporary events, to intervene in current debates and make claims about political strategy. The repeating of Lenin and the recovery of the Communist Idea are central to his work. These topics relate directly to matters of political actors (proletariat), political organization (party) and strategy (taking over and transforming the state). Even so, his remarks on the latter three topics lie scattered throughout his texts. The authors of this volume have set out to retrieve these comments and connect them. Most of them deny that there is

---

13 Žižek 2008a, 427.
14 Žižek 2010, 220.

something like a 'Žižekian theory of the state', which can be uncovered by simply connecting the dots. Rather, they have opted for a strategy of taking cues from some of Žižek's comments on the past, present and future state; subsequently thinking 'along his lines' to further develop these notions and finally examine them critically in terms of their internal coherence and critical potential. This leads the various authors in very interesting and diverging directions.

The contributors thus address questions that seek to identify revolutionary actors and outline the contours of revolutionary organization. If the proletariat is to be organized in a revolutionary party, while the Leninist party is to be reinvented, how then are we to envision this new type of party? If violence is an inherent part of the struggle for liberation, while it is acknowledged that Leninism can turn into Stalinism and mass terror, where then is the line to be drawn between liberating violence and repressive terror? If the proletariat is to take over power to subsequently 'transform the state', what does this mean and what strategies follow from it?

Reloading Lenin (and Lacan)

The first three contributors seek out to find answers in the links between Žižek's politics and its philosophical foundations. Žižek belongs to what Yannis Stavrakakis has called the Lacanian left.[15] The philosophical basis of his politics are formed by 'a highly original mixture of Marxism and Psychoanalysis', as Erik Vogt states in his contribution to this volume. In what way does Žižek's philosophy inform his politics and with what results? Vogt systematically discusses the philosophical foundations of Žižek's politics, since Žižek's 'first aim [...] is to lend a new explosive force to contemporary philosophy, so that it can inform genuine emancipatory politics'. Vogt aims to lay out the consistency of Žižek's program and the systematic way in which Žižek moves from philosophy to politics.

Žižek's philosophy also informs a political *attitude* that Žižek sums up through his call to 'dream dangerously'. In his argument, Lenin and Lacan feature prominently. Santiago Roggerone zooms in on this and places the (Lacanian) Act at the center of (Lenin's) call for a revolutionary seizure of power: 'For Žižek the essence of Lenin's thinking is that "you never get the guarantee; you must act. You must take the risk and act."' The principles of dreaming dangerously, acting and taking risks form the basis of Žižek's politics. At the same time, Roggerone admits that Žižek's 'definition of the proletariat remains elusive'. This also remains true of his definition of the political party and the state.

---

15 Stavrakakis 2007; McGowan 2013.

Žižek builds on Lenin's politics, one of its central claims being that revolutionary consciousness must be introduced to the proletariat from the outside. This seemingly leads Žižek to carve out a 'privileged conceptual space' for himself from where he defines the outlines of proper politics. Sina Talachian takes issue with what he deems the external mode of Žižek's politics, since 'this means that the actors who are actually engaged in a particular emancipatory praxis are not involved in the process of identifying the normativity that guides and gives content to it'. Furthermore, this way of thinking seeps into Žižek's claims on migration, tolerance and racism. Ignoring the agency of migrants and refugees leaves Žižek vulnerable to adopting 'static, monolithic categories of "Muslim" or "Pakistani"', even leading to the 're-producing and naturalizing of the marginalization of Muslims in the West'. This is particularly problematic 'in a context wherein Islamophobia is increasingly on the rise'.

There are clear links in these approaches to Žižek's thinking about political organization and the state. Žižek's philosophy is overtly political and serves as a basis for a form of politics that aims at radically changing the present order. His philosophy informs a consistent way to think about politics (Vogt), to assume a specific attitude that focuses on 'dreaming dangerously' and taking risks (Roggerone), while the philosophical basis of his politics may also inform a blind spot around issues that are not directly related to class, such as ethnicity and culture (Talachian).

Communist Politics and The State

Three contributions delve more deeply into the intricacies of Žižek's thinking about the state. Their assumption is that Žižek's politics can be analyzed in their own right. But what kind of states does Žižek envision when he speaks about the present or post-capitalist state? The authors do not aim to systematically draw out the contours of Žižek's state theory. Rather, the existence of such a theory is contested. Alex Del Duca states that 'what best characterizes Žižek's approach to the state is the glaring absence of any explicit approach at all'. Agon Hamza writes: 'Žižek has up to now never put forward a theory of the State'.

Geoff Pfeiffer takes this notion as an invitation to 'think along the lines' of Žižek and ask what such a state theory could look like. He picks up on a discussion between Žižek and his long time comrade Alain Badiou to investigate the characteristics of a post-revolutionary state. According to Badiou, there is no way to escape the power of the state, since every social order requires a state apparatus that maintains it. The Althusserian notion of science, however, allows one to recognize how states have grown historically and, therefore, which aspects of them can be changed. This, however, can only be done from a position of power. This is the reason why Žižek emphasizes that the goal of revolutionary struggle must be to take power, since 'the goal of this communist state-form is the total transformation of the state'. Thus, the capitalist state 'withers and dies' in favor of a 'renewed and emancipatory state-form'.

Žižek takes what is generally called the 'democratic deficit' as a point of departure to think about democracy and the dictatorship of the proletariat. The liberal democratic order excludes groups from decision-making, even when it claims that all have a say in democratic procedures. For Žižek, the moment when the excluded make themselves heard and lay claim to power, social order is undermined. This 'democratic explosion' harbors a 'terroristic element'. Marc de Kesel is willing to follow this logic, but asks where the boundaries between democratic violence and repressive terror lie: 'Even if one agrees with the idea that, within the process of a revolution, a phase of dictatorship is unavoidable, one does not really find in Žižek's thought indications how that dictatorship will turn into a state that recognizes its inner negativity.' This issue is all the more important, since here lies the boundary between the Leninist gesture and its Stalinist regression.

Overall, Žižek's theory of the state seems little developed. As a result, he fails to 'fully think through the difference between the democratic revolution against semi-feudal absolutism, on the one hand, and the socialist revolution under conditions of repressive tolerance and liberal democracy, on the other hand.' This raises concerns for Geoff Boucher, who fears that Žižek's undifferentiated conceptualization of the state and Leninism can give way to a form of politics that is 'ultimately about domination' and 'culminates in a rehabilitation of the politics of Mao'. For Boucher these findings are an appeal: 'Žižek needs to further develop his definition of the state, and distinguish between feudal and modern state dynamics if he is to develop a convincing theoretical alternative to neo-Maoism'.

The Two Žižeks: The Performer and the Leninist

Most contributors critically engage with Žižek's philosophy and politics, working on the assumption that these form an original and coherent whole. Alex Del Duca proposes a wholly different take on Žižek's work. His contribution starts with three explicit claims: 'Slavoj Žižek's relationship to so-called practical political theory has mostly been an ambiguous and obfuscated one. [...] Žižek's relationship to state theory and his track record of analyses of the state fall into a woefully similar pattern', and finally Žižek is '[f]ar from producing something legitimately novel in terms of content'. Del Duca takes the recent disenchantment of many radical activists and commentators with Žižek as his starting point, only to claim that 'it was never his goal to develop and popularize a new revolutionary politics'. Rather than 'providing the ultimate answers', Žižek's aim is more moderate, namely 'to re-inaugurate authority or, in other words, to modify the current politico-theoretical coordinates of Marxism'. According to Del Duca, Žižek's goal is not so much to reinvent or further develop Marxism, but rather to 'reclaim Marxism as a political practice.'

While Del Duca emphasizes the form of Žižek's political interventions, Agon Hamza insists on the consistency of Žižek's political program, which seems to oscillate between classical Marxism and its reinvention in the present. Hamza remains close to Žižek's political project, as he has worked together with him on several occasions. Hamza's contribution provides a good overview of Žižek's thinking about the state and political organization overall. In doing so, he shows the outlines of Žižek's ideas about the state and the political party. Conquering state power should be central to revolutionary politics, since it is the only body 'capable of radically transforming and reorganizing the whole of social life'. Hamza emphasizes that 'we must break with the taboos of the Left, so that we can re-envision socialist struggle for, and with, organizational tools that today are monopolized by the ruling class [...] such as the commodity form, the state-form, global logistics, informational networks'. He confirms Žižek's claim that the political party is the only form through which opposition can be turned into true politics. Although the main tenets of Žižek's thinking about political organization are thus elucidated, questions remain about the specifics of what this political party would look like.

Asking the Right Questions

The contributors to this volume acknowledge Žižek's prominence as a radical thinker. Žižek's investigations, claims and appeals with regard to political organization and strategy are highly controversial, but remain an important point of reference nonetheless. At the same time, the current chapters seem to document above all how Žižek struggles to identify revolutionary actors, to think the political party anew and conceptualize what it means to take power. The latter question informs Žižek's grave interest in the history of the Soviet Union and other communist regimes. New forms of political organization are necessary, as well as a renewed courage on the side of the left to 'dream dangerously' – which, among other things, means that the left should strive to not merely confront the state but to take over power. The search for these new forms of organization – and actors willing to adopt them – is not over.

In various settings, Žižek has claimed that 'the task of philosophy is not to provide answers'. Rather, the goal is 'to ask the right questions'.[16] This does not have to be an individual task. In fact, Žižek has initiated various collaborations, most impor-

---

16 Žižek ny.

tantly the conferences on *The Idea of Communism*. The response has been impressive, with various authors criticizing, supporting and/or building on Žižek's work, focusing on questions of revolutionary strategy and organization. This volume can be seen as part of that endeavor.

References

Judith Butler, Ernesto Laclau and Slavoj Žižek, 2000: *Contingency, Hegemony, Universality. Contemporary Dialogues on the Left*. London.

Butler, Rex, 2006: *Slavoj Žižek zur Einführung*. Hamburg.

Dean, Jodi, 2006: *Žižek's Politics*. London and New York.

Johnson, Alan, 2009: The reckless Mind of Slavoj Žižek. In: *Dissent* 56:4 (2009), 122-127.

Kirsch, Adam, 2008: The Deadly Jester. In: *The New Republic*, 3 December 2008.

Kriss, Sam, 2015: Building Norway. A Critique of Slavoj Žižek. https://samkriss.wordpress.com/2015/09/11/building-norway-a-critique-of-slavoj-

Kriss, Sam, 2015a: In Defense of Fantasy. A Further Response to Slavoj Žižek. https://samkriss.wordpress.com/2015/11/17/in-defence-of-fantasy-a-further-response-to-slavoj-

McGowan, Todd, 2013: *Enjoying What We Don't Have. The Political Project of Psychoanalysis*. Nebraska.

Riemer, Nick, 2015: How to Justify a Crisis. In: *Jacobin*, 10 May 2015. https://www.jacobinmag.com/2015/10/refugee-crisis-europe-

Sharpe, Matthew and Geoff Boucher, 2010: *Žižek and Politics. A Critical Introduction*. Edinburgh.

Stavrakakis, Yannis, 2007: *The Lacanian Left. Psychoanalysis, Theory, Politics*. Edinburgh.

Thompson, Peter, 2013: The Slavoj Žižek v Noam Chomsky Spat is Worth a Ringside Seat. In: *The Guardian*, 19 July 2013. https://www.theguardian.com/commentisfree/2013/jul/19/noam-chomsky-slavoj-zizek-ding-dong

Žižek, Slavoj, 2001: *Repeating Lenin*. Zagreb. http://www.lacan.com/replenin.htm

Žižek, Slavoj (ed.), Maximilien de Robespierre, 2007: *Virtue and Terror*. London.

Žižek, Slavoj (ed.), Mao Zedong, 2007a: *On Practice and Contradiction*. London.

Žižek, Slavoj, 2008: Confessions of an Unrepentant Leninist. http://www.lacan.com/zizbomarz.html

Žižek, Slavoj, 2008a: *In Defense of Lost Causes*. New York and London.

Žižek, Slavoj and Costas Douzinas, 2010: *The Idea of Communism*. New York and London.

Žižek, Slavoj, 2010: How to Begin from the Beginning. In: Slavoj Žižek and Costas Douzinas (eds.), *The Idea of Communism*. London and New York, 209-226.

Žižek, Slavoj and Costas Douzinas, 2013: *The Idea of Communism. Vol. 2*. New York and London.

Žižek, Slavoj, 2015: The Non-Existence of Norway. In: *London Review of Books*, 9 September 2015. http://www.lrb.co.uk/2015/09/09/slavoj-zizek/the-non-existence-of-norway

Žižek, Slavoj, 2015a: In the Wake of Paris Attacks the Left must Embrace its Radical Western Roots. In: *In These Times*, 16 November 2015. http://inthesetimes.com/article/18605/break ing-the-taboos-in-the-wake-of-paris-attacks-the-left-must-embrace-its

Žižek, Slavoj and Alex Taek-Gwang Lee, 2016: *The Idea of Communism. Vol. 3.* New York and London.

Žižek, Slavoj, ny: The Purpose of Philosophy is to Ask the Right Questions. http://bigthink.co m/videos/the-purpose-of-philosophy-is-to-ask-the-right-questions

Reloading Lenin (and Lacan)

Santiago M. Roggerone[1]

An Act Proper. Slavoj Žižek and the Persistence of Marxism

The career of Slavoj Žižek in the English-speaking world started in 1989, when the collapse of what existed of socialism at that time appeared imminent. Much of the success of *The Sublime Object of Ideology* (1989) – the first book that the Slovenian philosopher wrote entirely in English – is due to the singular combination between Hegelian dialectics and Lacanian psychoanalysis that it proposed as a way to update the ideas of the left, which were by then in serious crisis.[2] The notion of the Act, which Žižek adopted from Jacques Lacan – in order to refer to the radical abolition and transformation of the existing state of things by one particular subject –, plays an important role in this work. It functioned as a key tool for critiquing ideology, which was so central to the agenda of radical democracy.

Radical democracy was a revisionist Marxist project developed by Ernesto Laclau and Chantal Mouffe in the mid-1980s (1985), and initially Žižek was very supportive of it. Laclau and Mouffe argued that the politics of radical democracy should not focus on building consensus, but on accepting difference. This, then, was to form the basis for the political strategy of new social movements in neo-liberal times. Rather than taking over power, social movements should strive for hegemony by demanding that everyone should be given a voice.

Inspired by these ideas, Žižek's early works focused on the Act as merely a *symbolic act* which would form part of a practice through which capitalism would gradually be reformed. Symbolic and theatrical actions and events were to merely *show* that there were still people who resisted neo-liberalism. However, at the end of 1990s, Žižek's conception of the Act started to develop into a sort of synonym for revolution. Taking over power moved to the fore in his thinking. As a result, the Act evolved into a powerful analytical tool with which to explain historical and contemporary political changes, to assume a true proletarian position and forward revolutionary demands aimed at overthrowing capitalism. Žižek thus links the concept of the Act to what Alain Badiou calls the Communist Idea.[3]

In what follows, I will distinguish Žižek's Act proper from other notions, such as *symbolic act, passage à l'acte*, and *Acting-out*. This Act proper is so important for

---

1 Garrett Busshart reviewed a preliminary version of this chapter. I also thank Bart van der Steen and Marc de Kesel for their invaluable commentaries and suggestions.
2 Žižek 1989.
3 Badiou 2008, 115.

the Slovenian philosopher because it alludes to the revolutionary gesture through which a particular subject can provoke a radical break and a new beginning; in other words, it forms the basis of the rebirth of the Communist Idea. In order to define the contours of the Act proper, I will first assess the ontological materialistic foundations upon which Žižek's work is based. Subsequently, I will be able to introduce the three main components that make up the Žižekian Act: *the possibility of the impossible*, *la traversée du fantasme*, and *the fidelity to principles*. Finally, I will show how the Act informs Žižek's conceptualization of the proletariat, the party and radical emancipatory politics.

This chapter foremost constitutes an intellectual history that intends to reconstruct the development of Žižek's thinking and situate it within the theoretical and political coordinates of its time. In this respect, I follow Perry Anderson, for whom intellectual history basically means locating 'specific contradictions of argument where they occur, generally treating them not as random lapses but as symptomatic points of tension'.[4]

But before moving to the study of the ontological, materialistic foundations of Žižek's perspective, I must make a preliminary remark about his intentions. For although Žižek is not a Marxist, he has made a number of noteworthy interventions in the fields of Marxist theory and practice. In fact, Žižek has developed his conception of the Act precisely to deactivate one of the most difficult challenges for Marxism, namely the post-Marxist radical democracy project. In doing so, Žižek is attempting to refute the main post-Marxist challenges to Marxism. Paraphrasing Žižek himself, we might ask, is Žižek's intervention in this field not the very definition of an Act proper?

Žižek and the Lacanian Left

Žižek distinguishes himself from other contemporary thinkers that try to renew and revive Marxism by the fact that he himself is not strictly a Marxist. Even so, he plays a crucial role in what André Tosel has called the 'well-nigh impotent flowering of a thousand Marxisms'.[5] In this role, he is contributing to 'the renaissance of Marxism',[6] and some have dubbed him 'the unavoidable star' of the 'contemporary critical thinking' that emerged out of the crisis of Marxism.[7] Given all this, it is important to note that Zizek is *not* a Marxist, but rather an active member of the Laca-

---

4 Anderson 1992, X.
5 Tosel 2008, 42; see also Wallerstein 1991.
6 Bensaïd 2002, XV.
7 Keucheyan 2013, 182.

nian left.[8] At the same time, he is a Hegelian philosopher who is dedicated to developing a materialist theory of subjectivity.[9]

The fundamental premise of Žižek's interventions is that the conceptual framework developed by Lacan to explore the individual psyche can also be used to analyze and criticize culture and society. In this regard, Žižek's approach is similar to that of Claude Lévi-Strauss, who extrapolated the linguistic tools originally developed by Ferdinand de Saussure to analyze indigenous communities.[10]

Social reality is for Žižek what psychological reality was for Lacan. As a result of this, Žižek's materialistic philosophy is mainly articulated through Lacan's psychoanalytic vocabulary. Thus, when he attempts to explain what effects an Act can bring about, Žižek appeals to the Lacanian notion of *la doublure*: 'the redoubling, twist or curvature in the order of being which opens up the space for event'.[11] An Act can twist or curve the symbolic register of societal order. And when he explains the societal conflicts that open up the possibility of the Act, he refers to society – what philosophers call the order of being – as the symbolic order or the big Other.

This societal order is 'inconsistent, marked by an irreducible contingency', which is class struggle.[12] Class struggle leads to tensions, conflicts and plain short-circuits in the symbolic order. These short-circuits themselves make up events which subvert societal routines. Or, as Žižek states in *Organs without Bodies*: 'The [...] Event is *nothing but* [...] a cut/rupture in the order of Being on account of which Being cannot ever form a consistent All'.[13]

'Less than Nothing': Žižek's Ontology

Žižek recently dubbed his perspective 'a renewed Hegelian 'dentology' (the ontology of *den*, of 'less than nothing')'.[14] In works like *Less Than Nothing* and *Absolute Recoil*, he makes an ontological statement and claims that symbolic reality is overdetermined by something that is *more real than reality itself* – that is to say, by an excessive register that Lacan calls *the Real*. In the beginning, there is nothing (the void, the Real). Still, from this nothing emerges, not by addition but by subtraction, what Democritus described as δεν (*den*). According to Žižek, this might more precisely be translated as *othing*:

---

8   Stavrakakis 2007.
9   Johnston 2008.
10   Lévi-Strauss 1967; De Saussure 1977.
11   Žižek and Daly 2004, 137.
12   Žižek 2006, 79.
13   Žižek 2003a, 107.
14   Žižek 2014, 5.

Den is [...] not nothing without 'no', not a thing, but an *othing*, a something but *still within the domain of nothing*, like an ontological living dead, a spectral nothing-appearing-as-something. Or, as Lacan put it: 'Nothing, perhaps? No – perhaps nothing, but not nothing'.[15]

The *den*'s or *othings* are in fact little pieces of the Real, and in this form, like the latter, more real than reality itself. Following Lacan, Žižek claims that it is seemingly impossible to encounter the Real, to see reality for what it ontologically is – a non-totality of *othings*. In Lacan's work, this Real is always a trauma, an irreducible nucleus that cannot be explained, internalized or accepted. Therefore, the symbolic register prevents us from encountering the Real and works like a filter. Still, at the same time, our subjectivity is overdetermined by the Real.

For Žižek, these ontological statements form the basis of his social philosophy. Applying Lacan's concepts to society, he sees society as a symbolic order, regulated by fantasies (i.e. ideologies) which impede the encounter with the Real. For Žižek, the Real of capitalist society is class struggle, 'the fundamental social antagonism [...] that divides the social edifice from within'.[16] Class struggle determines the limits of what we can imagine and fixes the limits of all possible symbolizations. Yet, our understanding of class struggle is distorted and repressed by ideological fantasies.

In short, one could say that our contemporary society is a symbolic reality (late capitalism), overdetermined by a traumatic Real (the social antagonism of class struggle), distorted by an imaginary truth (the diverse ideological class perspectives) and retroactively organized by a Master(-signifier) in which subjects believe (neoliberal democracy).

According to this line of reasoning, it would be impossible to gain a true understanding of societal relations, since our view is distorted by the symbolic order and ideological fantasies. Žižek, however, proposes to explore the ideological fantasies that distort our vision. In fact, this is one of the goals of his work. According to Žižek, the symbolic order is riddled with inconsistencies (stemming from social antagonisms). The Act is the moment when someone picks up these inconsistencies, exploits them and uses them to subvert and undermine the existing symbolic order.

Žižek's notion of the Act is thus based on the thesis that it *is* possible to cross the fantasy of neo-liberal democracy, to confront the Real, to produce an encounter with the traumatic antagonism of class struggle – that is, to engage in class struggle – and take a side in it. The Act is so important because it reveals the fictitious character of the neo-liberal symbolic order and opens up opportunities to abolish it.

These are the basic contours of Žižek's ontology in which his conceptualization of the Act is grounded. Its political significance lies in the contrast to more Heideg-

---

15 Žižek 2012a, 59.
16 Žižek 2000, 124.

gerian conceptualizations of the Act – formulated by French intellectuals in the wake of the Paris revolts of May 1968. Impressed by these sudden and spectacular protests, the latter hailed the idea that the event bursts onto the stage; that a revolt can emerge out of nowhere. Žižek emphatically opposes the view that an event 'is something that emerges out of nothing'.[17] In his view, such a vision is 'too idealistic'.[18] As Žižek sees it, his work shares the same premise as that of philosophers such as Deleuze, the late Althusser and his comrade Badiou: 'The irreducibility of the event to some positive order of being'.[19] Thus, according to Žižek, people initiate events. His philosophical project, however, focuses on formulating a materialistic program that makes it possible 'to think the unity of being and event'[20] – that is, the relation between actors and the Act.

What, then, is the Act, and how can it be brought about? The Act signifies the moment when someone's intervention subverts the symbolic order. How can this be achieved? To explain this, Žižek again introduces a concept from Lacanian psychoanalysis and applies it to society: enjoyment or *jouissance*. Žižek speaks of enjoyment as that dimension which belongs to the field of the Real and 'we experience as "transgression"'.[21] In a perverted consumerist society like this one, where 'everything' is permitted, enjoyment becomes a hedonistic imperative. Paradoxically, in late capitalism, ideology obstructs the encounter with real enjoyment through an absurd and cynical invitation to enjoy. It has become an 'obscene call'. But precisely because of this, enjoyment or *jouissance* turns into a political-ideological factor. When someone attempts to achieve real enjoyment, that individual is likely to come into conflict with the symbolic order, unveil its inconsistency and through this experience confront the Real. As a result, the symbolic order can be revealed for what it truly is – a non-totality. In this setting, the realization of the Act becomes possible.

The Act and its Three Components

Originally, Žižek defined the Act as merely a symbolic act, an instrument that could be used as a tool with which to critique ideology. This definition was inspired by Laclau, and in later accounts, Žižek explained that in this period – the 1980s and early 1990s –, he still held firm to a 'liberal-democratic political stance', oscillating 'between Marxism proper and praise of "pure" democracy'.[22] According to him, it took him 'years of hard work to identify and liquidate these dangerous residues of

---

17 Žižek and Daly 2004, 136.
18 Ibid., 136-7.
19 Žižek and Daly 2004, 135-136.
20 Ibid.
21 Žižek 1992, 9-10.
22 Žižek 2002b, XVIII.

bourgeois ideology'.[23] One of the things Žižek did in order to accomplish this was the 'elaboration of the concept of act'.[24] As a result, Žižek redefined the Act into a concept that presupposes 'the possibility of a radical political transformation of the existing state of things'.[25] In this context, the Act becomes an '"excessive", trans-strategic intervention which redefines the rules and contours of the existing order'.[26] Conceptualized like this, the Act is 'increasingly linked to the actuality of communism'.[27] Thus, the Act transformed from a critical ideological procedure used to radicalize democracy into a theory with the aim of actualizing communism.

For Žižek, the Act is different from *Acting-out*, the *passage à l'acte* and the *symbolic act*, because the Act proper 'restructures the very symbolic coordinates of the agent's situation: it is an intervention in the course of which the agent's identity itself is radically changed'.[28] In this stance, Žižek builds on the work of Lacan, who in his 1967-8 seminar *L'acte psychanalytique* (unpublished), distinguished it from

> the hysterical acting out, the psychotic *passage à l'acte*, [and] the symbolic act. In the hysterical acting out, the subject stages, in a kind of theatrical performance, the compromise solution of the trauma she is unable to cope with. In the psychotic *passage à l'acte*, the deadlock is so debilitating that the subject cannot even imagine a way out – the only thing he can do is to strike blindly in the real, to release his frustration in the meaningless outburst of destructive energy. The symbolic act is best conceived of as the purely formal, self-referential, gesture of the self-assertion of one's subjective position.[29]

Only in the course of the Act proper can a subject change in a positive and sustainable way. The other acts all offer either elusive or destructive transformations. The Act proper is a radical intervention which both subverts the symbolic order and, in its course, changes the agent who initiates it. It consists of three components: the *possibility of the impossible*, *la traversée du fantasme*, and *the fidelity to principles*.

The Possibility of the Impossible

To subvert the symbolic order, the Act redefines what is deemed 'possible'. On this, Žižek states: 'An act does not simply occur within the given horizon of what appears to be "possible" – it redefines the very contours of what is possible'. And he continues to state that 'an act accomplishes what, within the given symbolic universe, ap-

---

23 Ibid.
24 Ibid.
25 Bosteels 2011, 176.
26 Žižek 2004, 81.
27 Bosteels 2011, 176.
28 Žižek 2001, 85.
29 Ibid., 84.

pears to be "impossible"'.[30] Even more so, the Act not only redefines what is deemed possible, but also what is deemed *necessary*.

To explain this point, Žižek frequently uses the Antigone myth and cinematographic examples such as the self-destruction of Keyser Söze in *The Usual Suspects* (1995). Confronted with opponents who are holding his family to ransom, Söze first kills his family before going after his enemies. In retrospect, we understand that the killing of his family was necessary for Söze to become truly free and achieve his goals. The Act does not only completely change the 'rules of the game' that Söze and his rival criminals 'play', but it also transforms Söze. Only after the Act has taken place do we see it as both possible and necessary – while before it seemed both 'impossible' and undesirable. Certainly, an Act is unlikely until it becomes inevitable – and is deemed inevitable only in retrospect.

What it is clear for those who act is that it is necessary to take great risks, to confront Hegel's *Nacht der Welt,* to take a step into the void of madness without any guarantee of success.[31] Only then, through confronting a dead end head on, through the violent encounter with both the big Other and oneself, is it possible to 'clear the terrain for a new beginning'.[32] If one is not willing to take such risks, one can only bring about false revolutions of the symbolic order, which change everything in such a way that nothing really changes. The Act is a foundational gesture that neutralizes the field of possible symbolization.

La traversée du fantasme

However, the alteration of the symbolic order is not sufficient to concede the status of the Act to a particular phenomenon. According to Žižek, 'a true act does not only retroactively change the rules of the symbolic space [and thus change what is deemed possible]; it also disturbs the underlying fantasy'.[33] Disturbing the underlying (ideological) fantasy which regulates the balance of the symbolic order is referred to as *la traversée du fantasme.*

In psychoanalytical therapy, the Act entails a re-elaboration of fantasy, which means a step-forward towards a cure – that is to say, towards the end of analysis, the adoption of the position of the analyst, and identification with the *sinthome*. When an Act occurs, its subject '*posits himself as his own cause*', and warns himself of the effects of his fantasies.[34] As a result, he or she who acts resolutely assumes responsibility for his or her actions. In doing so, he or she reveals the ideological character of

---

30   Žižek 2000, 121.
31   Hegel 1974, 204.
32   Žižek 2000, 121.
33   Žižek 1999, 200.
34   Ibid., 375.

the symbolic field which supports the elections which appear possible. This is the basis on which all authentic Acts must be founded.

Fidelity to principles

What is crucial to the Act is that it has no intrinsic temporality. According to Žižek 'the Act is only conceivable as the intervention of Eternity into time'.[35] The Act is the moment when the Real disturbs the symbolic order. The first is eternal, the latter contextual. As discussed above, in retrospect the Act was always both possible and necessary. This is why Žižek deems it a false question to ask under what circumstances the Act can be executed: '[W]e cannot establish the time of the explosion of the Event through a close 'objective' historical analysis (in the style of 'when objective contradictions reach such and such a level, things will explode')'.[36]

This explains why Žižek vindicates a so-called form of *decisionism* close to that which Rosa Luxemburg upheld 'against the revisionists' and states: '[T]here is no Event [i.e. Act] outside the engaged subjective decision which creates it – if we wait for the time to become ripe for the Event, the Event will never occur'.[37]

Thus, he who acts takes a risk, steps into a void and commits to it without symbolic legitimization, in a sort of Pascalian wager. He who acts seizes the moment because it is clear to him or her that acting tomorrow will be too late. The Act entails the firm conviction that no permission from the symbolic order is required. The moment to act must not be awaited; there is no such thing as the right time to act. There are no secret signs to be awaited, there is no guarantee of success. An Act consists of an opportunity that emerges or, rather, as the experience of the Russian Revolution reminds us, an opportunity that one causes to emerge and as such must be taken. Thus, to put it in the terms of Bosteels, the Act requires 'a stubborn fidelity to principles regardless of all consequences'.[38]

Vice versa, the Act implies that even if the cause is lost, it is necessary to demonstrate fidelity and forge ahead. As Žižek pointed out in *In Defense of Lost Causes*, the 'past defeats accumulate the utopian energy which will explode in the final battle: "maturation" is not waiting for "objective" circumstances to reach maturity, but the accumulation of defeats'.[39] This fidelity to principles can guide us, while we base our beliefs and actions 'on nothing more than ambiguous signs from the future'.[40]

---

35 Žižek 2012a, 427.
36 Žižek 2003b, 133.
37 Ibid., 134-35.
38 Bosteels 2011, 191.
39 Žižek 2008, 392.
40 Žižek 2012b, 135.

The Žižekian Act is thus founded on a materialistic ontology – that is to say, a *den*tology – and retroactively deems possible and necessary what early on appeared to be impossible. The Act disturbs the underlying ideological fantasies of the symbolic order, while it requires its bearers to fully commit to their deeds. In other words, the Act implies a movement of subjective destitution, while it allows for an instant during which the Real explodes the imaginary symbolic coordinates of the symbolic order.

Contrary to what may be expected, this theory of the Act is far from a post-Marxist variant of politics. Rather, Žižek is dedicated to laying the philosophical foundations of the Act. In this way, he attempts to neutralize the postmodern challenges launched against Marxism by philosophers such as Laclau. At the same time, Žižek's work implies a tacit alliance with the radical emancipatory politics associated with figures such as Lenin or even Trotsky.

In this regard, the motto that Žižek adopted in his political writings is emblematic: *Repeating Lenin*. In his afterword to a compilation of Lenin's writings, Žižek arrived at a firm conclusion: 'Today, more than ever, we should go back to Lenin'.[41] With this call to return to Lenin, Žižek explicitly rejects capitalism *and* (its fetishizing of) democracy. It informs his unrelenting critiques of multiculturalism and of left-liberal (or post-political) politics. Ultimately, it allows him to acknowledge the redemptive character of violence as he answers those who demonize the party by quoting Robespierre's reply to the Girondists: 'You want a revolution without a revolution!'.[42]

The main reason for this 'repetition' of Lenin is a very important affinity between Lenin and Lacanian ethics. For Žižek, the essence of Lenin's thinking is that

> you never get the guarantee; you must act. You must take the risk and act. I think that this is the Lenin that is truly a Lacanian Lenin. In the same way that Lacan says the analyst is authorized only by him – or herself –, Lenin's message is that a revolutionary *ne s'autorise que de lui-même*. That is to say, at a certain point you have to assume responsibility for the act.[43]

Even though Žižek promotes 'repeating', or reloading, Lenin,[44] he does not seek to be tied to the tight framework of Leninism. Rather, he calls the latter 'a thoroughly *Stalinist* notion'.[45] As Žižek sees it,

---

41 Žižek 2002a, 273.
42 Ibid., 297.
43 Žižek and Daly 2004, 164.
44 Budgen, Kouvelakis and Žižek 2007.
45 Žižek 2002a, 193.

[r]epeating Lenin does not mean a *return* to Lenin – to repeat Lenin is to accept that 'Lenin is dead', that his particular solution failed, even failed monstrously, but that there was a utopian spark in it worth saving. Repeating Lenin means that we have to distinguish between what Lenin actually did and the field of possibilities that he opened up, the tension in Lenin between what he actually did and another dimension: what was 'in Lenin more than Lenin himself'. To repeat Lenin is to repeat not what Lenin *did* but what he *failed to do*, his missed opportunities.[46]

It is along these lines that Žižek defends Trotsky and his pamphlet *Terrorism and Communism*, exactly that piece of writing which is often glossed over in the Trotskyite tradition. For Žižek, *Terrorism and Communism* represents the Trotsky of Party government and revolutionary terror – far-removed from the myth which conceives Trotsky as a democratic figure, supporter of psychoanalysis, friend of surrealists, and lover of Frida Kahlo. For Žižek, there is no Trotsky other than this cursed one, 'which disturbs the alternative 'either' (social-) democratic socialism or Stalinist Totalitarianism'.[47] In Žižek's eyes, this is the Trotsky that should be redeemed:

> Trotsky is the one for whom there is no room either in pre-1990 Really Existing Socialism or in past-1990 Really Existing Capitalism, in which even those that are nostalgic for Communism do not know what to do with Trotsky's permanent revolution – perhaps the signifier 'Trotsky' is the most appropriate designation of that which is worth redeeming in the Leninist legacy.[48]

Confronted with Stalinism – where '"Lenin lives forever" as an obscene spirit which "does not know it is dead", artificially kept alive as an instrument of power'[49] – Trotsky represents the site where Lenin lives 'in so far as he embodies [...] the "eternal Idea" of universal emancipation, the immortal striving for justice that no insults and catastrophes manage to kill'.[50]

The Eternal Idea of Communism

And with this eternal Idea we confront the decisive point of Žižek's radical emancipatory politics. Recently, his theory of the Act has been increasingly interwoven with what Badiou described as the communist hypothesis:

> The communist hypothesis remains the right hypothesis, as I have said, and I do not see any other. If this hypothesis should have to be abandoned, then it is not worth doing anything in the order of collective action. Without the perspective of communism, without this Idea, nothing in the historical and political future is of such a kind as to interest the

---

46 Ibid., 310.
47 Žižek 2008, 232.
48 Žižek 2002a, 305-306.
49 Žižek 2007, xxxii.
50 Ibid., xxxi.

philosopher. Each individual can pursue their private business, and we won't mention it again [...] But holding on to the Idea, the existence of the hypothesis, does not mean that its first form of presentation, focused on property and the state, must be maintained just as it is. In fact, what we are ascribed as a philosophical task, we could say even a duty, is to help a new modality of existence of the hypothesis to come into being. New in terms of the type of political experimentation to which this hypothesis could give rise.[51]

It is true that Žižek has dedicated a considerable number of pages to specifying his disagreements with Badiou. However, it is also undeniable that, since his break with Laclau, he has developed an increasingly strong bond with the French philosopher. Yannis Stavrakakis has correctly pointed out that 'one of the inspirations for Žižek's conceptualization of the act/event' is 'Badiou's work'.[52] In fact, the Slovenian philosopher indicates in *Less Than Nothing* that Badiou is '*the* theorist of the Act'.[53]

One of the reasons why this bond has grown ever stronger is the fact that Badiou revealed to Žižek the nature of 'the *politics of (universal) Truth*'.[54] For Žižek, this is the essence of 'politics proper', which he defines as

> the moment in which a particular demand is not simply part of the negotiation of interests but aims at something more, and starts to function as the metaphoric condensation of the global restructuring of the entire social space. There is a clear contrast between this subjectivization and today's proliferation of postmodern 'identity politics' whose goal is the exact opposite, that is, precisely the assertion of one's particular identity, of one's proper place within the social structure. The postmodern identity politics of particular (ethnic, sexual, etc.) lifestyles perfectly fits the depoliticized notion of society, in which every particular group is 'accounted for', has its specific status (of victim) acknowledged through affirmative action or other measures destined to guarantee social justice.[55]

In response to postmodern conceptions of the political, Badiou has developed a conceptual framework in which the Subject is buttressed by Fidelity to an Idea. In consonance with the French philosopher, Žižek has pointed out that those Ideas which are true are, at the same time, 'eternal, they are indestructible, always return every time they are proclaimed dead'.[56] One of these eternal ideas, which – because of its universality – cuts across specific historical worlds and particular horizons of meaning, is the Idea of communism.

According to Žižek, this Idea condenses 'the 'four fundamental concepts' at work from Plato to the medieval millenarian revolts and on to Jacobinism, Leninism and Maoism: strict *egalitarian justice*, disciplinary *terror*, political *voluntarism*, and *trust in the people*'.[57] Žižek defines the communist Idea as a 'platonic Idea which

---

51   Badiou 2008, 115.
52   Stavrakakis 2007, 122.
53   Žižek 2012a, 427.
54   Žižek 1999, 132.
55   Ibid., 208.
56   Žižek 2008, 5.
57   Žižek 2009, 125.

persisted, returning again and again after every defeat':[58] 'it survives the failures of its realization as a specter which returns again and again, in an endless persistence best captured in the [...] words from Beckett's *Worstward Ho*: 'Try again. Fail again. Fail better''.[59]

From this identification of communism as an eternal Idea, Žižek concludes 'that the situation which generates it is no less eternal, i.e., that the antagonism to which communism reacts will always exist'.[60] Following up on this, he insists on defining communism in a strictly Marxist sense: 'There are social groups which, on account of their lacking a determinate place in the "private" order of the social hierarchy, stand directly for universality'.[61] They are what Jacques Rancière calls the 'part of those who have no part'.[62] For this reason, Žižek emphasizes that it is imperative to show unconditional solidarity with this part of the no-part, as it embodies a singular universality.

Identifying Actors

But who or what embodies this part of no-part in contemporary global society? Laclau has criticized Žižek numerous times for his inability to define a 'concrete historical actor for his anti-capitalist struggle' or provide a 'theory of the emancipatory subject'.[63] Indeed, the Slovenian philosopher is often ambiguous or imprecise in his attempts to define the part of no-part of the social body.

In defense of Žižek, it must be said that, for him, politics is foremost about distinguishing between 'false' and 'true' points, 'false' and 'true' choices. Proper politics should 'bring back the third element whose obliteration sustains the false choice'.[64] The implications of this stance can be illustrated by the way Badiou and Laclau envision anti-capitalist struggle and the role of the state. While Badiou proposes moving away from the state, Laclau aims at transforming the state through radical democracy. In a sense, both resign themselves to conventional anti-capitalist polit-

---

58 Ibid., 126.
59 Ibid., 125.
60 Ibid., 88.
61 Ibid., 99.
62 Rancière 1999, 11.
63 Laclau 2005, 238.
64 Žižek 2008, 385-386.

ics.[65] Žižek, on the other hand, attacks the logic of *in* the state or *out* of the state. Rather, it is this logic itself that must be dismantled, rejecting it as a false choice.

Žižek's Leninism is an indicator that he is far from Laclau or Badiou. In his singular way, he remains faithful to the political project of Marxism. This is illustrated by the fact that he maintains – against Laclau – that the enemy today is called democracy and – against Badiou – that the dictatorship of the proletariat constitutes 'the only true choice'.[66]

Even so, his definition of the proletariat remains elusive. For Žižek, the present state of things compels us to radicalize the notion of the proletariat 'to an existential level beyond Marx's imagination'. What we need today is, according to Žižek, 'a more radical notion of the proletarian subject, a subject reduced to the evanescent point of the Cartesian *cogito*' and deprived of substantial content. For Žižek, the term proletariat 'has absolutely no content, no substantial consistence'. Emancipatory politics in the future 'will stem no longer from a particular social agent, but from an explosive combination of different agents'.[67] The proletariat is not a specific social group, but an Idea, which '"generates its own actualization" by way of motivating people to struggle for it'.[68] For this reason, Žižek prefers the notion of 'proletarian position' above proletariat.[69]

None other than the working classes reveal the contradictions within the symbolic order and show the Real (i.e. class struggle) which overdetermines and distorts it. Therefore, '*every* act is proletarian' and those who act uphold the proletarian position. According to Žižek: 'It is only from such a 'proletarian' position […] that an act can emerge'.[70] In response to Laclau, we can say that it follows from Žižek's conception of politics and the proletariat that he does not define a specific actor.

---

65 For Badiou, the main lesson of the failure of the Cultural Revolution in China is that the tradition of the communist party-state form is dead. As a consequence, Badiou thinks that, although politics still needs organization, it has to be a non-partisan and a non-programmatic one. For Badiou, political truth can only be achieved by being faithful to a local event, a local struggle, etc. He thus adheres to a version of postmodernity, where the only possible political act is a local act of resistance. Thus, paradoxically, Badiou has ended up coinciding with Laclau but through different paths: The first through a sort of autonomism, the second through gradual reformism. Both Laclau's radical democracy and Badiou's politics of subtraction are, thus, a retreat from the horizon of Marxism.

66 Žižek 2008, 412.

67 Žižek 2009, 92.

68 Žižek 2012a, 187.

69 Žižek 2009, 92.

70 Žižek 2012a, 434.

Another indicator of Žižek's support of Marxist politics is his defense of 'a strong body able to make quick decisions and realize them with the necessary harshness' – that is, the necessity of 'the tetrad of *people-movement-party-leader*'.[71] Nowadays, when people become politically active, they '"organize themselves" directly in movements'. However, the most that movements like Occupy Wall Street can create 'is an egalitarian space for debate where speakers are chosen by lottery and everyone is given the same (short) time to speak'. Žižek believes that these movements 'prove inadequate the moment one has to act, to impose a new order'. This is why he holds to the belief that 'something like a *Party* is needed',[72] as well as 'a *Leader*', who guarantees 'the unity of Party and people'.[73]

For Žižek, the party has the potential to become a true 'Master', which he defines as 'a vanishing mediator who gives you back to yourself, who delivers you to the abyss of your freedom'. And he states: '[W]hen we listen to a true leader, we discover what we want (or, rather, what we always already wanted without knowing it). A Master is needed because we cannot accede to our freedom directly'. Thus,

> a true Master is not an agent of discipline and prohibition, his message is not 'You cannot!', and not 'You have to...!', but a releasing 'You can!' – what? Do the impossible, namely what appears impossible within the coordinates of the existing constellation – and today, this means something very precise: you can think beyond capitalism and liberal democracy as the ultimate framework of our lives.[74]

Again, Žižek approaches the Party in Lacanian terms, but he gives it a twist. In his view, it is wrong to equate the position of the Party to 'that of the analyst in the analytical social link'.[75] The Party is not a therapist that guides a people to salvation. Rather, it is 'an open field of knowledge in which "all possible mistakes" occur (Lenin)'.[76] The Party is a place of confrontation and struggle. This is why, despite the electoral failure of Podemos in Spain and the betrayal of Tsipras in Greece, we still need a Party and a Leader. Only through a hard struggle against the Master itself can we achieve freedom.

Defining the Party in such a way causes Žižek to move beyond traditional Marxist claims. In fact, Žižek's premises do not adjust to the conception of historical materialism. Rather, they are inscribed in a materialistic ontology which is articulated through Lacanian motifs. As a philosopher, Žižek seeks to rehabilitate 'the philoso-

---

71 Ibid., 998.
72 Ibid., 1000.
73 Ibid., 1001.
74 Žižek 2014, 44-45.
75 Ibid., 47.
76 Žižek 2012a, 1000.

phy of *dialectical materialism*[77] and even proposes 'a new foundation for dialectical materialism'[78] through the vindication of a Hegelian-Lacanian position. If all this is considered, it becomes evident that Žižek's relationship with the paradigm of Marxism is far more ambiguous than it seems at first glance.

Ultimately, the Žižekian Act is determined by this ambiguity. It simultaneously rejects and accepts the postulates of Marxism; it contradicts and admits the problematic antagonism of class struggle; it questions and reaffirms the historical materialistic conception of social change. But in spite of its ambiguity – or perhaps: because of it – the theory of the Act constitutes a useful tool with which to neutralize the principal challenges to Marxism proper: radical democracy. Slavoj Žižek places 'radical 'unconditional' acts' against democracy, which will produce 'a radical refoundation of the social in a progressive direction', and as such function as 'models of ethico-political action'.[79] As these Acts are marked by 'the communist horizon',[80] they allow us to assume a truly radical emancipatory position (or proletarian position) and 'dream dangerously' in a 'new epoch of interesting times'.[81]

References

Anderson, Perry, 1992: *A Zone of Engagement*. London and New York.

Badiou, Alain, 2008: *The Meaning of Sarkozy*. London and New York.

Bensaïd, Daniel, 2002: *Marx for Our Times. Adventures and Misadventures of a Critique*. London and New York.

Bosteels, Bruno, 2011: *The Actuality of Communism*. London and New York.

Budgen, Sebastian, Eustache Kouvelakis and Slavoj Žižek, 2007: *Lenin Reloaded. Toward a Politics of Truth*. Durham.

Dean, Jodi, 2012: *The Communist Horizon*. London and New York.

Hegel, G.W.F., 1974: Jenaer Realphilosophie. In: Ibid., *Frühe politische Systeme*. Frankfurt.

Johnston, Adrian, 2008: *Žižek's Ontology. A Transcendental Materialist Theory of Subjectivity*. Evanston.

Keucheyan, Razmig, 2013: *Left Hemisphere. Mapping Critical Theory Today*. London and New York.

Laclau, Ernesto, 2005: *On Populist Reason*, London and New York.

Laclau, Ernesto and Chantal Mouffe, 1985: *Hegemony and Socialist Strategy. Towards a Radical Democratic Politics*. London and New York.

Lévi-Strauss, Claude, 1967: *Structural Anthropology*. New York.

---

77   Žižek 2006, 4.
78   Žižek 2014, 1.
79   Stavrakakis 2007, 134-5.
80   Dean 2012, 3.
81   Žižek 2011, 403.

Marchart, Oliver, 2007: *Post-Foundational Political Thought. Political Difference in Nancy, Lefort, Badiou and Laclau*. Edinburgh.

Rancière, Jacques, 1999: *Disagreement. Politics and Philosophy*. Minneapolis.

De Saussure, Ferdinand, 1977: *Course in General Linguistics*. Glasgow.

Stavrakakis, Yannis, 2007: *The Lacanian Left. Psychoanalysis, Theory, Politics*. Edinburgh.

Tosel, André, 2008: The Development of Marxism. From the End of Marxism-Leninism to a Thousand Marxisms – France, Italy, 1975-2005. In: Jacques Bidet and Eistache Kouvelakis (eds.): *Critical Companion to Contemporary Marxism*. Leiden and Boston, 39-78.

Wallerstein, Immanuel, 1991: *Unthinking Social Sciences. The Limits of Nineteenth-Century Paradigms*. Cambridge.

Žižek, Slavoj, 1992: *For They Know Not What They Do. Enjoyment as a political factor*. London and New York.

Žižek, Slavoj, 1999: *The Ticklish Subject. The Absent Center of Political Ontology*. London and New York.

Žižek, Slavoj, 2000: Class Struggle or Postmodernism? Yes, Please! In: Judith Butler, Ernesto Laclau and Slavoj Žižek (eds.): *Contingency, Hegemony, Universality. Contemporary Dialogues on the Left*. London and New York, 90-135.

Žižek, Slavoj, 2001: *On Belief*. London and New York.

Žižek, Slavoj, 2002a: Afterword: Lenin's Choice. In: Ibid (ed.), V.I. Lenin: *Revolution at the Gates. A Selection of Writings from February to October 1917*. London and New York, 167-336.

Žižek, Slavoj, 2002b: Foreword to the Second Edition: Enjoyment Within the Limits of Reason Alone. In: Ibid: *For They Know Not What They Do. Enjoyment as a Political Factor*. London and New York, xi-cvii.

Žižek, Slavoj, 2003a: *Organs without Bodies. Deleuze and Consequences*. London and New York.

Žižek, Slavoj, 2003b: *The Puppet and the Dwarf. The Perverse Core of Christianity*. Cambridge and London.

Žižek, Slavoj, 2004: *Iraq. The Borrowed Kettle*. London and New York.

Žižek, Slavoj, 2006: *The Parallax View*. Cambridge and London.

Žižek, Slavoj, 2007: Trotsky's *Terrorism and Communism*. Or: Despair and Utopia in the Turbulent Year of 1920. In: Ibid. (ed.), Trotsky, L.: *Terrorism and Communism*, vii-xxxii. London and New York.

Žižek, Slavoj, 2008: *In Defense of Lost Causes*. London and New York.

Žižek, Slavoj, 2009: *First as Tragedy, Then as Farce*. London and New York.

Žižek, Slavoj, 2011: *Living in the End Times*. London and New York.

Žižek, Slavoj, 2012a: *Less Than Nothing. Hegel and the Shadow of Dialectical Materialism*. London and New York.

Žižek, Slavoj, 2012b: *The Year of Dreaming Dangerously*. London and New York.

Žižek, Slavoj, 2014: *Absolute Recoil. Towards a New Foundation of Dialectical Materialism*. London and New York.

Žižek, Slavoj, and Glyn Daly, 2004: *Conversations with Žižek*. Cambridge.

Erik Vogt

The Philosophy and Politics of Slavoj Žižek

1. Introduction

Slavoj Žižek is one of the most prominent and controversial contemporary left-wing thinkers. His work aims on the one hand to articulate a radical critique of ideology, and on the other hand to re-invent the idea of communism. In doing so, his critique of ideology analyzes how ideologies function, in order to formulate a truly anti-capitalist strategy that goes beyond these ideologies. His writings on communism aim to give new meaning to central Marxist notions, such as class struggle, proletariat and the dictatorship of the proletariat. Through his appeal to 'reload' Lenin, Žižek aims to do nothing less than to place global revolution on the agenda of the radical left. Žižek's publications have reached a wide readership and have elicited time and again both intense criticism and approval. Because of this, his work is without doubt one of the most important contributions to contemporary radical emancipatory politics. This contribution aims to discuss and elucidate the two major strands of his thinking: his critique of ideology and his attempt to reload Lenin.

This contribution starts with a brief discussion of the central elements that make up Žižek's critique of ideology, which originates from a highly original mixture of Marxism and psychoanalysis. The concepts of (social) 'symptom' and 'fantasy' are crucial in this practice. A concise discussion of anti-Semitism illustrates the way in which Žižek's method works. Subsequently, I discuss Žižek's redefinition of class struggle and the Act, because Žižek's critique of ideology offers a means to analyze both historical and contemporary developments, while the concepts of class struggle and the Act offer ways to intervene.

According to Žižek, neither a multicultural politics of identity nor an adherence to liberal or radical conceptions of democracy can form the basis of a true anti-capitalist strategy. The chapters on multiculturalism and the fetish of (both liberal and radical) democracy reconstruct Žižek's thinking on both issues and show how they are interlinked. From these lines of reasoning, the contours of Žižek's politics become visible: one that reloads Lenin's politics and reinvents the idea of communism for the present era.

2. On Žižek's Biography

Slavoj Žižek was born on 21 March 1949 in Ljubljana, the capital of Slovenia. Between 1969 and 1981, he studied philosophy and sociology there, after which he moved to Paris to study psychoanalysis. In 1985, he returned to Ljubljana. At the beginning of his academic career, he was ignored and marginalized for his refusal to become a member of the communist party or to hold firm to the party line. For a brief period of time, he did join the party, but he left in 1988 to become active in several opposition movements. In 1990, he even ran for president, on the ticket of the liberal democratic party. He lost the elections, but instead was appointed as scientific ambassador for the Republic of Slovenia.

Since the 1990s, Žižek has held professorships at numerous universities in the United States, France, England and Germany. In 1992, he became professor of philosophy at the University of Ljubljana. From 2000 to 2002, he headed a research group at the institute for cultural sciences in Essen, and since 2005, he has been a member of the Slovenian Academy of Sciences and Arts. Furthermore, he heads the Society for Theoretical Psychoanalysis in Ljubljana. In addition to being a professor at the University of Ljubljana, he currently holds a professorship at the European Graduate School in Saas-Fee (Switzerland), and is international director of the Birkbeck Institute for the Humanities in London.

Slavoj Žižek has published more than seventy books, which were translated into numerous languages, and edits the book series *Analecta*, *Wo es war*, *SIC* and *Short Circuits*.

3. Critique of Ideology: Social Symptom, Fantasy and Anti-Semitism

The following chapter focuses on Žižek's critique of ideology, a method which he uses not only to analyze the essence and workings of ideology, but also to move beyond them. Žižek bases his method on a combination of Marxism and Lacanian psychoanalysis. The chapter starts with a discussion of how Žižek connects the Marxist concept of the fetishism of commodities with Lacan's elaborations on the fetishist denial. Through this discussion, concepts such as the (social) symptom and fantasy are explained. Finally, Žižek's analysis of anti-Semitism offers an illustration of his method.

Žižek's early elaborations on critiquing ideology stem from an original combination of Marxist and Lacanian concepts. Through this combination, Žižek aims to connect methods that explain social processes on the one hand and individual consciousness on the other, thus building on and at the same time deepening our understanding of Marx's fetishism of commodities.

Marx used the latter term to point out how inter-human relationships were mystified under capitalism. Under capitalism, social relations between humans are experienced as objective relations, for example, between employer and employee, between consumer and seller. People are reduced to the roles that they fulfil within society, while at the same time identifying to a high degree with these assigned roles. Because of this dynamic, social relations seem only all the more objective. Through the mystification of relations between people, larger social processes such as 'the economy' become an objective social power. The fetishism of commodities thus does not only inform inter-human relationships, but also society as a whole.

According to Žižek, the power of the fetishism has increased in the current stage of late capitalism, a term that he adopts from the Marxist economist Ernest Mandel and the cultural sociologist Fredric Jameson.[1] The term refers to the changes that capitalism has undergone since the 1970s. As industrial capital has been replaced by much more speculative and unstable financial capital, the borders between production, culture and private life are ever more obscured. This can be most clearly seen in the emergence of the 'knowledge economy', which has replaced industrial labor in many sectors. Scientists, call center employees, precarious workers in the culture and entertainment industries, and marketers all have to insert their creativity, their emotions and even identities in the labor process, where they become sources of surplus value. As a result, capitalist structures start invading the human psyche.

The aim of Žižek's method is to uncover how capitalism affects the individual psyche and analyze the dynamics between individual consciousness and social developments. In this attempt, he builds, among other things, on the work of the Marxist philosopher Alfred Sohn-Rethel (1899-1990). While Marx focused his analysis on social processes, Sohn-Rethel concentrated his efforts on assessing how these influenced the individual psyche. Being a member of the Frankfurt School, Sohn-Rethel premised his work on the fact that under capitalism products are made to be exchanged. As objects with use-value become products with (exchange) value, the value of the objects itself becomes a 'thing'; a process he termed *Realabstraktion*. In the case of an automobile, this means that a car transforms from a tool that helps to cover long distances over a brief period of time into a carrier of value. Both aspects

---

1   Mandel 1972; Jameson 1991.

of the car are just as 'real'. This process of turning objects into value gravely influences the unconscious of individuals.[2] It fundamentally changes the way in which we observe society. Because of this, the structure of human thinking can be deciphered by analyzing it from the perspective of commodity exchange, or, put otherwise, to properly understand individual consciousness, one must start with a proper analysis of capitalism.

An even more important source of influence for Žižek is the French psychoanalyst Jacques Lacan (1901-1981). While Marx concentrated his work on analyzing social developments, and Sohn-Rethel focused on how these processes influence individual consciousness, Lacan starts his analysis at the individual level. Žižek aims to combine these three viewpoints to construct an analytical framework that connects social developments and individual consciousness. From Lacan's work, Žižek adopts concepts such as fetishism and the fetishist denial, which in a fascinating way complement Marx's interpretation of the fetishism of commodities.

Just as the fetish of commodities mystifies inter-human relationships, the Lacanian concept of fetishism refers to a distortive process through which things are no longer seen for what they really are. Lacan's fetish refers to the situation in which an individual realizes in a traumatic way that his desires inherently stem from a deficit. As the individual searches for a symbolic replacement for this deficit (in the form of another object), the true cause of desire is not recognized and is, instead, linked to the presence of something else. Thus, someone who suffers from love sickness eats chocolate, while others respond to economic decline with increasing racist sentiments.

As an illustration of the above, one could say that fascist anti-Semitism (to which we will return later) pointed towards 'the Jew' as a fetish: the fascist image of the Jew served to draw attention away from class struggle, which was the true cause of 'deficit'; the true cause of social and political disruption. The latter was denied by fascism, which instead presented 'the Jew' as the real cause.

Žižek thus employs psychoanalytical concepts to explain social developments. Yet in doing so, he does not simply project individual psychological concepts onto social realities. Rather, one of the core concepts of Lacanian psychoanalysis is exactly that individual psychology is non-existent. Since individuals cannot be studied in isolation from other people or inter-human relations, Lacan saw himself not so much as a psychoanalyst but rather as a social philosopher, who always linked the individual to the social.[3]

---

2 Žižek 1989, 16-21.
3 Johnston 2010, 85-91.

The starting point of Žižek's critique of ideology is the notion that late capitalist society cannot be conceptualized as a coherent whole. Rather, society is torn by contradictions, the most important of which is class struggle, with the result that 'society' does not exist. Given society's torn and split nature, the concept of a coherent, inclusive whole is an idea, a construct.

Building on this notion, Žižek sees ideologies as attempts to artificially create a coherent society through the practice of exclusion. By excluding certain subjects, society creates itself into a closed and coherent whole. Fascist anti-Semitism worked in such a way. As fascism tried to create an organic society characterized by harmonious relations between all classes, 'the Jew' became the embodiment of everything that endangered such a society. By stating that Jews imported class struggle into society, the fascists suggested that class struggle could be eradicated by liquidating 'the Jew'. The regime presented society as a coherent and harmonious whole that was threatened from the outside by a clearly identifiable group. Excluding others is a means of trying to attain social totality and consistency, even if this result can never be achieved. In Žižek's terminology, the excluded groups are referred to as the social symptom, which refers to the fact that the excluded groups are not the source but rather the result of social conflict.

Žižek's critique of ideology, then, serves in the first place as a means of uncovering these mechanisms of exclusion and analyzing them. According to Žižek, the social symptom is thus an element that 'is necessary for that field [for instance, society] to achieve its closure, its accomplished form'.[4] Consistency is created through exclusion. However, this process can also be reversed. Žižek sets out to show that this consistent, harmonious whole is an illusion. The torn and split nature of society should, then, form the foundation of a new form of emancipatory politics. It is at this point that Žižek's approach moves from an analysis to a criticism of ideology. As the mechanisms of exclusion point out the sources of society's torn and split nature (since they show what society needs to exclude to attain a supposedly harmonious form), one could resist or even reverse this process and thus forward the social conflicts on which society is built. By revealing society's exclusive nature and subsequently resisting such exclusion, 'one necessarily includes a specific case which breaks its unity, lays open its falsity'.[5]

An example of this method is the critique of the so-called universal freedoms of bourgeois society. Seemingly, universal freedoms such as the freedom of speech, trade, the printed press and organization legitimize the liberal capitalist social order. However, it cannot only be easily shown that there are various opinions that cannot

---

4 Žižek 1989, 21.
5 Ibid.

be freely expressed; the so-called universal freedoms are in reality only enjoyed by a small elite that has the time, energy, financial means and security to use them. As the liberal public sphere explicitly suppresses political dissidence and implicitly excludes those who are economically dependent, the fault lines of the social order are revealed. Demands that this situation be changed have the potential to subvert the bourgeois capitalist order.

Žižek thus proposes a strategy that strikes out at the heart of the social order. Such a strategy is both highly potent and necessary, but Žižek does not hesitate to point out its limits, since ultimately it remains captured within the logic of exclusion and social symptoms. Žižek has repeatedly elaborated on how the strategy of revealing the exclusive nature of ideology often reinforces such mechanisms rather than abolishing them. In the case of fascist anti-Semitism, for example, many attempts at refuting its ideology were premised on pointing out other, 'real' causes for social disruption: the problem is not 'the Jews', but capitalism, or, in the case of bourgeois freedoms: the problem is not freedom, but social inequality. These strategies, however, merely lead to changes within the mechanism of exclusion. What is excluded changes, but the mechanism remains the same.[6]

Because of this, the method described is only one part of two complementary strategies. The first offers a strategy for critiquing ideology within the boundaries of the system, while the second offers a way to move beyond it. To do the latter, Žižek complements the concept of social symptom with Lacan's 'fantasy'.

Fantasy

Lacan introduced the concept of fantasy in opposition to the social symptom. In psychoanalysis, the symptom gives meaning to an original deficit (eating chocolate thus becomes a response to love sickness). The psychoanalyst can help a patient by explaining the nature of the symptom, so that the patient can ultimately be reconciled with the deficit. The belief, however, that every deficit can be articulated, explained and thus resolved is what Lacan calls the fantasy.

According to Lacan, every individual experiences traumas, emotions and longings that cannot be articulated and thus cannot be explained or reconciled. Lacan terms these non-articulable forms of enjoyment, longing and desire *Jouissance*. Attempts by the psychoanalyst to explain and reconcile these emotions are inherently limited, and therefore have the potential to question the position of the psychoana-

---

6   Ibid., 73-74.

lyst. They even have the potential to explode the frames of reference of the individual who is experiencing these emotions.[7]

A similar dynamic unfolds on a social level. Ideologies aim to resolve social problems by identifying a fundamental cause, explaining its effects and offering a solution (the exclusion of the social symptom). These attempts, however, are doomed to fail because on a social level too traumas and emotions exist that cannot be articulated. Since they resist interpretation, they cannot be reconciled. The misconception that ideologies can explain all societal wrongs and offer solutions to them is what Žižek calls the social fantasy. In a similar way as in psychoanalysis, the social fantasy has the potential to disempower ideologies and explode a society's frame of reference. Žižek builds on this line of reasoning to develop a true revolutionary strategy.

Anti-Semitism

If every social symptom is based on social fantasy, this must be taken into account in the practice of critiquing ideology. As a result, the latter should proceed following two subsequent steps. For Žižek, the first step is discursive. It revolves around 'the "symptomal reading" of the ideological text'.[8] Its goal is to show that ideologies refer to social symptoms instead of the real causes of social tensions and conflicts. The second step sets out to extract the core of enjoyment (*Jouissance*), to show how ideologies are based on and thus manipulate pre-ideological enjoyment.

The second step thus focuses on the fantasy. Žižek's goal is not to seek out another social symptom, but to reveal the dynamics that produce the symptom, so that the cycle can be broken. To Lacan, *Jouissance* was something that preluded ontology: since it could not be articulated or explained, it existed on a pre-conscious level. On a social level, *Jouissance* exists on a pre-ideological level and therefore has the potential to disrupt the fantasy. Žižek illustrates this method in his analysis of anti-Semitism.

For Žižek, anti-Semitism represents the paradigm of racist ideology. It sets out to 'define' 'the Jew' by means of 'over-determination'. In anti-Semitism, the Jew becomes the embodiment of various character traits that cannot logically be reconciled; 'the Jew' is regularly described as both 'dirty *and* intellectual, voluptuous *and* impo-

---

7 Lacan's definition of the fantasy is much more complex and encompassing. However, the scope and limited size of this contribution does not allow us to go into the topic much further, as we will focus on the influence of Lacan's ideas on Žižek's work. According to Lacan, the fantasy structures our desires and delimits them. Because of this, the fantasy operates ultimately as a safety barrier against desire itself. For more information on this, see Lacan 1966/67 and Widmer 1997.

8 Žižek 1989, 125.

tent', as 'capitalist *and* Bolshevik'.[9] Accordingly, 'the Jew' becomes a caricature of social antagonisms. If the mechanisms that produce this caricature are revealed, the process is, at least partially, undone.

The various character traits projected onto the image of 'the Jew' are merely externalizations of the conflicts unfolding within society. They serve to transform social conflicts into an apparent conflict between society on the one hand and 'the Jew' as an external, corrupt influence on the other hand. By doing so, they create the illusion that late capitalist society would be a harmonious whole if only this corrupting entity were removed. At the same time, 'the Jew' as the social symptom reveals society as an exclusionary entity, and since it shows what needs to be excluded from society to create an assumed whole, it points out where the fault lines of social conflict reside in class conflict created by capitalism.

The fantasy in which anti-Semitic ideology is grounded is the ideal of a harmonious and whole society. Since late capitalist society is unable to achieve such a state, the anti-Semitic construction of 'the Jew' becomes

> [T]he embodiment of a certain blockage – of the impossibility which prevents society from achieving its full identity as a closed, homogeneous totality. [...] Far from being the positive cause of social negativity, *the 'Jew' is a point at which social negativity as such assumes positive existence.*[10]

In other words, the anti-Semitic image of the Jew is not only a social symptom but also refers to something that cannot exist under late capitalism: a harmonious, coherent society. Žižek therefore concludes that 'we must recognize in the properties attributed to the "Jew" the necessary product of our very social system; we must recognize in the "excesses" attributed to "Jews" the truth about ourselves'.[11]

Conclusion

Žižek's critique of ideology presupposes that '(late capitalist) society' does not exist. Because society cannot become a closed whole, this state needs to be achieved through the exclusion of others. Because of this, two concepts become central in Žižek's method: the social symptom and social fantasy.

The social fantasy is the misconception that the conflicts within society can be explained, and its origin identified and therefore resolved, after which society reaches it true form: a harmonious whole. Ideology, then, becomes the power that seeks out an entity to which it connects all social tensions. The entity that supposedly disrupts social harmony is the social symptom. Under fascism, this symptom is 'the

---

9   Ibid.
10 Ibid., 127.
11 Ibid., 128.

44

Jew'. He becomes the source and embodiment of all social problems. For Žižek, anti-Semitism is the ultimate example of how the social fantasy works. The fantasy, however, not only forms the basis of anti-Semitism, but also – as will be discussed below – of postmodern multicultural identity politics and even certain orthodox Marxist visions of a harmonious communist society.

At the conclusion of his analysis, Žižek states that it does not suffice to include the social symptom within the social order. Such an act would leave the basic contours of the social order unchanged, and merely give way to the production of another social symptom. Instead, the social order needs to be disrupted and disjointed by a contradiction that can destabilize the social order as a whole. Žižek identifies this central contradiction as class struggle. This conclusion forms the bridge between his critique of ideology and his political program.

4. Class Struggle and the Act

According to Žižek, society is torn by class struggle to such an extent that it cannot be envisioned as a consistent whole. The only way for society to reach a state of social harmony and wholeness is by excluding parts of itself. Because of this, he terms society a 'non-whole'. This term makes explicit that there is nothing outside late capitalist society that could force a rupture or disrupt the status quo. Rather, the 'rupture' or 'catastrophe' – i.e. class struggle – is already inscribed into capitalism.

From this, Žižek concludes: 'If there is no outside or limit to capitalism, no objective breakdown or collapse, capitalism is also nothing, has no inside; the breakdown has already occurred'.[12] In a different context, he adds that the Marxist class struggle is 'the perfect example of what Lacan means by not-all, no exception but precisely for this reason you cannot totalize it'.[13]

The following section discusses Žižek's definition of class struggle and the Act. How does he define class struggle? Who are the ones who embody the proletariat; those who are inciting the class struggle? And how do individual actions relate to social context in this struggle?

Class Struggle

According to Žižek, class struggle is the central conflict that 'designates the very antagonism that prevents the objective (social) reality from constituting itself as a self-

---

12 Butler 2006, 206-9.
13 Žižek 2005, 73.

enclosed whole'.[14] Because of this, class struggle is not simply yet another social symptom. This view informs his definition of class struggle, the proletariat and the Act.

Early Marxists remained captured within the framework of phantasmatic mechanisms of exclusion. For them, the capitalist class or capitalism as an economic system embodied the social symptom. In doing so, they employed a sociological view of society, according to which the industrial workers were equated with the proletariat. Žižek steers away from these conceptualizations of capitalism and the proletariat, and instead proposes a new conceptualization of capitalism and class struggle. Instead of approaching class struggle as a social process, he defines it as a political struggle. One's position in the class struggle is not to be defined according to one's position in the production process, but instead on the basis of the extent to which one decides to resist capitalism. Žižek thus states:

> Every position we assume towards the class struggle, even a theoretical one, is already a moment of the class struggle. It involves taking sides in the class struggle, which is why there is no impartial objective standpoint enabling us to delineate class struggle [...] In this precise sense, we can say [...], that class struggle doesn't exist since there is no exception, no element eluding it.[15]

As a result, the industrial worker is no longer central in the class struggle:

> Although there is a link between the working class as a social group and the proletariat as the position of the militant fighting for universal Truth, this link is not a determined causal connection, and the two levels are to be strictly distinguished. To be proletarian involves assuming a certain subjective stance [...] that, in principle, can occur to any individual [...] any individual can be touched by grace and interpellated as a proletarian subject.[16]

Remaining loyal to class struggle means staying true to the collective struggle, seizing every 'symptomatic' point that marks the rifts within the late capitalist order and identifying with them. Only by focusing on the rifts that grow immanently from the system itself, and by identifying with those groups who are being excluded by the present social order, does one become able to mobilize oneself for what Žižek refers to as the Act: the moment in which the 'concrete universal' asserts itself and directly intervenes in the structures of late capitalism. Before we discuss the definition of the Act, we must focus our attention on the concrete universal.

---

14 Ibid., 263.
15 Žižek 2005, 73.
16 Žižek 2006, 199.

Žižek subscribes to the central claim of Marxism that there is one antagonism ('class struggle') which 'predominates over the rest'. Class struggle does not merely refer to the struggle of factory workers for better working conditions, it is the struggle against capitalism itself. It is not simply another social symptom, since only the Marxist notion of class struggle can reflect on the difference between the symbolic order – late capitalist liberal democratic society – and what is being excluded: 'Class antagonism certainly appears as one in the series of social antagonisms, but it is simultaneously the specific antagonism which "predominates over the rest, whose relations thus assign rank and influence to the others"'.[17]

In contrast to gender, race or cultural identity, class lays bare the contradiction that determines all the others. It supersedes the other conflicts within society, since identity politics aim at transforming antagonisms into differences, while class struggle seeks to transform antagonism into disruption and, ultimately, a radically different society. Therefore, class struggle determines the horizon on which present identity politics take shape. It structures the field in which various groups struggle for recognition. Every struggle is thus inscribed into class struggle and no conflict can withdraw itself from it.

Žižek accordingly defines the proletariat as the collection of those who remain committed to collective struggle, together with those who are most affected by social exclusion, since this is where the cracks in the system appear. The moment when groups start to identify with the 'wretched of the earth', their struggle not only gains a universal and humanist component, but also becomes loaded with an explosive power.

Society's deficit, its inability to reach a state of wholeness, is in a way rendered into something tangible through its production of excluded groups. By means of the identification of the social symptom, the inherently antagonistic character of late capitalist society is made visible. Because of this, the 'excesses' within a 'normally' functioning society must be made into the starting point of political intervention. Since these antagonisms cannot be resolved within the system, such a strategy has the potential to disrupt the social order as a whole.

It is for this reason that Žižek identifies 'the inhabitants of slums in the new megalopolises'. They are not only 'the "true" symptom of slogans such as "Development", "Modernization", and the "World Market" [...] a necessary product of the innermost logic of global capitalism', while many of their characteristics 'fit the good old Marxist determination of the proletarian revolutionary subject.'[18]

---

17 Bulter, Laclau and Žižek 2000, 320.
18 Žižek 2006, 268.

Žižek continues his argument by stating:

> [T]hey are 'free' in the double meaning of the word even more than the classic proletariat ('freed' from all substantial ties; dwelling in a free space, outside state police regulation); they are a large collective, forcibly thrown together, 'thrown' into a situation where they have to invent some mode of being-together, and simultaneously deprived of any support in traditional ways of life, in inherited religious or ethnic life-forms.[19]

It is not Žižek's intention to gloss over the 'decisive break' between the slum dwellers and the classic Marxist definition of the working class. Rather, he acknowledges the difference by stating that

> [W]hile the latter [the classical Marxist working class] is defined in the precise terms of economic 'exploitation' (the appropriation of surplus-value generated by the situation of having to sell one's labor-power as a commodity on the market), the defining feature of the slum-dwellers is socio-political, it concerns their (non-)integration into the legal space of citizenship with (most of) its incumbent rights – to put it in somewhat simplified terms, much more than a refugee, a slum-dweller is a homo sacer, the systematically generated 'living dead' of modern capitalism. The slum-dweller is a kind of negative of the refugee: a refugee from his own community [...] pushed into a space beyond control.[20]

In that sense, the slum dweller forms a category that exists partly within and partly outside capitalism.

The explosively growing number of slum dwellers, who are produced outside, at the fringes and even within the global capitalist order, provide a devastating statement on the failure of capital to transform any remainder into surplus. As the inhabitants of slums live as 'homo sacer', as the 'living dead', they illustrate how new forms of apartheid are based on the present dialectics of class.[21] It is exactly at the site of the slum where the fate of 'impossible' politics is being decided.[22]

Class struggle embodies the principle that Hegel laid out in the 'concrete universal'. In contrast to the 'abstract universal' – which is produced by abstracting from the concrete to ascertain what disparate parts have in common – the concrete universal remains true to individual particularities. The abstract universal concepts of mankind and book stand against the concrete universal concepts of man and book. The concrete universal does not possess a shared, uniform character. It has no distinct identity. Instead, it is at those points where society is torn and cracks emerge in the social order that (the possibility of) universality asserts itself. This universality is embodied by the proletariat.

---

19 Ibid., 269.
20 Ibid.
21 Vighi 2010, 21.
22 Žižek bases his statements on this topic on the excellent publications of Mike Davis (2007).

The Act

Žižek connects class struggle to the Act, which refers to those acts that subvert the symbolic order. An example is the Russian Revolution, after which 'nothing was as it was before'. The old ways of viewing and interpreting the world – the symbolic order – no longer functioned, with the result that a new symbolic order was required. The Act is thus a gesture that short-circuits and disrupts, that displaces the coordinates of the symbolic order. The Act targets the fault lines of society. It is at the cracks in the symbolic order that opportunities for politicization of the social order reside. These considerations lead Žižek to ask: 'Are we still able to commit the *act proper* [...]? Which social agent is, on account of its radical dislocation, today able to accomplish it?'[23]

His questions point at the relation between those who act and the context in which they are active. For Žižek, the point is that revolutionaries should free themselves from the illusion that revolution can only take place once the laws of societal development have created the objective opportunities for it. Revolution is not to be envisioned as the outcome of an objectivist logic of passing through various 'stages of history'. Rather than following the classic Marxist paradigm that states that all the conditions must be in place before revolution becomes a possibility, Žižek claims that these conditions are always already in place. Žižek maintains that 'the catastrophe' is unfolding within late capitalism, which leads him to conclude that class struggle – the Act that relocates the coordinates of the symbolic order – has already taken place. The point is merely to realize this and draw the ultimate conclusion from it.

Critique of Ideology and the Act.

In his discussion on revolution and the conditions which allow for a revolution, Žižek refers to the concept of repeating the past, a concept which links his critique of ideology to his definition of the Act. The goal of the critique of ideology is, after all, to assess the possibility of an Act that can disjoint the symbolic order.

In this context, Žižek refers to the Jewish Marxist philosopher Walter Benjamin, who also envisioned revolution as something that had always already been possible. In Žižek's words, the revolution 'represents an impossible moment of the *past* – a past which was never fully experienced as the present'.[24] Benjamin, just as Trotsky, envisioned the years after the First World War as a failed chance for a revolution. Accordingly, he interpreted the political crisis of the 1920s and 1930s as a result of

---

23 Žižek 2006, 118.
24 Žižek 2001, 334.

this failed movement. The opportunities for revolution are always present; only after an attempt to conduct a revolution, can it be assessed whether it was possible or not. Revolutionaries should not wait, but anticipate.

Žižek illustrates this point by referring to 'Lenin's choice'. For Žižek, Lenin's choice illustrates how the right circumstances for the Act can even be forced onto the symbolic order. Lenin's decision to incite a revolution was based on a 'premature' Act, which was forced onto the world. By people seizing a social symptom and exploiting it to the full, the 'right conditions' for a revolution were in fact created. In Lenin's strategy, the critique of ideology thus played a central role.

Žižek has been criticized repeatedly for his interpretation of the Act. Yet, his interpretation is in no way 'an "irrational" self-grounded gesture, a metaphysical free act cut off from all strategic considerations that locate it within a specific socio-political'.[25] Rather, Žižek aims to elucidate the relation between the Act and the social-political situation, because the Act is neither made possible by social political conditions, nor inserted into the present from a mysterious extra-societal field. Instead, the Act is possible through the unveiling of society's torn and inconsistent nature and the critique of all ideologies that respond to this situation as insufficient.

It has often been claimed that Žižek advocates a form of individualism through his proposal to repeat Lenin. This proposal would reduce the Russian Revolution to Lenin's Act alone.[26] In this way, Žižek would falsify history and not take full account of the complex of developments and events that brought about the revolution.[27] Žižek's definition of the Act should, however, not be interpreted as a violent and psychotic act of rendering the symbolic order inoperative. Rather, he sees the Act as the outcome of a continuous repetition of attempts to intervene in the impasse on which society is based.

Žižek is not concerned with individual acts of heroism, for he embeds his Act in the context of new collective forms of politics. According to him, interventions are only possible when the relation between socially excluded groups and (potentially) 'revolutionary collectives' is concrete and dialectical. Žižek therefore analyzes contemporary forms of political organization according to the extent in which they have the potential to become a 'proletarian subject'. Žižek's politics thus do not consist of cheap social romanticism, but of the realization of this potential through hard (theoretical) work and committed struggle.

Žižek's theory thus combines an appeal to universality and contingency (a possible but not necessary outcome per se of an action or process), which allows him to connect the concepts of a critique of ideology, class struggle and the Act and load them with a new and explosive philosophical political power. For Žižek, the claim

---

25 Žižek 2007, 238.
26 Sharpe and Boucher 2010, 226-9.
27 Robinson and Tormey 2005, 104.

that an Act cannot be reduced to objective circumstances means that these circumstances are always already present. The goal of his theory and method is not to assess if the objective conditions allow for radical change, but to show – through the critique of ideology – that society is torn and split, making it possible to Act and thus to disjoint the coordinates of the present symbolic order. The goal of his method is, thus, to identify the opportunities to Act and subvert the present order.

5. Critique of Multiculturalism

The torn and split nature of society informs Žižek's choice to break with the politics of (radical) democracy. According to Žižek, such politics is ultimately curtailed by multiculturalism, which for him is 1.) an agent of Capital, 2.) oscillates between politically neutralizing ethics of diversity and a new fundamentalist/terrorist form of racism, and 3.) blocks the road to a politics of truth, i.e. politics based on humanist universalism. Instead of being based on the principles that people have in common, multiculturalism focuses on issues that divide them. Ultimately, multiculturalism gets stuck in a politics of identity and recognition, which is exactly what Žižek tries to overcome.[28]

According to Žižek, multiculturalism is an agent of capital because it reinforces capitalist logic. It is not a coincidence that multiculturalism has come to reign supreme only in the era of late-capitalism. In fact, it has become a decisive factor in the triumph of global capitalism. Žižek acknowledges that multiculturalism has significantly contributed to the recognition of ethnic, sexual and other previously marginalized identities. Yet, at the same time, this development has strengthened the view that conflicts over identity can be resolved within the boundaries of capitalism. In the struggle for recognition by various groups, the capitalist order is rarely questioned.

All kinds of minorities (for instance, homosexuals, migrants, transsexuals) are formally accepted as long as they subject themselves to the capitalist system. As a result, the economy itself is left as a site for political struggle. Economic equalities are left untouched, as long as all sorts of identities are accepted within the capitalist system. Such politics thus furthers 'the acceptance of capitalist economic relations as the unquestionable framework'.[29]

---

28   Dean 2006, 115-119.
29   Žižek 2006, 174.

Upon closer examination, however, the tolerance at the heart of multiculturalism is actually 'a disavowed, inverted, self-referential form of racism'.[30] Although multiculturalism claims not to impose its own values upon other cultures, it nonetheless assumes a position from which it recognizes or disqualifies those cultures. Multicultural respect and tolerance for other cultures itself has become the essence of its superiority, while at the same time it looks down upon those cultures that have not yet reached such a state of development. Multiculturalism perpetuates colonialist attitudes when it distinguishes between natives and newcomers, while upholding the idea that the Other is, in its core, different.

For Žižek, the multicultural perspective mirrors the perspective of Capital in a diametrical way. For while multiculturalism concentrates on the supposed essence of Otherness, Capital focuses on its superficial appearance, seeking to extract surplus from marketed externalities which are presented as curiosities; 'pre-modern ecological wisdom, fascinating rites, and so on'.[31] At the end of the day, however, multiculturalism and Capital constitute two sides of the same coin, basing politics on essence and surplus extraction on the appearance of Otherness. In this way, the cultural imperialism inherent in multiculturalist politics constitutes the precise mirror image of global capitalism. Žižek summarizes his point when he writes:

> In the same way that global capitalism involves the paradox of colonization without the colonizing Nation-State metropole, multiculturalism involves patronizing Eurocentric distance and/or respect for local cultures without roots in one's own particular culture.[32]

... and racist intolerance

Multiculturalist tolerance soon reaches its limits, however, when the Other organizes his or her enjoyment (*Jouissance*) beyond the boundaries of the multicultural symbolic order. The populist attack on non-European (Muslim) migrants in Austria, for example was based on the accusation from its inception that they were on the one hand stealing 'Austrian enjoyment' (by threatening Austria's specific cultural and religious practices), while at the same time having supposed access to a secret kind of enjoyment which, from an 'Austrian' perspective, could only be characterized as 'perverse' and 'non-natural' (for instance, their religious practices or the way they organize relations between the sexes). At this point, the limits and hypocrisy of multiculturalist politics become obvious, for as soon as the Other is on the verge of in-

---

30 Žižek 1999, 216.
31 Ibid., 219.
32 Žižek 2006, 170-171.

fluencing our ways of life instead of the other way around, multiculturalist tolerance ends and feelings of superiority are given full reign. If push comes to shove, multiculturalism is not willing or able to deliver on its promise: namely acceptance of difference. In practice, the multiculturalist ideal of tolerance only addresses those who are already supposed to share similar outlooks on life and society. The Other, who does not share this ideal, all the same becomes a subject onto which racist fantasies are projected that render the Other as irrational, violent, uncivilized and as being obsessed by 'obscene' enjoyment.

Žižek mainly focuses his attention on the hatred towards the 'enjoyment' of the Other, since through such a focus (the hatred towards) our *own* enjoyment becomes visible. Accusations of the Other allegedly 'stealing our enjoyment' simultaneously bring out the Other of our own interiority into the open. Again, inner conflicts are externalized and projected upon others – conflicts which have their origin in the torn and split condition of society. Ironically, multiculturalism rejects the concept of all individuals and societies as being split. It recognizes the differences between cultures, but not the fissures and fault lines *within* cultures. Given this, it becomes ever more logical to view multiculturalism as the result of the increasing fissures and cracks within society's symbolic order.

According to Žižek, both multiculturalism and cultural racism operate according to the same logic, as both focus on the 'otherness' of non-European migrants. It is this fantasy of the non-European Other that supplies the negative basis for both racism and multiculturalism. For Žižek, the apparent opposition between the two must be considered as only a difference in degree. He furthermore notices that both ideologies foreclose the path to radical social change.

Multiculturalism obscures the logic of Capital and reduces conflicts (class struggle) to contention over the recognition of various cultural identities. Through these debates, however, both the differences and the inequalities among people are maintained.

As an alternative to multiculturalism, Žižek forwards class struggle and true solidarity with the wretched of the earth, those who are the worst hit by capitalism's excesses. Instead of multiculturalism's apparent focus on tolerance and dialogue, he claims that 'the only authentic communication' stems from 'solidarity in a common struggle'; a struggle that is based on the realization 'that the deadlock which hampers me is also the deadlock which hampers the Other'.[33]

---

33 Žižek 1999, 220.

In his critique of multiculturalism, Žižek builds, among other things, on the concept of *négritude* that was put forward by Franz Fanon (1925-1961) in the 1950s.[34] According to Fanon, *négritude* was first of all an essentialist acknowledgment of black self-identity, employed by blacks as a subversive reaction to racist colonialism. The problem of such an acknowledgment, however, lies in the fact that ultimately it is nothing more than the reversal of colonial racism. This is why Fanon argued that fixed identity claims should be dropped. Instead, he argued, the point is to acknowledge that cultural and racial identities are always fragile and that they are marked by an insurmountable split – an *inner* difference – which creates an openness towards the Universal. The goal should not be to acknowledge and accept one's identity, but to overcome it, and to find a new form of politics focused on humans as a universal category.[35]

In multiculturalist politics, however, cultural differences are not only left intact, but they are also deprived of their (potentially) subversive character, since the recognition of difference usually goes hand in hand with a legal discourse aimed at guaranteeing individual identities, i.e. avoiding discrimination, racist maltreatment and abuse (which is often conditioned by identification with the victim's identity). Identity politics therefore not only stimulates the establishment of an ever growing and more complex police apparatus, it also prevents genuine politicization.

For Žižek, multiculturalism and global capitalism form two sides of the same coin. Multiculturalism ultimately deprives difference of its potential to provoke, destabilize and even liberate, and instead renders difference a state where it is easily absorbed within global capitalism. Globalization, therefore, does not truly threaten local identities, as is often claimed. Rather, the Universal is threatened by globalization. While capitalism plays people off against one another, multiculturalism fosters the differences between people instead of pointing out their common interests.

6. Beyond Multiculturalism: Critique of Liberal Democracy

The observation that multiculturalism reinforces the position of capital, instead of weakening it, brings Žižek to the conclusion that the task of radical politics today is to link a critique of capitalism to a critique of liberal democracy. Since liberal democratic politics and late capitalist economics are inextricably linked, class struggle

---

34 'Négritude' is a French literary and philosophical movement that resisted French colonial racism and its intellectual hegemony, by fostering the self-consciousness of African people by emphasizing their common origin.

35 Fanon 1981, 263-267; Vogt 2011, 206-252.

must have both an economic and a political dimension. According to Žižek, the concept of liberal democracy must be called into question, precisely because it is so intimately connected with capitalist private property.

The most important opponent of general emancipation is therefore not only (or, at least, not directly) capital, but also liberal democracy. Žižek has repeatedly claimed that the struggle against late capitalism is critically limited or even blocked by the conviction that this struggle has to be fought in the liberal democratic arena. Again, such a way of doing 'politics' reduces social and political conflicts to a kind of difference that can be mediated within the boundaries of capitalism: namely parliamentary debates and attempts to find compromises.[36]

Debating Laclau

According to Žižek, liberal democracy is the dominant 'post-political' way of organizing consensus and governing the global capitalist order. The term 'post-politics' refers to the situation in which all significant political agents both subscribe to liberal democratic procedures and the logic of global capitalism, thus moving past the true political conflict, which revolves around the acceptance or rejection of capitalism (and, thus, liberal democracy). Radicalizing our understanding of democracy does not suffice to move beyond this deadlock. Ultimately, such a revised understanding will still remain captured within the principles of liberal democracy. This, then, is Žižek's central critique of the 'radical democracy' project that was developed by Ernesto Laclau.

Ernesto Laclau (1935) is an Argentine philosopher who received fame for his *Hegemony and Socialist Strategy* – authored with Chantal Mouffe – in which he argued for a strategy focused on achieving hegemony (a dominant role in the political sphere through a strong influence on common opinion) through political debate.[37] Initially, Žižek was strongly in favor of such a strategy, but in later years he distanced himself ever more from Laclau's strategy. In Žižek's critique of radical democracy, the contours of his own 'Leninist' politics become ever clearer.[38]

Laclau's strategy is premised on the idea that 'society' cannot be observed as an objective totality. Rather, the ways in which people view society are the result of political conflicts. Just like Žižek, Laclau thus claims that society is a construction, an idea. In this way, Laclau departs from essentialist approaches to society, which not

---

36 For Žižek's early criticism of democracy, which is still in line with Laclau's radical democracy, see: Dean 2006, 102–104.

37 Laclau and Mouffe 1985.

38 I repeat some of Dirk Jörke's remarks about radical democracy and hegemony. Jörke 2004, 168–169.

only form the basis of many orthodox Marxist theories, but also of liberal political theories.

According to Laclau, there is no direct link between social reality and our views or interpretations of society. Rather, ideologies explain the world: they supply an image of how society should be and why it is not like that. Fascism, for instance, sees the ideal society as harmonious and devoid of social conflicts, and identifies 'the Jew' as the reason why society has not reached such a state. According to Laclau, however, it is impossible to confront ideologies with social reality, and thus render the former inoperable, because the latter (social reality) is itself always already a construction. Therefore, the goal of political struggle should be to make its own ideology dominant (hegemonic). Politics is therefore above all a communicative process.[39]

The pursuit of hegemony is the main goal of Laclau's politics. His politics are post-Marxist since he departs from a traditional definition the working class as the primary revolutionary actor. An ideology based on the emancipatory potential of class struggle could become hegemonic, but does not have to become so, and is ultimately one ideology amongst others. Laclau's politics thus depart from class struggle to focus on political struggle; its focus lies on debate and dialogue, with the result that antagonism (class struggle) is transformed into agonism (political debate). Although Laclau is a socialist, he considers his theory to cover the general political process. For him, politics is always a fight for hegemony. At the same time, his theory is normative because, according to him, political conflict can only be hashed out through debate and dialogue.

Žižek has vehemently criticized Laclau's politics and theory, mainly because he argues that it is implicitly based on an acceptance of global capitalism. If the radical democratic project is 'anchored in the new structures of contemporary capitalism', as Laclau states, does that not imply that radical democracy is only possible in the contemporary (capitalist) situation'?[40] If this is the case, then it follows that Laclau's theory is not a general theory: '[it] explains why, today, "radical democracy" is the proper choice, while it also explains why in a different situation another choice would be more appropriate'.[41] Žižek's goal is not to find ways of doing politics within the framework of global capitalism, but to find ways to move beyond it.

Furthermore, Žižek criticizes the radical democracy project for not questioning the mechanisms of exclusion it purports. Laclau's concept of radical democracy transforms antagonism into mere agonistic struggles, that is, into a highly formalized processes of political debate and dialogue. Such politics excludes those who are not capable of debating politics in such a way from the political arena, as well as those

---

39 Butler 2006, 59-70.
40 Žižek 2003, 94.
41 Ibid.

who downright 'reject the democratic rules of the game'.[42] Žižek's main criticism of Laclau's strategy is based on the fact that 'the self-organization of the excluded is radically different from that of those whose identity is admitted into the "legitimate" social body'.[43]

Universality and the Democratic Trap

Žižek's critique is thus not so much directed at Laclau's strategy as such, but rather at its implied presuppositions. For Žižek, it lacks a proper anti-capitalist perspective and does not reflect on its exclusionary effects. Finally, Žižek takes Laclau to task for turning the impossibility of a coherent society (within global capitalism) into an imperative that is valid under all circumstance. It is this principle that informs Laclau's decision to focus on agonism and to keep antagonism at a distance – thus avoiding the 'totalitarian' temptation to instigate radical change. For Žižek, this signifies a lack of determination. While he concentrates his theoretical work on class struggle and the Act – i.e. strategies aiming at abolishing capitalism – Laclau limits himself to strategies of political struggle *within* the framework of capitalism.

In Žižek's view, Laclau's radical democracy project falls into the classic 'democratic trap':

> Many 'radical' leftists accept the legal logic of 'transcendental guarantee': they refer to 'democracy' as the ultimate guarantee of those who are aware that there is no guarantee. That is to say: [...] since every [political] act involves the risk of a contingent decision, nobody has the right to impose his or her choice onto others – which means that every collective choice has to be democratically legitimized. From this perspective, democracy is not so much the guarantee of the right choice as a kind of opportunistic insurance against possible failure [of political acts].[44]

To put it differently: in an abstract way, Laclau reduces politics to the regulation of competition between various ideologies, rather than allowing for struggle and the ultimate victory of one over the others.

Žižek refuses to put liberal democracy on a pedestal, if only because it is the formal political system of capitalism.[45] As part of his argument, he refers to the emergence of new forms of racism and fundamentalist violence *within* liberal democracy, for example through the rise of populist parties and governments, which leave the democratic system formally intact. For Žižek, this shows that liberal democracy and fundamentalism are not so much opposites, but rather share the same logic. Both

---

42 Ibid., 92.
43 Ibid., 91.
44 Ibid., 87.
45 Ibid., 87.

suppress, albeit in different way, real political struggle and emancipatory movements. Instead, militant movements fighting for universalism form the hallmark of
genuine politics.[46]

Chancing the leap beyond liberal democracy and capitalism, then, becomes the
primary concern in Žižek's politics. In an elucidating passage, he reflects on the
problem of democracy, Lenin's choice and the concept of going beyond democracy:

> The problem with democracy is that, the moment it is established as a positive formal
> system regulating the way a multitude of political subjects compete for power, it has to
> exclude some options as 'non-democratic', and this exclusion, this founding decision
> about who is included in and who is excluded from the field of democratic options, is not
> itself democratic. This is no mere matter of formal games with the paradoxes of metalan-
> guage, since, at this precise point, Marx's old insight remains fully valid: this inclusion/
> exclusion is overdetermined by the fundamental social antagonism ('class struggle'),
> which, for that very reason, cannot ever be adequately translated into the form of demo-
> cratic competition. The ultimate democratic illusion – and, simultaneously, the point at
> which the limitation of democracy becomes directly palpable – is that one can accom-
> plish social revolution painlessly, through 'peaceful means', by simply winning elec-
> tions. It is this illusion that is formalist in the strictest sense of the term: it abstracts from
> the concrete framework of social relations within which the democratic form is operative.
> Consequently, [...] one should nonetheless insist on the Marxist lesson [...] about politi-
> cal democracy's reliance on private property. In short, the problem with democracy is not
> that it is democracy but that it is a form of state power involving certain relationships of
> production. Marx's old notion of the 'dictatorship of the proletariat', reactualized by
> Lenin, points precisely in this direction, trying to provide an answer to the crucial
> question: what kind of power will there be after we take power?[47]

7. Dictatorship of the proletariat

Four Antagonisms

Žižek continually emphasizes the importance of developing a critique of political
economy, for only in this way can we conceive interventions that 're-politize' the
economy and aim radically at subjecting capitalist production processes to social
control. To do so, it is necessary to reveal the explosive contradictions on which
global capitalism is based. For Žižek, the only relevant question is:

> [D]o we endorse this 'naturalization' [i.e. depoliticization as described above in the con-
> text of multiculturalism] of capitalism, or does contemporary global capitalism contain
> antagonisms which are sufficiently strong to prevent its indefinite reproduction?[48]

---

46 Dean 2006, 95-105.
47 Žižek 2004, 180.
48 Žižek 2008, 421.

Žižek argues that there are four social antagonisms which threaten the survival of capitalism: ecological catastrophes, the conflict between (intellectual) property and the increasing digitalization of society, the tensions caused by new technological and scientific developments (first of all biogenetics and the capitalist appropriation of genetic data), and finally the emergence of new forms of social exclusion.[49] For Žižek, the most important antagonism, which forms the basis of the others, is the fourth one:

> [I]t is the antagonism between the Excluded and the Included which is the zero-level antagonism, coloring the entire terrain of struggle. Consequently, only those ecologists are Included who do not use ecology to legitimize the oppression of the 'polluting' poor, trying to discipline the Third World countries; only those critics of biogenetic practices who resist the conservative (religious-humanist) ideology which all too often sustains this critique; only those critics of intellectual private property who do not reduce the problem to a legalistic issue.[50]

Politicization of the Masses and of the Party

Žižek defines class struggle as picking up the struggle with the socially excluded, since their presence marks the fault lines in the capitalist order, while solidarizing with them lends the struggle a universalist and revolutionary character. The precondition for politics to be genuine is that they are based on this premise. For Žižek, the wretched of the earth are in the first place the slum dwellers: '[T]he "destructured" masses, poor and deprived of everything, situated in a non-proletarianized urban environment, constitute one of the principal horizons of the politics to come'.[51] They possess the potential to form social collectives that are capable of ending the global capitalist system. Only the politicization and organization of these masses can resist the dominance of global capital and its twin, multiculturalism.[52] Only in this context can one speak of (the repetition of) the idea of communism.

According to Žižek, the Leninist legacy has *not* yet been superseded. Rather, he claims that Leninist concepts such as the Party and the dictatorship of the proletariat must be repeated and reloaded, and thus become a relevant response to the present order.[53] For Žižek, 'politics without the organisational form of the party is politics without politics'.[54] Without a party, the revolts against capitalism remain limited to temporary uprisings. Only the kind of politics that takes the organisational form of a

---

49 Ibid., 421-424.
50 Ibid., 428.
51 Žižek 2008, 426.
52 Ibid., 425.
53 Žižek does not argue in favour of taking over the party structure. Rather, he subjects the old (Stalinist) idea of 'party' to radical criticism. See Žižek 2000, 102-108.
54 Žižek 2002, 132.

party is able to overcome the cycle of explosive situations, surpass the return to normality, and build up a new order against the global capitalist disorder.

Yet, Žižek's communism and communist politics differ on essential points from the Soviet politics of old. These differences are primarily linked to the role Žižek ascribes to the state. According to him, the Soviet state and its party politics failed because they were unable to revolutionize the bourgeois state. This failure led to the deformation of communist politics into bureaucratic rule and dictatorship. For Žižek, the failure of communism was 'above all and primarily the failure of anti-static politics'. What failed was the attempt 'to break out of the constraints of the State, to replace statal forms of organisation with "direct" non-representative forms of self-organization ("councils").'[55]

While historical communism tried to conquer the state, the state's main opponent now is capitalism: 'The focus on capitalism is crucial if we want to re-actualize the communist Idea: today's "worldless" dynamic capitalism radically changes the very coordinates of the communist struggle – the enemy is no longer the State to be undermined from its point of symptom torsion, but a flux of permanent self-revolutionizing'.[56] What Žižek points towards is the fact that late capitalism cannot be controlled or subjected by the state.

This new situation requires a new form of politics. Neither withdrawal from the state– the anarchist strategy, which aims at creating an ever larger rift between the state and the direct forms of political organization, – nor the simple struggle for state power and governmental structures suffice in the battle against global capitalism, since ultimately both strategies leave the state form untouched. Therefore, Žižek argues for a strategy which appropriates state power in order to transform its nature and apparatus: '[T]he goal of revolutionary violence is not to take over the State power, but to transform it, radically changing its functioning, its relation to its base'.[57]

As an example of such politics, Žižek referred in 2008 to the government of Hugo Chávez in Venezuela:

> The course on which Chavez embarked from 2006 is the exact opposite of the postmodern Left's mantra regarding de-territorialization, rejection of statist politics, and so on: far from 'resisting state power', he *grabbed* power (first by an attempted coup, then democratically), ruthlessly using the state apparatuses and interventions to promote his goals; furthermore, he is militarizing the favelas, organizing the training of armed units. And [...] now that he is feeling the economic effects of the 'resistance' to his rule by capital [...], he has announced the constitution of his own political party! Even some of his allies are skeptical about this move: does it signal a return to the politics of the party-state? However, one should fully endorse this risky choice: the task is to make this party func-

---

55 Žižek 2010a, 219.
56 Ibid.
57 Ibid., 220.

tion not like the usual (populist or liberal-parliamentary) party, but as a focus for the political mobilization of new forms of politics (like the grassroots communal committees).[58]

Dictatorship of the Proletariat and the Role of the Party

Žižek argues for a form of emancipatory politics that is premised on class struggle and the collective appropriation of the means of production. According to him, such politics requires a party and a dictatorship of the proletariat. Žižek, however, redefines these Leninist concepts and situates them in a new context to reload their revolutionary potential.

Žižek's dictatorship of the proletariat implies a radical reformation of the state based on new popular forms of participation. As examples, Žižek refers to the Morales government in Bolivia, the Maoist government in Nepal and the government of Chávez in Venezuela. These governments did not take power by force, but by 'fair' elections. However, this went hand in hand with massive mobilization of the population, with the result that once they were in power, their rule did not remain within the limits of state routine, and instead often acted beyond the limits of liberal democracy.

In all these examples, Žižek emphasizes the central role that institutional-organisational parties play in such mobilization, which aims at moving beyond liberal democracy and restricting the freedom of capital. Accordingly, political theorist Jodi Dean points out that in Žižek's texts, the party is no longer ascribed the role of leader, but of catalyst. It disjoints ideological coordinates and paralyses hegemonic ways of thinking, in order to act in such a way that allows for the development of new forms of society. The party is no longer the representative of the working class or the embodiment of objective historical developments, directing where society should go. Instead, it offers the proletariat a way out of capitalism. It is in this context that Žižek pleads with people to 'give a chance to the dictatorship of the proletariat' and to challenge liberal democracy.

In order to refute accusations of favoring new forms of totalitarianism, Žižek emphasizes that the terms 'democracy' and 'dictatorship of the proletariat' are for him merely '*formal* concepts'. In doing so, Žižek cites Lenin, who characterized (liberal) democracy as bourgeois dictatorship, as dictatorship of the bourgeoisie. Or, more precisely put: 'What he [Lenin] meant is that the very *form* of the bourgeois-democratic state, the sovereignty of its power in its ideologico-political presuppositions, embodies a "bourgeois" logic.'[59] Žižek deems liberal democracy 'a form of dictator-

---

58 Žižek 2008, 427.
59 Žižek 2008, 412.

ship' because in its institutional form it represents 'the excess of state representation over what it represents'[60] This is to say that the dictatorial side of democracy is 'palpable when the struggle turns into the struggle about the field of struggle itself'.[61] Žižek quotes Walter Benjamin, who writes: 'while democracy can more or less eliminate constituted violence, it still has to rely continuously on constitutive violence.'[62] Both liberal democratic and dictatorial state forms suffer from a democratic deficit and rely on force to uphold their order.[63] But while democracy also has dictatorial characteristics, the dictatorship of the proletariat, too, has its origin in a 'democratic explosion'.[64]

The Democratic Explosion

For Žižek, the 'dictatorship of the proletariat' does not describe a state form in which the proletariat would be the (new) ruling class. Instead, the term 'dictatorship of the proletariat' stands for 'the tremulous moment when the complex web of representations is suspended due to the direct intrusion of universality into the political field'. And he continues: 'From ancient Greece, we have a name for that intrusion: democracy', which leads him to conclude that

> [T]he 'dictatorship of the proletariat' is another name for the violence of the democratic explosion itself. The 'dictatorship of the proletariat' is thus the zero-level at which the difference between legitimate and illegitimate state power is suspended, in other words, when state power as such is illegitimate.[65]

In Žižek's terminology, the 'dictatorship of the proletariat' is the moment in which the existing representational structures are neutralized by the *demos*, i.e. by those who present themselves as excluded from social totality and who, for that reason, represent its very totality, and thus intervene directly in the political field. Žižek's reconnection of the terms democracy and dictatorship with *demos* is meant to solve the problem of democracy becoming immune to its own egalitarian-'terroristic' logic. Democracy always disrupts the social order in an explosive way, after which it becomes institutionalized in the shape of liberal democracy, after which the antagonism which stood at the heart of the democratic explosion is suppressed. This is why liberal democracy, according to Žižek, 'cannot reach beyond pragmatic utilitarian inertia, it cannot suspend the logic of the "servicing of goods" (*service des biens*)'.[66]

---

60 Ibid.
61 Ibid.
62 Ibid.
63 Žižek 2009, 240.
64 Žižek 2008, 416.
65 Ibid.; Žižek's italics.
66 Ibid., 378.

Proponents of radical democracy claim that under democracy there is no longer a substantial authority or actor who, in an *a priori* way, could rightly claim the center of power. Žižek disagrees in that he states: 'We still have a "Big Other" in the guise of this empty form itself, of a neutral frame [...] which guarantees the translation of antagonism into agonisms – political struggles in a democracy never reach the level of radical antagonism'.[67] For Žižek, the 'dictatorship of the proletariat' is the solution for a form of emancipatory politics attempting 'to reintroduce into this democratic field the radical antagonism'.[68] It stands for politics that recognizes neither a substantial nor a formal Other. From the perspective of the problem of power, this means that the 'dictatorship of the proletariat', the 'totalitarian excess', is 'on the side of the "part of no part", not on the side of the hierarchical social order'.[69] The dictatorship of the proletariat does claim the center of power in an a priori way, but in doing so places itself in a historical tradition of democratic movements, while solidarizing with the wretched of the earth.

The dictatorship of the proletariat, therefore, implies not only new state forms but also a new social order:

> [T]o put it bluntly, ultimately, the people are in power in the full sovereign sense of the term, in other words, it is not only that their representatives temporarily occupy the empty place of power, but, much more radically, they "twist" the very space of state representation in their direction.[70]

As an example, Žižek refers to the October Revolution:

> [T]he revolution stabilized itself into a new social order, a new world was created and miraculously survived for decades, amid unthinkable economic and military pressure and isolation [...] Against all hierarchical orders, egalitarian universality directly came to power.[71]

8. By way of conclusion

Since the late 1980s, Žižek has presented himself as a radical political thinker whose first aim is to lend a new explosive force to contemporary philosophy, so that it can inform genuine emancipatory politics. He does so by combining a Marxist critique of political economy with (Lacanian) psychoanalysis. According to Žižek, the current post-political state of late capitalism does not indicate that emancipatory politics and class struggle have become insignificant or superseded concepts. Rather, his cri-

---

67 Žižek 2010, 392.
68 Ibid., 393.
69 Žižek 2008, 379.
70 Ibid.
71 Žižek 2010a, 217.

tique of global capitalism stems from a universalist commitment to a form of politics that solidarizes with the wretched of the earth as a way to end the rule of global capitalism. As he reinterprets Leninist concepts of the party and the dictatorship of the proletariat, he does not simply reproduce old leftist dogmas. Instead, he places them in a new context to reload their revolutionary potential. The reloading of Leninist politics is about favoring new forms of organization and new forms of politics, the characteristics of which still have to be determined. In a dialogue with activists of the Occupy movement, Žižek declared:

> There is a long road ahead, and soon we will have to address the truly difficult questions – not questions of what we do not want, but about what we *do* want. What social organization can replace the existing capitalism? What type of new leaders do we need?[72]

This chapter was originally published in German in: Bart van der Steen et al (eds.), *Linke Philosophie Heute. Eine Einführung zu Judith Butler, Antonio Negri und Slavoj Žižek* (Schmetterling: Stuttgart, 2012).
We thank the publisher for their permission to publish a translated version of the chapter in this volume.
Translation by Bart van der Steen and Marc de Kesel.

References

Butler, Rex, 2006: *Slavoj Žižek zur Einführung*. Hamburg.

Butler, Judith, Ernesto Laclau and Slavoj Žižek, 2000: *Contingency, Hegemony, Universality. Contempory Dialogues on the Left*. London and New York.

Davis, Mike, 2007: *Planet of Slums*. London and New York.

Dean, Jodi, 2006: *Žižek's Politics*. London and New York.

Fanon, Frantz, 1981: *Die Verdammten dieser Erde*. Frankfurt am Main.

Jameson, Fredric, 1991: *Postmodernism. Or: The Cultural Logic of Late Capitalism*. Durham (NC).

Johnston, Adrian, 2010: *Badiou, Žižek, and Political Transformations. The Cadence of Change*. (Evanston (Ill.).

Jörke, Dirk, 2004: Die Agonalität des Demokratischen: Chantal Mouffe. In: Oliver Flügel et al. (eds.), *Die Rückkehr des Politischen. Demokratietheorien heute*. Darmstadt, 164-184.

Lacan, Jacques, 1966/1967: *Livre XIV. La Logique du Fantasme*. Paris.

Laclau, Ernesto and Chantal Mouffe, 1985: *Hegemony and Socialist Strategy. Towards a Radical Democratic Politics*. London.

---

72 Žižek 2011.

Mandel, Ernest, 1972: *Der Spätkapitalismus. Versuch einer marxistischen Erklärung*. Frankfurt am Main.

Robinson, Andrew and Simon Tormey (2005), A Ticklish Subject? Žižek and the Future of the Left. In: *Thesis Eleven* 80, 94-107.

Sharpe, Matthew and Geoff Boucher, 2010: *Žižek and Politics. A Critical Introduction*. Edinburgh.

Vighi, Fabia, 2010: *On Žižek's Dialectics. Surplus, Subtraction, Sublimation*. London and New York.

Vogt, Erik, 2011: *Slavoj Žižek und die Gegenwartsphilosophie*. Vienna and Berlin.

Widmer, Peter, 1997: *Subversion des Begehrens. Eine Einführung in Jacques Lacans Werk*. Vienna.

Žižek, Slavoj, 1989: *The Sublime Object of Ideology*. London and New York.

Žižek, Slavoj, 1999, *The Ticklish Subject. The Absent Center of Political Ontology*. London and New York.

Žižek, Slavoj, 2000, *The Fragile Absolute. Or: Why the Christian Legacy is Worth Fighting for*. London and New York.

Žižek, Slavoj, 2001, *Did Somebody Say Totalitarianism? Five Interventions in the (Mis)Use of a*

Notion. London and New/York.

Žižek, Slavoj, 2002: *Die Revolution steht bevor. Dreizehn Versuche über Lenin*. Frankfurt am Main.

Žižek, Slavoj, 2003: *Iraq. The Borrowed Kettle*. London and New York.

Žižek, Slavoj, 2004: From Purification to Subtraction: Badiou and the Real. In: Peter Hallward, (ed.), *Think Again. Alain Badiou and the Future of Philosophy*. London/New York, 165-181.

Žižek, Slavoj, 2005: *Interrogating the Real*. London and New York.

Žižek, Slavoj, 2006: *The Universal Exception*. London and New York.

Žižek, Slavoj, 2007: Afterword: With Defenders like These, Who needs Attackers? In: Paul Bowman and Richard Stamp (eds.), *The Truth of Žižek*. London and New York, 197-255.

Žižek, Slavoj, 2008: *In Defence of Lost Causes*, London and New York.

Žižek, Slavoj, 2010: *Living in the End Times*. London and New York.

Žižek, Slavoj, 2010a: How to Begin from the Beginning. In: Costas Douzinas and Slavoj Žižek (eds.), *The Idea of Communism*. London and New York, 209-226.

Žižek, Slavoj, 2011: Occupy first. Demands come later. In: *The Guardian*, 26 October 2011 https://www.theguardian.com/commentisfree/2011/oct/26/occupy-protesters-bill-clinton

Sina Talachian

The Normative Structure of Žižek's Leninist Project

Introduction*

Slavoj Žižek's project of reviving a Leninist strain in Marxian and more broadly radical political thinking contains an explicit critique of reformism, and those who are skeptical about an externally derived normative conception of emancipatory praxis.[1] For Žižek, the latter view negates the necessity or even possibility of revolution of an emancipatory kind, a staple of classical Marxist theory and praxis embodied by arguably its most influential theorists, Lenin and Mao – figures whom Žižek has written admiringly about for exactly this reason.[2] According to Žižek, they understood, as we should now, that it is not the notion of a revolution that is utopian, but rather the belief in the durability of the bourgeois democratic state and the capitalist system that sustains it. As he says:

> The ultimate answer to the criticism that radical Left proposals are utopian should thus be that, today, the true utopia is the belief that the present liberal-democratic capitalist consensus can go on indefinitely, without radical change. We are therefore back with the old '68 slogan *'Soyons réalistes, demandons l'impossible!'*: in order to be a true 'realist', we must consider breaking out of the constraints of what appears 'possible' (or, as we usually put it, 'feasible').[3]

Renewing the radical Left's belief in the possibility, or rather the absolute *necessity*, of revolution rather than reform is the first key element of Žižek's project of reviving Leninism. As such, Žižek places himself in a long tradition of radical Left thinking that goes back to well before Rosa Luxemburg's famed pamphlet on the subject.[4] The second key element emanates from the first, and concerns Žižek's understanding of what he defines as the 'liberal Left' and at times simply 'the Left', which he ties to reformism.[5] It is a 'sad predicament of today's Left', Žižek laments, that the latter have accepted the 'Cultural Wars (feminist, gay, antiracist, etc., multiculturalist struggles) as the dominant terrain of emancipatory politics', while what is

* I am grateful for helpful comments provided on earlier versions of this text by the editors of this volume, Bart van der Steen and Marc de Kesel, as well as Titus Stahl and Sergio Mariscal.
1 Žižek 2002b, 299.
2 Žižek 2002a; 2007a.
3 Žižek 2002b, 302.
4 Luxemburg 1973.
5 Žižek 2002b, 308.

needed is 'conceiving of capitalism neither as a solution nor as one of the problems, but as *the* problem itself'.[6] For Žižek, any rejection of his particular conception of revolution automatically condemns one to the category of reformism. Any other emancipatory praxis is defective as a consequence of positing 'culture' as the 'dominant terrain' on which to act.[7]

Žižek's project of reviving Leninism thus relies on an implicit normative standpoint in two respects. It defends the necessity of revolution as opposed to reform, and it upholds a distinctly class and economics-focused Leninist understanding of the emancipatory political praxis that is required to realize it. As Žižek says, 'today, more than ever, we should return to Lenin: yes, the economy is the key domain, the battle will be decided there.'[8] Such a project negates the contextual specificities that various emancipatory struggles involve, as well as alternative understandings of class and the social/cultural sphere which are forwarded by advocates of, for example, intersectionality theory.[9] Moreover, as should be obvious, the adoption of such a Leninist perspective is not empirically given or imposed by the existing social and political constellation. Rather, it is a normative choice, one that is justified by normative arguments that reveal the exact nature of the sources of normativity that Žižek draws upon to get his Leninist revival project off the ground. The project relies on two central claims: 1) that there is some notion of post-capitalism that can serve as the normative basis of emancipatory political praxis, and 2) that such praxis ought to adopt a Leninist perspective which focuses on economics if it is to be *truly* emancipatory rather than defective in some crucial way.[10] My aim in this essay is to critically investigate these two central claims which undergird Žižek's project of reviving Leninism. In the process, I intend to uncover the specific mode of emancipatory political praxis it embodies – one that is *external* rather than *immanent*. I will subsequently contrast this external mode with the immanent mode of social critique, which is practiced by those working in the tradition of the Frankfurt School of critical theory, thereby revealing the flaws of the former.

The sources of normativity underlying Žižek's project relate to distinctive conceptions of the state and revolution. To draw out the political significance of Žižek's normativity, it is useful to provide a brief historical overview of the immanent and external modes of political theory and praxis within the Marxian tradition. The externality of normativity can be traced back to Kautsky's distinction between trade

6   Ibid.
7   Žižek 2007b, 77-78.
8   Žižek 2002a, 7-8. See also: Žižek 2002b, 308.
9   See: Keucheyan 2013, 187-188; Honneth 2007, though there are many disagreements among adherents of intersectionality theory, and the approach remains – like Žižek's Leninist view of class and capitalism –essentially contested. For an excellent overview of the approach and some of these disagreements see: McCall 2005.
10   Žižek 2002b, 308.

union and class consciousness, which Lenin adopted.[11] According to this view, class consciousness was only accessible to Marxist intellectuals who had been organized in the vanguard Party of the proletariat.[12] Through their privileged access to this external space, which then contained the proper emancipatory sources of normativity, the Marxist intellectuals could introduce it to the working class 'from without'. This externalist model saw its worst excesses under Stalinism, when the privileged access to normativity was employed as the justification to enact all sorts of repressive, anti-emancipatory policies – all in the name of realizing emancipation.[13] This contrasts sharply with immanent models of political praxis that can also be found in the Marxian tradition, like the council communist, as developed by Anton Pannekoek. Rather than carving out a privileged space for the Marxist intelligentsia and ascribing only epistemically inferior, spontaneous trade union consciousness to workers, Pannekoek located the source of normativity *within them*, in accordance with the credo that the emancipation of the working classes must be conquered by the working classes themselves.[14] The distinction between external and immanent modes of political praxis thus has a long history, and its political significance is crucial, which is why I am interested in analyzing the normative structure of Žižek's Leninist project.

Before I proceed with the investigation, a clarification of a key concept and a brief note on method are necessary. The concept concerns that of 'the emancipatory'. Its basic, 'thinly' defined version provides the shared normative standard which I employ to conduct my critical investigation of the normative structure underlying Žižek's Leninist project. By emancipation I mean the normative ideal that encompasses what Žižek and the broader radical (Marxian) Left is normatively committed to, and hence underlies its political praxis. The normative ideal of emancipation in its basic form is succinctly captured in Horkheimer's classic description of the distinction between traditional and critical theory: A critical theory 'serves a practical purpose', seeking human 'emancipation from slavery', acting as a 'liberating [...] influence', and working 'to create a world which satisfies the needs and powers' of human beings.[15] This 'thin' conception of our shared emancipatory normative commitments is 'thickened' in our fleshed out conceptions of the proper kind of emancipatory praxis to pursue, as in Žižek's Leninist project. My aim in this essay is to investigate whether the 'thick' normativity contained in Žižek's Leninism infringes on the 'thin' standards that underlie emancipatory praxis, thereby negating the project's

---

11 Lih/Lenin 2006, 120.
12 The distinction is drawn by Lenin in his *What is to be Done?*, though it should be noted that Lenin was relying primarily on Kautsky in doing so and its significance was not as strong as some interpreters have claimed. See: Lih/Lenin 2006, 19-20; 613-614.
13 Habermas 1973, 36, 197.
14 Pannekoek 2003, 149-152.
15 See Horkheimer 1972, 246; Bohman 2015. This ideal is traceable to Marx. See: Celikates 2011.

pretensions to emancipation by carrying anti-emancipatory elements and implications. I believe this to be case, which problematizes the value of adopting Žižek's model for emancipatory praxis in the present. My investigation, which leads to this conclusion, begins by locating the sources and nature of the normativity underlying Žižek's project, which I do in the first section. In the second, I scrutinize these sources of normativity and reveal their anti-emancipatory implications. I conclude with a brief discussion of the alternative, *immanent* modes of political praxis.

Now for the brief note on method. One of the many challenges facing a proper critical analysis of Žižek's work is his, at times, admirable and, at other times, frustrating insistence on eschewing traditional norms of academia. This relates in particular to norms generally adhered to in the 'analytic' tradition of philosophy, which are summed up as at least a nominal insistence on clarity of style, coherence and consistency of argument.[16] In my view, such a conception of philosophy and academia more broadly is often overly and needlessly restrictive, often excluding ways of thinking that are valuable in their own right, and capable of carrying important, crucial insights concerning the subjects they address. This is one reason to admire Žižek's work. At the same time, his refusal to adhere to generally proscribed norms is also the source of much frustration. It is not uncommon that an argument contained in one text is presented in a different and contradictory fashion in another – or even in another section of the same text. John Gray, an interminable critic of Žižek's work, has lamented the difficulty of grasping hold of him given his 'inordinate prolixity, the stream of texts that no one could read in their entirety, if only because the torrent never ceases flowing'.[17] Žižek recently got into a public spat with Chomsky over similar issues.[18] This methodological note is meant to clarify – in accordance with some of the aforementioned analytic norms that I feel bound by – that in this critical investigation of Žižek's project of reviving Leninism I do not aim to exhaust the totality of Žižek's views on the various topics discussed as part of that project. Rather, I aim to locate, clarify and critique the externalist normative structure that underlies the project by contrasting it with the immanent structure underlying contemporary Frankfurt School critical theory, which in my view contains a superior 'Marxian' account of the normative sources of emancipatory political praxis that elides what I see as fatal flaws contained in Žižek's.[19]

---

16 Beany 2013.
17 Gray 2012.
18 Thompson 2013.
19 I use the term 'Marxian' to denote the broadly post-foundational thinking in the tradition as represented by the likes of Laclau, Mouffe and Castoriadis, whereas I reserve the term 'Marxist' for its foundationalist aspects. Žižek represents an interesting case in this context of use. He is certainly not foundationalist in the classical sense in many of his writings – most notably being critical of foundationalist epistemology and ontology in his theory of ideology – yet his project of reviving Leninism bears the marks of a foundationalist logic and conceptual structure.

The Ambiguity of Žižek's Post-Capitalism as an External Source of Normativity

The emancipatory political praxis proposed by Žižek represents a particular mode of social critique. Several modes of such a praxis can be distinguished, the most relevant for the purposes of this essay being the immanent and external ones.[20] Each of these possesses a distinctive normative structure, with a particular ontology, epistemology and conception of normative justification or reflexivity emanating from it.[21] As Stahl explains,

> [...] any theory, which attempts to draw on normative standards within objective social reality [...] must solve three distinct problems. First [...] [it] must plausibly explain the sense in which such immanent standards 'exist'. [...] Second, even given a justification for the assumption of immanent norms on the level of social ontology, it is unclear what type of epistemic access social critics have to the relevant normative potentials immanent to social reality. Third, and finally, it is an open question as to what kind of critical authority an immanent critique that draws upon them can aspire to.[22]

While the description refers to the immanent mode of political praxis or critique in particular, the same three elements underlie the external mode,[23] of which Žižek's Leninist project is an exemplification. In Žižek's project there is no room for the immanent mode, as it is perceived as being intrinsically defective because it stays within the purview of present-day capitalist society, from which it seeks to derive its sources of normativity. By doing so, for Žižek it becomes mortally infected by present society's dominant norms and standards, collapsing into utopian reformism.[24] In order to revive the belief in the absolute necessity of revolution, following in the footsteps of the likes of Lenin and Mao, Žižek's project has to accept the legitimacy of an *external* reference-point from which to draw the normative standards of its emancipatory praxis – one that by virtue of its externality remains untainted by the norms of present-day liberal-democratic capitalist society.[25]

Žižek is generally seen as a theorist of the event. Such events are disclosive, opening up avenues that were unimaginable or thought closed off by the liberal-democratic capitalist consensus. However, it is unclear exactly what type of event

---

20 Stahl 2013a, 2-3. The other is the internal mode, which derives its sources of normativity from present-day society but in an uncritical way, without appeal to the emancipatory elements that reside in it. For a detailed discussion see Stahl 2013a, 6-7.
21 Stahl 2013b, 534.
22 Ibid.
23 Though each element differs with respect to its particular conceptual configuration in relation to the mode concerned. So it is that immanent critique and praxis rely on a *social* ontology, wherein the sources of normativity are posited to be contained in a given community, whereas external critique and praxis lacks this by virtue of its reliance on an external reference point as the source of normativity.
24 Žižek 2009a, 74-75, 77-79.
25 Žižek 2002b, 302.

Žižek has in mind when he appeals to it as the potential source of emancipatory praxis and normativity. He has referred to the Green and Occupy movements, the Arab Spring and simply 'the New' as candidates for such events.[26] The source of his normativity is thus contained in the future, Utopian potentiality that resides in such revolutionary events. If they fail to materialize, they are mere *events-in-themselves*, useless passions that need to transform into *events-for-themselves* in order to be truly revolutionary. What this means concretely for Žižek – and this is where the Leninist revivalism can be seen most clearly – is that the contingent, unstable, fleeting event has to be stabilized and regularized in some way, turned into a realized passion.[27] We only know of two successful instances of this happening in the modern era: the Russian and Chinese Revolutions. As St. Paul stabilized the Christ-event by forming the stable and lasting structures of the Church – thus giving life to Christ's teachings – so Lenin and Mao stabilized their respective Revolutionary Events by forming the stable (at least for a considerable period of time) structures of the Soviet and Maoist states – thus giving life to Marx's eleventh thesis, which states: 'The philosophers have only interpreted the world in various ways; the point is to change it.'[28] It is therefore no wonder that Žižek so often harkens back to the memory of 'really existing socialisms' and their ideological and political originators when he confronts the utopianism of reformism, and counters it with a call for a renewed *revolutionary utopianism*.[29]

There are, however, significant problems with this particular definition of revolutionary events and the political praxis that emanates from it. The notion itself is not particularly novel, but rather derived from the Leninist and more broadly classical Marxist understanding of the proletariat as a class, and its enacting of revolution as the culmination of class struggle, which aims to transcend its being as such. This process is also known as the transformation of the proletariat as a class-*in-itself* – when it is beholden to the liberal-democratic capitalist consensus – to a class-*for-itself*, when it breaks free from these constraints and, in the Leninist and classical Marxist model, obtains class as opposed to false consciousness.[30] In another context, Žižek describes this as moving from the particular to the universal, which is concomitant with the stabilization of the revolutionary event and the class-for-itself that has been realized within and through it.[31] The progression of the one to the other, the inferior to the superior, is perceived as a veritable ontological promotion.[32]

26 Žižek 2008a, 270-71; Žižek 2012, 88.
27 Žižek 1999, 236.
28 Marx 1976, 5. See: Žižek 2002b, 191; Žižek 2007a, 2.
29 Žižek 2009a, 216-19; Žižek 2002b, 3-4.
30 Žižek 2007a, 58; Žižek 2009a, 12.
31 Žižek 2008b, 152.
32 Bourdieu 1985, 726.

This definition of the event, which undergirds Žižek's Leninist conception of political praxis, is ridden with either determinist or voluntarist assumptions that reveal the problematic nature of his reliance on an external source of normativity as a justificatory mechanism (the future, Utopian, as yet unrealized post-capitalist realm of the *for-itself*). Bourdieu offered a concise diagnosis of the Leninist class-in-itself/for-itself structure and the fatal lacuna that lies at the heart of it, which applies to the Žižekian event as well and so is worth quoting at some length:

> More often than not, Marxism either summarily identifies constructed class with real class (in other words, as Marx complained about Hegel, it confuses the things of logic with the logic of things); or, when it does make the distinction, with the opposition between 'class-in-itself', defined in terms of a set of objective conditions, and 'class-for-itself', based on subjective factors, it described the movement from one to the other (which is always celebrated as nothing less than an ontological promotion) in terms of a logic that is either totally determinist or totally voluntarist. In the former case, the transition is seen as a logical, mechanical, or organic necessity (the transformation of the proletariat from class-in-itself to class-for-itself is presented as an inevitable effect of time, of the 'maturing of the objective conditions'); in the latter case, it is seen as the effect of an 'awakening of consciousness' (*prise de conscience*) conceived as a 'taking cognizance' (*prise de connaissance*) of theory, performed under the enlightened guidance of the Party. In all cases, there is no mention of the mysterious alchemy whereby a 'group in struggle,' a personalized collective, a historical agent assigning itself its own ends, arises from the objective economic conditions.[33]

As shall be seen in the following section, the reductive economic determinism described (albeit it 'in the last analysis') also seeps into Žižek's Leninist project, emanating from its externalist normative structure. Returning to the event that is at the core of Žižek's Leninism; the realm of the *for-itself* is left normatively underdetermined. Žižek wishes to maintain an externalist normative structure that relies on a conception of post-capitalism, which requires a detailed account of this post-capitalist alternative and the moment (revolution event) that leads to its formation if normative standards (and political praxis) are to be drawn from it. As Stahl notes, '[w]hile there are many types of social critique which do not directly aim at justifying some standard and then using this standard as a reason [...] at some point the question becomes inevitable as to how we can distinguish between standards that are not only justified but in regard to which we can have a legitimate expectation that others should accept them and standards for which this is not the case', adding: 'This is especially true if the addressees of the critique have beliefs about norms and justificatory reasons which do not coincide with those of the critic'.[34]

This is exactly what Žižek has little interest in providing, since it would infringe on his eschewing of 'thick' Utopianism. In this, Žižek stays true to the notion that

---

33 Ibid., 726-727.
34 Stahl 2013a, 5.

the future communist state of affairs need not, and in fact *ought* not, be described in detail since this would infringe on the (historical) materialist view that this future communist state of affairs is established through the free agency of future actors. They do so as they see fit, per the requirements of their specific context, which we as actors stuck in the present cannot possibly predict or even begin to grasp given the epistemic gulf that separates us from them. In fact, when describing examples of such revolution events, Žižek highlights the contingency of their occurrence and their indeterminacy. These things make them what they are; emancipatory potentials for realizing another, post-capitalist world.[35] By thus eliding the Scylla of an unrealistic 'thick' Utopianism, he falls victim to the Charybdis of normative incoherence by relying on an ambiguously defined conception of post-capitalism as the source from which normative standards are to be sought to justify emancipatory, Leninist political praxis.

This observation concerning the vagueness of Žižek's political project is hardly novel. Therborn describes an acrimonious exchange Žižek had with Laclau over it: 'Like that of most other radical philosophers today, Žižek's anti-capitalist project is very vague; this provoked an ill-tempered exchange between him and Laclau, each accusing the other of a political project meaning "nothing at all"'.[36] In fact, it is worth citing Laclau's comments in full as it succinctly summarizes what has already been argued with respect to the externalist nature of the normative structure underlying Žižek's Leninist project:

> Žižek takes a patently anti-capitalist stance, and asserts that the proponents of postmodernism 'as a rule, leave out of sight the resignation at its heart – the acceptance of capitalism as "the only game in town", the renunciation of any real attempt to overcome the existing capitalist liberal regime' [...] The difficulty with assertions like this is that they mean absolutely nothing. I understand what Marx meant by overcoming the capitalist regime, because he made it quite explicit several times. I also understand what Lenin or Trotsky meant for the same reason. But in the work of Žižek that expression means nothing – unless he has a secret strategic plan of which he is very careful not to inform anybody. Should we understand that he wants to impose the dictatorship of the proletariat? Or does he want to socialize the means of production and abolish market mechanisms? And what is his political strategy to achieve these rather peculiar aims? What is the alternative model of society that he is postulating? Without at least the beginning of an answer to these questions, his anti-capitalism is mere empty talk.[37]

Instead of answering these questions, Žižek's project amounts to an appeal to the radical Left to capture power by exploiting revolution events that may lead to it, and ensuring they keep power once they have taken it.[38] The references to Lenin and

---

35 Žižek 2012, 89.
36 Therborn 2008, 148.
37 Laclau 2000, 205-6.
38 Žižek 2002b, 191; Žižek 2007a, 2.

Mao's example are meant to counter the fear of taking illiberal, anti-emancipatory measures to this end. Yet it is never clarified what exactly the limits of these measures ought to be, if any, and how people can be convinced of their necessity lacking any normative justification, and the ability to draw on normative standards that may feasibly do so. 'Give me Stalin and St. Paul' is seemingly the only answer that is provided.[39]

Laclau fails to appreciate, however, what the source of this conspicuous lacuna in Žižek's political theory is, and why it has been left unfilled since it was identified by his early critics.[40] The reason why Žižek is unperturbed by this is exactly because it is the vagueness and ambiguity of the notion of post-capitalism that forms the source of normativity underlying his Leninist project. To clarify, consider again Stahl's three normative elements of a mode of critique or political praxis – the ontological, epistemological and justificatory.[41] Žižek's adoption of the external mode means that a privileged conceptual space is carved out for himself from where he identifies the normative standards in which its praxis is grounded. In reality, these standards refer to a vague post-capitalist ideal (the ontology), to which only he has epistemic access (the epistemology), and for which there is no justificatory burden as it is wholly detached from present-day society and the practices (including the emancipatory) it contains.[42] This means that the actors who are actually engaged in a particular form of emancipatory praxis are not involved in the process of identifying the normativity that guides and gives content to it. The vagueness and ambiguity emanating from the external source of normativity therefore never become a pressing issue for Žižek that has to be resolved. The risks of such an endeavor are a narrow conception of emancipation and a structural reflexivity deficit, which together provide fertile grounds for the rise of anti-emancipatory tendencies, as was the case in classical Marxism and its Leninist incarnation.

For Lenin, the taking of anti-emancipatory (repressive) measures was necessary to maintain the revolution event and the post-capitalist potential it carried within it (i.e., the young Soviet regime). As a result, it was his very understanding of emancipation that was compromised by the narrowness of his approach towards it. Since his praxis, however, lacked a reflexive mechanism, due to its externalist normative structure, these tendencies were not recognized or alleviated. Instead, Leninism was transformed into a state ideology premised on an exclusionary logic that reached its height under Stalin. Before participating in furthering this logic, Trotsky had astutely foreseen its presence in Leninist praxis. It was captured succinctly in the following statement, written when he was still Lenin's opponent: 'Lenin's methods [of

---

39   A line from Leonard Cohen's song *The Future*.
40   Therborn 2008, 148.
41   Stahl 2013a, 534.
42   Ibid., 6.

"hard" centralism and mistrust of the working class] lead to this: the party organization substitutes itself for the party, the central committee substitutes itself for the organization, and, finally, a "dictator" substitutes himself for the central committee.'[43] The danger of anti-emancipatory tendencies arising is thus all the more present when the externalist normative structure of Leninism is adopted as one's own. Habermas noted in this regard:

> [I]f indeed the old Utopias of the best possible social order and eternal peace, the highest degree of freedom and perfect happiness, contain the underlying rational themes of a theory, no matter how distorted into a derivative myth, as their implicit basis; and if praxis must legitimate itself in terms of this theory, because it has now been invested with the mantle of a state ideology—then one may cautiously raise the consideration [...] whether ultimately such a system does not have a corrective for such dangers at its disposal.[44]

Such a corrective, reflexive mechanism is lacking in Žižek's Leninist project, and when it is missing or underdeveloped – as in all external as opposed to immanent modes of critique – the fleshed out, 'thick' normativity that informs a particular political project and the praxis expressed by it runs the risk of violating the 'thin' normative commitment to emancipation. This, then, renders the praxis politically impotent and – what is worse – reproduces the very anti-emancipatory practices it aims to combat and transcend.

The first key element of Žižek's Leninism – its appeal to a post-capitalist referential point as a source of normativity on which to base a belief in the absolute necessity of revolution – thus does not advance genuinely emancipatory political praxis. Rather, it is cut off from the concerns of the actors who are involved and engaged in them, instead imposing on them normative standards drawn from a vaguely and ambiguously defined conception of post-capitalism. The potentiality of anti-emancipatory tendencies arising out of this normative structure has now been discussed theoretically, but what about its actuality? There have, in fact, been exemplifications of this by Žižek in recent years, which not only indicate the impotence of his Leninist revival project, but also more worryingly its reproduction of the very anti-emancipatory pathologies that the radical Left is committed to opposing and transcending with its emancipatory praxis. These are brought to light by the second key element of Žižek's Leninist project, which emanates from the first: its reliance on a reductionist, class and economics-focused conception of political praxis.

---

43 Deutscher 1987, 90.
44 Habermas 1973, 198.

The Primacy of the Economic and the Danger of Anti-Emancipatory Tendencies

The fundamental problem of politics that hyperfocuses on economics is that it is based on an *a priori* conception of the category of 'the economic'. This is exemplified both by liberal (in the political philosophical sense) and classical Marxist political theory. In both conceptions, 'the economic' is stripped of all social content and suspended into the airy realms of abstraction through the magical filter of 'rational choice theory' or Marxist 'laws of economics and history'.[45] In both cases, 'the economic' is governed by immutable laws of (human) nature, which are by virtue of this capable of yielding objective (anormative) definitions of the social world. The shared ontology and epistemology of liberal and Marxist conceptions of the economy causes both to overlap in certain crucial respects. For example, classical Marxism can be seen as having originated a modern rational choice theory, not only in the economic but also the social and cultural (superstructural) sense.[46] At the same time, liberalism (and in particular neo-liberalism) has outdone Marxism in its fanatical belief in the immutability of economic laws, in particular those of capitalism, which are perceived and presented as laws of (human) nature.[47]

However, although their logics may overlap in many ways, the normative ends to which their conceptions of political praxis are oriented clearly do not. As discussed in the previous section, Žižek's Leninist revival project hinges on the critique of capitalism and the concomitant call for an absolute revolution to break with the liberal-democratic capitalist consensus that sustains it.[48] As was also noted, there is both a determinist and voluntarist aspect to this conception of political praxis. The transformation is, on the one hand, seen as a consequence of the aforementioned immutable Marxist laws of economics and history, while, on the other hand, it is seen as the result of the actions of the Party and its symbolic representative – a St. Paul, Lenin or Mao.[49] While Žižek routinely claims there is a dialectical relation between the two, it is the economic that holds a primary role within this conceptual structure, providing the basis on which active transformation can be grounded.[50] Alongside references to the dialectical, the phrase 'in the last analysis' or a variation thereof is often employed by adherents of Leninist praxis as a means of eliding the reductionist/determinist critique. The economic is primary, *but only in the last analysis!* As with references to post-capitalism, it is never explicated what exactly this means an-

---

45 For a highly illuminating account and critique of the rational actor model see: Bowles and Gintis 2013. For critical accounts of the Marxist model see: Habermas 1973; Baudrillard 1975; Bourdieu 1985 and Castoriadis 1978.
46 Cohen 1978; Elster 1986.
47 Bourdieu 1998; Ibid. 2005.
48 Žižek 2002b, 302.
49 Bourdieu 1985, 726-727.
50 Keucheyan 2013, 187; Laclau 2000, 205-206.

alytically. How exactly does it affect the conceptual structure of the classical Marxist – carried on in Žižek's Leninist – understanding of political praxis in such a way that it avoids collapsing into reductionism/determinism? Žižek has nothing novel to offer on this question.

He simply reproduces the classical Marxist view, presenting the economic as the primary means of furnishing the grounds for and possibility of emancipatory praxis – *the* mechanism propelling events-in-themselves toward events-for-themselves.[51] The category of the economic and the semantic field that revolves around it – terms like 'class', 'proletariat', 'bourgeoisie', 'means of production', 'base', 'superstructure' – are thus presented as an objective, anormative lens through which politics can be seen as it really is. We are left with the ambiguity inherent in the classical Marxist and Leninist model, adopted by Žižek, that the economic is the necessary but not sufficient condition for revolution. Since the 'sufficient' conditions are considered to be unknown and contingent (like the coming into being of a St. Paul or Mao), the objectively known, universally valid and anormative economic conditions naturally take center stage in the political praxis that emanates from this model. The crucial question of normativity is relegated to an epiphenomenal afterthought and is, moreover, left underdetermined when it is acknowledged at all (i.e., the ambiguity of Žižek's conception of post-capitalism).[52]

The notion that there is such an *a priori* and anormative objective set of laws of economics and history in my view yields false illusions about the prospects and nature of political praxis. It is not only analytically inadequate as it fails to capture the complexity and 'messiness' of politics, reducing it to easily recognizable elements of the *a priori* classificatory scheme of the economic.[53] It also carries within it anti-emancipatory implications, which have been expressed by Žižek with increasing frequency over the past decade. These anti-emancipatory tendencies lead Žižek to risk reproducing the very anti-emancipatory pathologies that the radical Left aims to eradicate. This is most clearly exemplified in Žižek's rejection of 'the cultural' understanding of political praxis.

One of Žižek's claims to fame among the radical Left is his vociferous rejection of a form of political praxis that focuses on the cultural, by which he means the by now familiar caricature of 'identity politics', which is centered on issues of gender, sexuality, ethnicity, religion etc. If one limits one's political praxis to social and cultural identities, Žižek claims, the economic factor fades into the background, which makes the praxis defective since it turns the praxis into a kind of reformism that is satisfied with merely adjusting the liberal-democratic capitalist consensus. Rather,

---

51 Laclau 2000, 205-206.
52 Bourdieu 1985, 727.
53 Which includes such concepts as 'proletariat', 'bourgeoisie', 'class-in-itself', 'base', 'superstructure'—all of which are imbued with normativity, but from within the conceptual scheme are presented as objective and anormative descriptions of the social world.

he argues, the goal should be to overthrow capitalism, thereby removing the root causes of the marginalization and oppression inflicted on those who embody such social/cultural identities.[54] Žižek's main problem with a culturalist conception of emancipatory political praxis is its disavowal of the universal. Social and cultural identities are by their very nature particular, embodied by smaller clusters of actors, whereas the economic – reductively defined in Žižek's Leninist project – is universal, extending to the proletariat as a whole, cutting across social/cultural lines.[55] The central role of the category of the economic in Žižek's political ontology is on full display here. It provides universality and through this the realistic prospect of eliminating anti-emancipatory structures and practices. Again, the post-capitalist realm justifies the emancipatory political praxis that leads to its realization. As Laclau aptly noted, the economic is thus introduced 'as a sort of *deus ex machina* to play the role of the good guy against the multicultural devils'.[56]

This circular structure, whereby the normative question is evaded through a reference to immutable, anormative aspects of nature (the economic), which in turn legitimizes one's normative position (the need for post-capitalism to realize emancipation), was lucidly identified by Castoriadis in his later readings of Marx. The economic, he argues, cannot fulfill this double role, for the very concept of 'need' that lies at the basis of economics is a normative one: 'What are the needs and capacities that a society ought to create, toward which it ought to prepare/educate individuals, and on what basis and by what means are these needs and capacities to be created – this question cannot be eliminated [...] Paradoxically, the question grinds to a halt with the philosopher of history, Marx – and I would add also with Žižek.[57] The economic cannot be separated into its own domain, from where it is only accessible to those who are sufficiently trained in the arcane arts of Marxist economics. Instead, it must be perceived as a social phenomenon always already infused with normativity. When approached in this way, the question of normativity takes center stage in debates about the economic and therefore also in one's conception of political praxis. As a result, both become *truly political*. As Castoriadis notes,

> To propose another institution of society raises the issue of a political project and a goal, which can certainly be discussed and argued, but cannot be grounded in some kind of Nature or Reason (even if these were the nature or reason of history). Surpassing the limit requires understanding a 'banality': value (even economic value), equality, justice are not concepts that one could ground, construct [...] in and by theory. They are political ideas/significations concerning the institution of society as such that could not be and that we would not want to be an institution that is anchored in a natural, logical, or tran-

---

54 Žižek 2007b, 77-78.
55 Žižek 2009a, 44-45, 147.
56 Laclau 2000, 205.
57 Castoriadis 1978, 725.

scendent order. [...] Thus it is for 'value' and 'equality', including the domain that seems to be the most 'rationalizable' of all, the 'economy'.[58]

My claim here is that we need to dissolve the essentializing and reductive category of the economic. Social and cultural forms of oppression and marginalization are not to be approached as separate and distinct domains in their own right – detached from any economic considerations –, but rather as inextricably intertwined with economic inequalities. A useful aid with which to clarify the nature of the conceptual structure that underlies such a view can be found in Wittgenstein's notion of family resemblances, denoting an overlapping network of similarities revolving around certain key elements (economic, social, cultural – and the myriad of forms contained within these categories), without, however, being reducible to them.[59] There have been many prominent attempts made by radical Left theorists to introduce some order to this complexity – such as Bourdieu's critical sociology and those working on intersectionality – but, as expected, disagreements abound.[60] These disagreements, one could say, are reflective of the very messiness and complexity of the political and its intrinsically normative nature. Since the adoption of a particular conception of emancipatory political praxis is a normative one, appealing to the radical Left's shared 'thin' normative commitment to emancipation, how can it be justified in contradistinction to Žižek's externalist model, which relies on a vague conception of the post-capitalist and a reductionist conception of class and the economic?

Honneth provides an answer to this question by revealing the anti-emancipatory pathologies that are induced by a lack of recognition with respect to social and cultural factors.[61] Put simply, he claims that since the realization of autonomy is the goal of emancipation, anything that distorts or impedes it is problematic from that standpoint. Given that the realization of autonomy does not only rely on economics but is also fundamentally dependent on the recognition of social and cultural identities, the adoption of an economics-focused conception of emancipatory political praxis is intrinsically flawed from the perspective of emancipation.[62] The crux of Honneth's position is that any conception of emancipation, no matter how thinly defined, by necessity has to include a recognitional component if it is to take this commitment to emancipation seriously. What is at stake is the very realization of autonomy that this commitment is premised on. Honneth appeals to a normative ideal in his work too – that of the autonomous actor – but it is both clearly defined and rooted immanently in our own social practices.[63] The question of whether or not actors take

---

58 Ibid., 737.
59 Baker and Hacker 2009, 91, 239.
60 For Bourdieu's approach, see his: *Pascalian Meditations* (2000). For an overview of intersectional thinking, see: McCall 2005.
61 Honneth and Anderson 2005.
62 Ibid., 129-30.
63 See Honneth 2007; Honneth 2014.

it up as a viable conception of emancipatory praxis is independent of any kind of *a priori* anormative mechanism attached to a vague notion of post-capitalism. Rather, its adoption is a consequence of its ability to address actors (who engage in emancipatory practices) and present them with both an adequate account of anti-emancipatory pathologies and the ability to engage in emancipatory praxis to oppose and eliminate them. The actors can, in turn, contribute their own insights and/or change their practices accordingly. This reflexivity provides this mode of political praxis with an immanent normative structure.[64]

Žižek's Flirtations with Orientalism and Islamophobia

The lack of such a reflexive mechanism in Žižek's Leninist political project has caused him to make some highly problematic political interventions in recent years. Among the more controversial of these has been the application of his aforementioned critique of multiculturalism to the place of Islam and Muslims in the West, which has come up with increasing frequency in political debates in the West since 9/11.[65] Muslim communities in the West constitute a systematically marginalized group. They are disproportionately victimized by law enforcement and intelligence agencies, who take advantage of their increased legal authority in the wake of 9/11 to target them specifically. The profiling of Muslims under the guise of 'anti-terrorism activity' has become the norm, while populist right-wing movements have gained substantial support throughout the Western world based primarily on their anti-Muslim animus or Islamophobia.[66] Muslims in the West are a *racialized* group, meaning that their social being is perceived as being reducible to its purely physical, bodily attributes. These physical characteristics, which are but a reified abstraction, are then universalized into the standard norm of what it means to be Muslim.[67] This essentializing of Muslims goes hand in hand with the naturalization of universalized negative aspects that go into the making up of this image of *the* 'Muslim'. Edward

---

64 Stahl 2013a, 4-5, 7.
65 Fekete 2009, 43-44.
66 Fekete 2009, 43-44. I use the term 'Islamophobia' in the sense proposed by Erik Bleich: 'I propose that Islamophobia can best be understood as *indiscriminate negative attitudes or emotions directed at Islam or Muslims.* Because not all criticism constitutes Islamophobia, terms like *indiscriminate* – or cognates like *undifferentiated* or *unnuanced* – cover instances where negative assessments are applied to all or most Muslims or aspects of Islam. [...] Viewed in this way, Islamophobia is also analogous to terms like racism, sexism, or anti-Semitism' (2012: 182).
67 Here, I follow Sally Haslanger's proposed method of identifying racialized groups in a *contextual* sense, which elides the problem of falling into essentialism, 'strategic' or otherwise. See Haslanger 2000, 36-37.

Said uncovered parts of this image in his *Orientalism*, which includes such elements as lazy, depraved and violent.[68]

It is therefore not surprising that in dominant Western discourses Muslim communities are the standard object of critique, exclusively taking on the external approach which can best be described as a form of ideology *production* and symbolic violence.[69] The fact that journalists, pundits, and intellectuals in general engage in this type of activity should not come as a surprise to critical theorists, who should be familiar with the problematic nature of externalized normative standards being reified and universalized at the expense of whatever group finds itself on its opposite end. The Muslim is backward, the West enlightened, and so it is with barbarism/ civilization, violent/peaceful and lazy/active.[70] The maintaining of such hierarchies, i.e., the creation of social meanings that have these inscribed within them, is the aim of symbolic violence as Bourdieu shows with respect to masculine domination. The dominant social meanings so constructed form the space in which the critical theorist and those on the radical Left must formulate their own emancipatory critique and praxis, which therefore cannot but be affected by it, even if the intention is otherwise. Muslim communities and the social practices emanating from them which are the object of this critique do not exist in a vacuum; they are structurally positioned in a society both in a material and symbolic or social sense. Given that their structural positioning is one of systematic marginalization, any external critique which appeals to a position of superiority in opposition to that of the inferiority of the object of critique risks reproducing its marginalized status. To clarify this with a similar case, take African-American communities who are often the victims of external critiques couched in the most virtuous language of uplifting and emancipation. Not only is this ineffective as a means of adjusting practices within such communities due to the distance involved between the critic and the actors it is aimed at – a consequence of its externalist normative structure –, it is also patronizing and paternalistic. It reinforces biases on the part of those who engage in this type of critique and those who perceive it 'from the outside' of the community, for the community is marginalized in dominant social contexts.[71] When they are confronted with such cases, a typical evasion maneuver among externalist critics of Muslims is to say that they do not constitute a race, which is an attempt to deny the racialization of Islam in the West. Even if that were valid, it does not undermine the point that Muslim communities in the West are structurally disadvantaged and subject to symbolic violence, as elaborated above.[72]

---

68 Said 1979, 253, 307.
69 Bourdieu 1985, 732-734.
70 Bourdieu 2002, 28.
71 For a critique of external critiques aimed at the African-American community see: West 1993.
72 Fekete 2009, 43-44.

Yet it is undoubtedly also the case that there are problematic or deficient social practices present in Muslim communities, just as there are in others. However, it is only in *how* they are critiqued that the danger of reproducing their marginalized status resides. Take the example of patriarchal practices in some Muslim communities. Those who have created the image of 'the Muslim' as inherently misogynistic naturally have no qualms about referring to an external normative standard when criticizing these communities on this score. In fact, it is a common strategy in reproducing the symbolic violence directed at Muslims – and Muslim men in particular – by portraying them as intrinsically misogynistic and in need of enlightenment by Westerners, described by Spivak as 'white men saving brown women from brown men.'[73] Needless to say, to universalize and essentialize patriarchal relations to Muslim nature in such a fashion is problematic from a normatively emancipatory perspective, but that is the social context in which the critical theorists must formulate their critique. How can they escape the dominant social meaning when they formulate their critique of patriarchal relations in parts of Muslim communities in an externalized manner? Careful and constant referral back to the normative standards they employ may ward off their critique and praxis becoming entirely tainted by this context, but it is inscribed in the very logic of the external mode of critique that there is a distance between the critic and the object of critique – and it is this distance that is filled in not only by the externalized standards employed by the critic but also by the broader social context in which the critique is produced – a society wherein Islamophobia is increasingly becoming mainstream.[74] There has been unease about how to approach certain problematic social practices emanating from Muslim communities by feminists and Marxists precisely for this reason. Take the issue of the veil, which has given rise to heated responses from feminists and secularists, with one side arguing that one must not play into dominant Islamophobic narratives and portraying Muslim women purely as victims who lack agency and are forced to wear the veil by men, and the other arguing that it is an intrinsic sign of masculine domination that needs to be fought against.[75] The latter type of critique is externalist, excluding the concerns of the actors involved in favor of a pre-established norm distant from them.[76]

The same externalist mode of praxis and critique informs Žižek's interventions in the discourse concerning Islam and Muslims, leading to his reproducing and natural-

---

73 Spivak 1988, 297.
74 Fekete 2009, 43-44.
75 Alia Al-Saji 2010.
76 That is not to say that it is impossible to formulate an immanent critique of this practice. In fact, there are many Muslim feminists and others who have done exactly this, in so doing ensuring their critique is more receptive to the targets of the critique while also eliding the danger of reproducing the marginalization and essentialization of Muslims. For a particularly illuminating account of this kind, which touches on the issue of the veil and others related to gender discrimination in some Muslim communities, see: Barlas 2002.

izing of the marginalization of Muslims in the West. For example, in discussing the Rotherham child sex abuse case of 2014, wherein groups of young predominately British-Pakistani men were found guilty of committing sexual offences against young girls, Žižek did not shy away from indulging in essentializing and Orientalist rhetoric about Muslims and Pakistanis, writing: '[…] we are dealing with the "political unconscious" of the Pakistani Muslim youth – not with chaotic violence, but with a ritualized violence with precise ideological contours: a youth group that experiences itself as marginalized and subordinated taking revenge on vulnerable women of the predominant group. And it is fully legitimate to raise the question of whether there are features in their religion and culture that open up the space for the brutality against women'.[77] The positing of static, monolithic categories of 'Muslim' or 'Pakistani' imbued with misogyny is nefarious, particularly in a context wherein Islamophobia is increasingly on the rise.[78] Similar Orientalist tropes were employed in Žižek's recent commentary on the Syrian refugee crisis: 'Should we tolerate migrants who prevent their children going to state schools; who force their women to dress and behave in a certain way; who arrange their children's marriages; who discriminate against homosexuals? We can never be tolerant enough, or we are always already too tolerant.'[79] In his recently published book on the subject, *Against the Double Blackmail*, he explicitly constructs a hierarchy between the lower, barbaric, unenlightened Muslim and the higher, civilized, enlightened Westerner: 'Furthermore, it is a simple fact that most of the refugees come from a culture that is incompatible with Western European notions of human rights.'[80] While discussing the New Year's Eve sexual assaults in Cologne of 2015, allegedly committed by suspects of North-African origin, Žižek again, as in the Rotherham case, ascribes misogynist attitudes to the nature of Muslim men, who want to 'wound our sensitivities' by engaging in carnivalesque violence against Western women.[81] How should we resolve this? Žižek explains in typical externalist fashion: 'The difficult lesson of this entire affair is therefore that it is not enough simply to give voice to the underdogs as they are now: in order to enact actual emancipation, they have to be *educated* (by others and by themselves) into their freedom.'[82] Here, Spivak's phrase comes to mind, 'white men saving brown [and white] women from brown men.'[83] It goes without saying that anyone normatively committed to emancipation opposes such misogynistic practices (this is even true of the 'liberal multiculturalists'). Suggest-

---

77 Žižek 2014.
78 For an analysis and critique of the claim that misogyny is an intrinsic part of Islam see: Abu-Lughod 2002.
79 Žižek 2015.
80 Žižek 2016, 98.
81 Ibid., 95-96.
82 Ibid., 96.
83 Spivak 1988, 297.

ing, however, that the refugees and their 'culture' are reducible to such practices, while the Westerner represents the enlightened obverse of it, reconstructs a hierarchy that emanates from a long history of Orientalist categorization of the Muslim Other.[84] It resonates with and thereby gives force to the Islamophobia that is increasingly on the rise in the West, contributing to naturalizing and reproducing the marginalization of Muslims – inflicting symbolic violence on them.[85]

It may seem curious that someone who must be familiar with the works of people like Said, Chakrabarty, Spivak and Scott is indulging in such dangerous rhetoric concerning ethnic and religious minorities and refugees with a Muslim background, especially since they are among the most marginalized and vulnerable groups in Europe today.[86] While it may appear to be an aberration, separate and distinct from Žižek's overarching project of reviving Leninism, I believe it is rooted in the externalist normative structure that underlies it. When the reflexive link between the commitment to emancipation is severed from the actors to whom one's critique and praxis is addressed, and the praxis evolving from the commitment is normatively reliant on an ambiguously defined conception of post-capitalism, which is in turn legitimized by an *a priori* reductive conception of the economic – the corrective mechanism that filters out potential anti-emancipatory aspects of one's praxis no longer functions.[87] This explains why Žižek can end up in the seemingly paradoxical situation of forwarding a radically utopian conception of post-capitalism as the only hope for realizing genuine emancipation, while at the same time espousing anti-emancipatory rhetoric as exemplified in his critique of 'liberal multiculturalism' and its supposed tolerance for an essentialized conception of Muslims.

It is instructive to look a little more closely at this critique of multiculturalism as the 'cultural logic of multinational capitalism' from which these aforementioned interventions emanate, as it reveals all the elements of the reductive and externalist normative structure that underlies Žižek's broader Leninist project, of which it is a component part.[88] As Pieterse discerningly observes with respect to the critique:

A familiar line of criticism dismisses multiculturalism as the cultural wallpaper of late capitalism [...] The multiculturalism = late capitalism view overlooks that cultural differences matter also prior to capitalism, recognizes but one variety of multiculturalism and one variety of capitalism, 'late capitalism', and by assuming that 'identity can wait' reproduces class reductionism. These forms of 'multiculturalism from above' [note the reference to normative externality as opposed to immanence – ST] do not address power relations and if we accept that multiculturalism is about the renegotiation of hierarchies and power relations in postimperial and postcolonial settings, these managerial multicul-

---

84   Said 1979, 253, 307.
85   Bourdieu 1985, 732-734.
86   Balibar 1991; Scott 2007; Modood 2007; Spivak 1988; Chakrabarty 2000.
87   Stahl 2013a, 4-5, 7; Habermas 1973, 198.
88   Žižek 1997.

turalisms [sic] miss the point. Alternative options are critical, transformative or revolutionary multiculturalism.[89]

The blindness to these alternative conceptions of multiculturalism, and its reduction to one crudely defined form, is but an expression of a routinized process that lies at the heart of Žižek's Leninism, informing the conceptions of normativity and economic and political praxis contained within it. The existence of emancipatory conceptions of multiculturalism and a more broadly recognitional account that brings into view the social/cultural in one's emancipatory praxis invalidates Žižek's view that a rejection of his economics-focused conception of emancipatory praxis necessarily leads to the acceptance of the liberal-democratic capitalist consensus.[90] This, then, undermines the very *raison d'être* of his revival project – which is perhaps even more fatal for its political praxis than the already diagnosed political impotence and the presence of anti-emancipatory tendencies within it.

A Concluding Note: Prospects of an Immanent Mode of Emancipatory Critique and Praxis

Throughout this critical investigation of Žižek's Leninist project, I have employed the immanent mode of political praxis and critique as its counterpart. It derives its strengths over Žižek's and other externalist models by eliding the central problems identified with it. These are, firstly, the reliance on an external, vaguely and ambiguously defined post-capitalist reference point as the source for its normative justification, leading to political impotence due to its epistemic distance from actors and communities in the present. Secondly, it suffers from blindness to the anti-emancipatory tendencies that emanate from its externalist normative structure, due to its lack of an adequate reflexive mechanism. Since there is no necessary relation between one's acceptance of Žižek's Leninist mode of praxis and critique and one's commitment to an anti-capitalist emancipatory project, raising the specter of liberal-democratic reformism cannot justify the former.

How does the immanent alternative fare in these respects? An immanent mode of praxis and critique derives its norms from the emancipatory potentials contained in present-day society.[91] By virtue of this, it contains a robust reflexive capacity that constantly subjects these norms to critical evaluation in accordance with the 'thin' normative standard of emancipation shared at least nominally by all who identify with the radical Left. It therefore has no need for an external reference point as a source of normative standards and, by virtue of this, elides the problems of political

---

89 Pieterse 2004, 41.
90 Žižek 2007b, 77-78.
91 Stahl 2013a, 2.

impotence and of reproducing anti-emancipatory pathologies due to its reliance on a vague and ambiguous external source of normativity.

Such an immanent method is not alien to the Marxian tradition; it is in fact derived from it by its adherents, in particular those working in the Frankfurt School tradition; though, as noted in the introduction, its political expression goes back to council communists like Pannekoek.[92] More recently it has been the preferred mode of critique of Habermas and Honneth, and has more recently been taken up and further developed by theorists like Celikates, Stahl and Jaeggi.[93] However, while immanent modes of critique and praxis seek to address and overcome the problems and dangers that reside in external modes, it is not without its own difficulties. One of the obvious challenges is how exactly to identify the proper normative standards needed to sustain one's emancipatory critique and praxis in present-day capitalist societies, given that one's horizon is limited to it. Whilst the eschewing of a reductive conception of the economic opens up spaces to locate such norms, there are nevertheless strict boundaries imposed on one's search. This wards off an overly Utopian and vaguely defined conception of the post-capitalist, but at the same time renders even more complex the question as to how one can identify the precise content of a truly emancipatory praxis and the normativity that informs it.[94]

The result is a vast plurality of forms of praxis and critique, each containing its own particularly identified normative standards. Such a plurality of forms of emancipatory praxis is a logical outcome of a conception of politics that is fundamentally *contextualist*, which is one of the key strengths of an immanent approach. Still, Žižek has a point when he warns of the danger of thereby losing sight of a commonly shared, universal emancipatory praxis that links these particular praxes as part of a broader political project – whether it is premised on a reductive conception of the economic or not – which could carry much greater transformative potential.[95] It is as yet unclear whether a form of emancipatory praxis premised on an immanent normative structure is capable of yielding such a universal project for the twenty-first century. However, it appears much more likely to do so than any externalist model given its recognizable and justifiable norms as a basis for its praxis and its intrinsically inclusive nature. The latter aspect especially, emanating from the reflexive mechanism that is embedded within its structure, befits our age in which a reductive conception of the economic has been largely rejected and the social/cultural sphere has

92   Celikates 2011; Pannekoek 2003, 149-152.
93   Stahl 2013b; Honneth 2001; Celikates 2011; Jaeggi 2009.
94   Titus Stahl is currently engaged in a detailed study to provide a cohesive answer to this question—of how exactly the appropriate norms sustaining critical theory and praxis are to be identified immanently, within a given community's totality of social practices—drawing on, among other things, insights from practice theory and Wittgenstein's philosophy. See also his earlier work which develops the basic elements of such a conception of an immanent critique. See: Stahl 2013c.
95   Žižek 2002b, 302; Žižek 2007b, 77-78.

been opened up as a distinctive space for political, emancipatory praxis.[96] What is most important, however, is that it avoids reproducing and naturalizing the marginalization of already marginalized groups in society, inflicting symbolic or real violence on them, as shown by Žižek's indulgence in Islamophobia and the history of Leninism as a state ideology.

There are other areas in which work should and is being done to further explicate and enhance the immanent mode of critique and emancipatory praxis. A particularly striking lacuna is the neglect of the historical dimension among those who adopt and defend it as a method. If norms are to be derived from present-day society, then obviously understanding the way in which these norms came into being and developed into what they appear to be now is of fundamental importance to one's political praxis.[97] This requires serious engagement with the philosophy of history and historical analysis more generally – an area Frankfurtian critical theory has always been found lacking in[98] – and with the philosophy and sociology of action and practice theory, which is concerned with illuminating the nature of normative practices, clarifying how actors come to engage in them and how they can be adjusted.[99] Perhaps most importantly – with regard to Žižek's 'we need *theory* and *philosophy* more than ever' – it is crucial to actually engage in immanent emancipatory political praxis so as to gain practical, direct experience in what it is like in all its vast richness of forms that cannot be fully captured or grasped in abstract concepts, however refined

---

96 Yet here lurks another danger to which Žižek's Leninism serves as a warning sign. I have made my disagreements with Žižek's outright rejection of the social/cultural and adoption of a reductive conception of the economic clear, but he is right to critique fetishized conceptions of identity and the concomitant social/cultural realm, wherein it is detached from any aspect of the material or economic (Žižek 2009a, 44, 147; Žižek 2013, 136-137). In these instances, it is no longer the legitimate, emancipatory concern for recognition that is expressed, but rather what Bourdieu termed 'the semiological vision of the world' (2004), which 'is fueling the fantastical belief, typical of "campus radicalism", that one changes the world by changing words, that the subversion of terms, categories, and discourses suffices to subvert or dent objective structures of domination' (Bourdieu 1996-1997, 201-202). However, as the work of adherents of the immanent mode of critique and praxis such as Stahl, Celikates and Jaeggi shows, an understanding of the nature of emancipatory praxis involving the inextricably connected social/cultural and economic realms does not require the adoption of a Leninist praxis and all that it involves, nor an outright rejection of the importance of recognitional aspects of emancipation.

97 Honneth has recently made an attempt to grapple with the historical (2014), but with him too it remains limited in scope, never fully engaging with the insights offered by the philosophy of history.

98 For this, see: Allen 2016, xv-xvi, 3. As Allen notes, the likes of Habermas and Honneth merely adopt a Hegelian conception of historical progress as their meta-theory of history wherein they base their normativity, while engaging only very generally in any kind of detailed historical analysis. Such a progress-oriented philosophy of history is, moreover, burdened by Eurocentric assumptions, and is therefore in need of decolonization, hence Allen's attempt to 'decolonize critical theory' (2016).

99 In this, one can build on the work already done by theorists like Stahl (2013a; 2013b) and Boltanski, with his pragmatic sociology of critique (2011).

they may be.[100] Though I am inclined to take a contextualist position on the 'theory versus practice' question, which is never an either-or proposition, Žižek's affording of priority to the theoretical rather than the practical aspect of praxis – a perfect expression of what Bourdieu termed the 'scholastic disposition' developed and valorized in academia – serves as a useful corrective to those who are part of the radical Left's hyper-activist milieu.[101] But in general the Western radical Left appears to be overburdened by an excess of high (critical) theory and a dearth of political action, a symptom of its excess in cultural capital more generally. The question of how one can identify the proper normative standards for an emancipatory critique is first and foremost 'not a question of theory but a *practical* question', to quote Marx's second thesis.[102]

References

Abu-Lughod, Lila, 2002: Do Muslim Women Really Need Saving? Anthropological Reflections on Cultural Relativism and its Others. In: *American Anthropologist* 104:3 (2002), 783-790.

Allen, Amy, 2016: *The End of Progress. Decolonizing the Normative Foundations of Critical Theory.*

Al-Saji, Alia, 2010: The Racialization of Muslim Veils. A Philosophical Analysis. In: *Philosophy and Social Criticism* 36:8 (2010), 875-902.

Baker, Gordon P. and P.M.S. Hacker, 2009: *Wittgenstein. Rules, Grammar and Necessity.* Chichester, (UK) and Malden, MA.

Balibar, Étienne, 1991: Is There a 'Neo-Racism'? In: Ibid. and Immanuel Wallerstein, *Race, Nation, Class. Ambiguous Identities.* London, 17-28.

Barlas, Asma, 2002: *'Believing women' in Islam. Unreading Patriarchal Interpretations of the Qur'an.* Austin.

Baudrillard, Jean, 1975: *The Mirror of Production.* St. Louis.

Beaney, Michael, 2013: What is Analytic Philosophy? In: *Oxford Handbooks Online.* http://www.oxfordhandbooks.com/view/10.1093/oxfordhb/9780199238842.001.0001/oxfordhb-9780199238842-e-039

Bleich, Erik, 2012: Defining and Researching Islamophobia. In: *Review of Middle East Studies* 46:2 (2012), 180-189.

Bohman, James, 2016: Critical Theory. In: *Stanford Encyclopedia of Philosophy.* https://plato.stanford.edu/entries/critical-theory/

Boltanski, Luc, 2011: *On Critique. A Sociology of Emancipation.* Cambridge.

Bourdieu, Pierre, 1985: The Social Space and the Genesis of Groups. In: *Theory and Society* 14 (1985), 723-744.

---

100 Žižek 2013, 32.
101 Bourdieu 2000, 12.
102 Marx 1976, 3.

Bourdieu, Pierre, 1998: Neo-liberalism. The Utopia (Becoming a Reality) of Unlimited Exploitation. In: Ibid and Richard Nice, *Acts of Resistance. Against the Tyranny of the Market*. New York, 94-105.

Bourdieu, Pierre, 2000: *Pascalian Meditations*. Stanford.

Bourdieu, Pierre, 2001: *Masculine Domination*. Stanford.

Bourdieu, Pierre, 2004 : *Science of Science and Reflexivity*. Chicago.

Bourdieu, Pierre, 2005: *The Social Structures of the Economy*. Cambridge.

Bowles, Samual and Herbert Gintis, 2013: *A Cooperative Species. Human Reciprocity and its Evolution*. Princeton.

Castoriadis, Cornelius, 1978: From Marx to Aristotle, from Aristotle to Us. In: *Social Research* 45:4 (1978), 667-738.

Celikates, Robin, 2011: Karl Marx. Critique as Emancipatory Practice. In Ruth Sonderegger and Karin de Boer (eds.), *Conceptions of Critique in Modern and Contemporary Philosophy*. New York, 101-118.

Chakrabarty, Dipesh, 2000: *Provincializing Europe. Postcolonial Thought and Historical Difference*. Princeton.

Chomsky, Noam, 2002: *Pirates and Emperors, Old and New. International terrorism in the real world*. Cambridge, MA.

Cohen, Gerald Allan, 1978: *Karl Marx's Theory of History. A Defence*. Princeton.

Deutscher, Isaac, 1987: *The prophet armed. Trotsky, 1879-1921*. New York.

Elster, Jon, 1986: *An introduction to Karl Marx*. Cambridge.

Gray, John, 2012: The violent visions of Slavoj Žižek. In: *The New York Review of Books*, 12 July 2012. http://www.nybooks.com/articles/2012/07/12/violent-visions-slavoj-zizek.

Fekete, Liz, 2009: *A Suitable Enemy. Racism, Migration and Islamophobia in Europe*. London.

Habermas, Jürgen, 1973: *Theory and Practice*. Boston.

Haslanger, Sally, 2000: Gender and Race. (What) Are They? (What) Do we Want Them to Be? In: *Noûs* 34:1 (2000), 31-55.

Honneth, Axel, 2001: Reconstructive Social Critique with a Genealogical Reservation. On the Idea of Critique in the Frankfurt School. In: *Graduate Faculty Philosophy Journal* 22:2 (2001), 3-11.

Honneth, Axel and Joel Anderson, 2005: Autonomy, Vulnerability, Recognition, and Justice. In: John Christman and Joel Anderson (eds.), *Autonomy and the Challenges to Liberalism. New Essays*. Cambridge, 127-149.

.Honneth, Axel, 2007: *Disrespect. The Normative Foundations of Critical Theory*. Cambridge.

Honneth, Axel, 2014: *Freedom's Right. The Social Foundations of Democratic Life*. New York.

Horkheimer, Max, 1972: Postscript. In: Ibid., *Critical Theory. Selected Essays*. New York, 244-252

Jaeggi, Rahel, 2009: Rethinking Ideology. In: Boudewijn Paul de Bruin and Christopher F. Zurn (eds.), *New Waves in Political Philosophy*. London, 63-86.

Keucheyan, Razmig, 2013: *The Left Hemisphere. Mapping Critical Theory Today*. London.

Laclau, Ernesto, 2000: Structure, History and the Political. In: Judith Butler, Ernesto Laclau and Slavoj Žižek: *Contingency, Hegemony, Universality. Contemporary Dialogues on the Left*. London, 182-212.

Langer, Lorenz, 2014: *Religious Offence and Human Rights. The Implications of Defamation of Religions*. Cambridge.

Lih, Lars T. (ed.), V.I. Lenin, 2006: *Lenin Rediscovered. What is to be Done? in Context*. Leiden and Boston.

Luxemburg, Rosa, 1973: *Reform or Revolution*. New York.

Marx, Karl, 1976: Theses on Feuerbach. In: Karl Marx and Friedrich Engels, *The Collected Works of Karl Marx and Frederick Engels. General works, 1844-1895. Volume 5* (3-5). Moscow.

McCall, Leslie, 2005: The Complexity of Intersectionality. In: *Signs. Journal of Women, Culture and Society* 30:3 (2005), 1771-1800.

Modood, Tariq, 2005: *Multicultural Politics. Racism, Ethnicity and Muslims in Britain*. Minneapolis.

Pannekoek, Anton, 2003: *Lenin as Philosopher. A Critical Examination of the Philosophical Basis of Leninism*. Milwaukee.

Pieterse, Jan Nederveen, 2004: Ethnicities and Multiculturalisms. Politics of Boundaries. In: Stephen May, Tariq Modood and Judith Squires (eds.), *Ethnicity, Nationalism and Minority Rights*. Cambridge, 27-49.

Said, Edward, 1979: *Orientalism*. New York.

Scott, Joan Wallach, 2007: *The politics of the veil*. Princeton.

Song, Sarah, 2007: *Justice, Gender, and the Politics of Multiculturalism*. Cambridge.

Stahl, Titus, 2013a: What is Immanent Critique? In: *SSRN Working Papers*, 1-20. http://ssrn.com/abstract=2357957.

Stahl, Titus, (2013b): Habermas and the Project of Immanent Critique. In: *Constellations*, 20:4 (2013), 533-552.

Stahl, Titus, 2013c: *Immanente Kritik: Elemente einer Theorie sozialer Praktiken*. Frankfurt.

Spivak, Gayatri Chakravorty, 1988: Can the Subaltern Speak? In: Cary Nelson and Lawrence Grossberg (eds.), *Marxism and the Interpretation of Culture*. Urbana ,271-313.

Therborn, Göran, 2008: *From Marxism to post-Marxism?* London.

Thompson, Peter, 2013: The Slavoj Žižek v Noam Chomsky Spat is Worth a Ringside Seat. In: *The Guardian*, 19 July 2013. https://www.theguardian.com/commentisfree/2013/jul/19/noam-chomsky-slavoj-zizek-ding-dong.

West, Cornel, 1993: *Race matters*. Boston.

Žižek, Slavoj, 1989: *The Sublime Object of Ideology*. London.

Žižek, Slavoj, 1997: Multiculturalism. Or: The Cultural Logic of Multinational Capitalism. In: *New Left Review* no. 225, 28-51.

Žižek, Slavoj, 1999: *The Ticklish Subject. The Absent Centre of Political Ontology*. London.

Žižek, Slavoj, 2001: *Repeating Lenin*. Zagreb.

Žižek, Slavoj, 2002a: Introduction. Between the Two Revolutions. In Ibid. (ed.); V.I. Lenin, *Revolution at the Gates. A Selection of Writings from February to October 1917*. London, 1-14.

Žižek, Slavoj, 2002b: Afterword. Lenin's Choice. In: ibid (ed.); V.I. Lenin, *Revolution at the Gates. A Selection of Writings from February to October 1917*. London, 165-336.

Žižek, Slavoj, 2007a: Introduction. Mao Zedong: Marxist Lord of Misrule. In: ibid (ed.); Mao Tse-Tung, *On Practice and Contradiction*. London, 1-28.

Žižek, Slavoj 2007b: A Leninist Gesture Today. Against the Populist Temptation. In Sebastian Budgen, Eustache Kouvélakis and Slavoj Žižek (eds.), *Lenin Reloaded. Toward a Politics of Truth*. Durham, 74-98.

Žižek, Slavoj, 2008a: *For They Know Not What They Do. Enjoyment as a Political Factor*. London.

Žižek, Slavoj, 2008b: *Violence. Six Sideways Reflections*. New York.

Žižek, Slavoj, 2009a: *First as Tragedy, Then as Farce*. London.

Žižek, Slavoj, John Milbank and Creston Davis, 2009b: *The Monstrosity of Christ. Paradox or Dialectic?* Cambridge, MA.

Žižek, Slavoj, 2012: *The Year of Dreaming Dangerously*. London.

Žižek, Slavoj and Yong-june Park, 2013: *Demanding the impossible*. Cambridge.

Žižek, Slavoj, 2014: Rotherham Child Sex Abuse. It is Our Duty to Ask Difficult Questions. In: *The Guardian*, 1 September 2014. https://www.theguardian.com/commentisfree/2014/sep/01/rotherham-child-sex-abuse-difficult-questions

Žižek, Slavoj, 2015: The Non-Existence of Norway. In: *London Review of Books*, 9 September 2014. http://www.lrb.co.uk/2015/09/09/slavoj-zizek/the-non-existence-of-norway

Žižek, Slavoj 2016: *Against the Double Blackmail. Refugees, Terror and other Troubles with the Neighbours*. London.

Communist Politics and The State

Geoff Pfeifer

Political Ontologies of the State. Žižek, Badiou, and the Idea of the Revolution from the Outside.

One way of beginning to understand Žižek's conception of the state is by looking at the differences between his view and that of his long-time interlocutor, French philosopher Alain Badiou. In 2012's *Less Than Nothing*, Žižek takes Badiou to task for 'ontologizing' the state in his mature system.[1] According to Žižek, Badiou makes no distinction between the state and society. In fact, Badiou reduces the state to nothing more than the ideological (and ultimately military) guarantee of the static social order – as repressive and exploitive as it may be. Because of this, Badiou is unable to conceptualize a state beyond coordinates of the bourgeois capitalist form of the state. This conceptual weakness in Badiou's account is the result, as Žižek puts it, of his movement from 'history to ontology'.[2] Instead of thinking about the historical nature of particular states (and their differing historical forms), Badiou offers a non-historical, static concept of the state that is nothing more than that which acts as both a repressive and an ideological apparatus; the agent that produces (and reproduces) the view that a given social order is both just and without alternative. This leaves Badiou in the unfortunate position of being unable to conceive of revolution or a revolutionary practice without also seeing it as completely oppositional to – or outside of – the state form as such.

Žižek goes on to argue that even Marx does not end up at such a problematic stalemate with regard to the state. Though there is of course Marx's controversial notion of the 'withering of the state' under proper communism, the state that 'withers' is the bourgeois capitalist state, not the state form itself. So in this way, the state in the form of political activity, simply becomes something else: a body in which all participate. Thus, communism does not lead to the total absence of the state, but rather to its transformation into a body that does not simply serve the needs of one social class.

Badiou and Žižek have, thus, two different notions of the way in which revolutionary politics takes place outside of the state as it exists now. This has far-reaching implications for the ways in which they conceptualize such politics. In an attempt to better understand Žižek's own view of this 'outside' and how it differs from that of

---

1   Žižek 2012, 841-42.
2   Ibid., 842.

Badiou, I will explore the ways in which Badiou forgets an important insight of his one-time teacher and collaborator, Louis Althusser, namely the fact that ideology is something that is ever-present (even in a post-revolutionary situation) and is in fact a *necessary* component of any social organization whatsoever (even a revolutionary one). This is a position, I will argue, with which Žižek is in agreement, with the result that for him the state (as the foundation and support of ideology and ideological apparatuses) becomes a necessary component of revolutionary practice. By triangulating the views of Badiou, Žižek, and Althusser and looking at their similarities and differences, we can gain a better understanding of Žižek's overall position vis-à-vis the idea of the state and its role in emancipatory and revolutionary politics.

Badiou

To gain a better understanding of Badiou's conception of the state, a logical starting point is his seminal *Being and Event*. This text famously begins with the claim that 'there is no one, only the count-as-one'.[3] For Badiou, this is a foundational ontological claim about the nature of reality. The world (and its contents) as we understand it at any given time is the result of an 'operation' – or a set of operations – which Badiou identifies here as the 'count-as-one'.[4] It is through this operation that individuals, objects, institutions, and so forth come to have a kind of oneness, consistency, and are ultimately made meaningful in particular ways. In other words, the count-as-one operation does the work of making these kinds of things 'legible' (i.e. understandable, sensible) in a given time and place. What underlies this oneness, that is, what 'is' outside of (or prior to) the operation of the count, is what Badiou terms 'Being-*qua*-being,' or 'the multiple without one'.[5] This is what reality (or society) ultimately is: an infinite, inconsistent, incomplete, and unstructured multiplicity that is necessarily divided and contradictory.

Only by bringing order to such an inconsistent multiplicity (through the operation of counting) can a 'situation' be brought about. A 'situation' is a place in which Being-*qua*-being becomes legible in the particular way that it does at a particular time and in a particular place.[6] So 'situations' are temporally located places in which series of multiples are 'presented' as consistent and in such a way that makes them legible. Here is Badiou:

> Let's fix the terminology: I term *situation* any presented multiplicity. Granted the effectiveness of the presentation, as situation is a place of taking place, whatever the terms of

3 Badiou 2005, 24.
4 Ibid.
5 Ibid., 35.
6 Ibid., 23-30.

multiplicity in question. Every situation admits of its own particular operator of the count-as-one. This is the most general definition of a *structure*; it is what prescribes for a presented multiple, the regime of its count-as-one.[7]

We might think here, very broadly, of the ways in which the contemporary capitalist situation counts-as-one individuals according to their economic and other related properties. Under this regime of the count (or 'structure' as Badiou puts it in the quote above) we have (again very generally) various categories of workers that are counted, for instance, by the types of work that they do – blue-collar, white-collar, full-time, part-time, contingent, precarious, informal and so forth – and other categories of individuals who are non-workers but are also counted in relation to their status as laborers insofar as they make up the varieties of non-laboring individuals that are made possible by this particular counting operation – from the super wealthy who need not work to those who lack work for various reasons, to those who are, in some places anyway, prohibited from working (i.e., the very young, 'illegal' immigrants, et cetera).

What is nice about a simple example like this is that it allows us to see how it is that Badiou understands the claim that outside the structure of the situation in which things and individuals are counted-as-one in particular ways, there is an infinite/inconsistent multiplicity of non-ones. It is easy to see, for example, that individuals certainly can be counted this way (in relation to their status as workers/laborers in capitalist societies) but this is not the only way that such individuals can be counted-as-one. Indeed, there are multiple ways in which such individuals could be counted that have nothing to do with economics or job status. Moreover, these ways of counting-as-one are inconsistent with one another. For instance, individual humans can also be counted by other counting regimes based on religion, political affiliation, familial status, gender, biological sex, and so on.

We can now begin to see how, for Badiou, individuals are foundationally not-one. Badiou's view is that all things (not only individual humans) are subject to the same conditions. Nothing is a 'one' foundationally, but rather all things, foundationally, are shot through with inconsistencies, and contradictions. As such, they are neither fixed nor whole. It is, however, the counting regime that brings about fixity and consistency. The former in that it fixes the *ways* in which multiples are counted, and the latter because the counting regime, in Badiou's parlance, 'subtracts' all of the other possible modes of counting-as-one. So again, the structure of the counting operation 'subtracts' all of the multiple ways of counting that are inconsistent with the way a given structure counts. In doing this, the count-as-one subtracts or covers over the foundational inconsistency at the heart of multiplicity itself.

---

7 Ibid., 24.

The example given above, of the ways in which individuals can be counted by capitalism in relation to the status of their working lives, opens a window to another important feature of Badiou's general (or ontological) conception of both situations and the functioning of the law of the count here: it shows us the ways in which the counting operation is *asubjective*, as it is not the result of the subjective choices of individuals themselves. The differing categories and statuses of work/labor discussed above pre-exist any one individual and are, rather, categories into which we are inserted and into which we insert ourselves through our own activity and understanding.

It is here then, in relation to these last two points, that Badiou's understanding of the state becomes important. It is the 'state' of the situation that acts as the enforcer of the particular regime of the count-as-one. The state does this, according to Badiou, by acting to 're-present' the counted multiples that a given situation has presented in being structured by the law of the count.[8] There is, however, always the possibility that the foundational non-oneness (or inconsistent multiplicity) itself bubbles to the surface, with the result that the counting operation comes to be seen for what it is (as non-foundational). Hence, its legitimacy can be challenged, destabilized, and ultimately, toppled. It is the state as Badiou understands it that prevents this:

> The state is a sort of meta-structure that exercises the power of counting over all the subsets of the situation. Every situation has a state. Every situation is the presentation of itself, of what composes it, of what belongs to it. But it is also given as a state of the situation, that is, as the internal configuration of its parts or subsets, and therefore as representation.[9]

When Badiou says that the state 'represents' and codifies the subsets of counted multiples in a given situation, what he is getting at is that the state, in its re-presentation, ensures that all presented multiples have a place in the situation, that there is nothing – no unpresented inconsistency or set of inconsistent multiples – that can act to disturb the structure. In this way, then, the state for Badiou acts, to refer again to Althusser, both as a repressive apparatus – that is, it works to force all presented multiples into the categories delineated by the law of the count, repressing anything that is inconsistent with that law – and also as an ideological apparatus: it makes the situation and its structure appear as if it is foundational full stop, that there is nothing underneath or outside of this structure; that this particular structure is the eternal way of things rather than something which is the result of the counting operation itself. This is why, for Badiou, any truly revolutionary politics – indeed anything that can be properly called politics – must happen at a distance from the state and is a

---

8 Ibid., 94.
9 Badiou 2005a, 143-144.

process through which the state's power is called into question via making the limits (or the 'measure', as Badiou puts it in the quotation below) of its power visible. Politics, then, becomes a process of exposing the ideological nature of the state's work and the limits of its power:

> Politics puts the state at a distance, in the distance of its measure [...] The state is in fact the measureless enslavement of the parts of the situation [...] Freedom here consists in putting the State at a distance through the collective establishment of a measure for its excess.[10]

Badiou claims that politics happens at a distance from the state because it is the state itself – as an ontological entity – that is constantly working in such a way as to stabilize the situation, to make it appear as though there are no alternatives, and, ultimately, to undercut any possibility of change. While this is true at the level of ontology in Badiou's system, this can also be read as evincing Badiou's conception of the political state. A truly political act – or 'event' in Badiou's language – exposes the weaknesses of the structure's count (by displaying its measure, or its limit) and thereby challenges the power of the state, in whatever state form there is. As Alberto Toscano has put it, for Badiou, 'politics invariably takes its departure from an excess – the hidden excess of singularity subtracted from but absolutely dominated by the law of a situation – and it is aimed at inhibiting or terminating another excess, the excess of domination, the excess of the state.'[11]

Again, we can see that, on a Badiouan accounting of things, a truly political act/ event opens up a space in which the inconsistent multiplicity becomes legible and thus offers a challenge to the workings of state domination insofar as it exposes the ideological limits of the state's activity and reveals the truth of the situation (that it is not all there is, that there are other ways of counting, other ways of organizing, etc). For Badiou, this truth is universal or non-historical, because in that moment of truth something is revealed that is not bound to that time and place or to that law of the count (for any situation whatsoever).

As Badiou puts it in *Logics of Worlds*, 'a truth is an exception to what is'.[12] To be sure, for Badiou, such truth-events, though they form the foundation of the possibility of the destruction of the domination of the state, should not and cannot, after such destruction, simply become the new place from which a new order arises (with a similar structure to the old one). Here again is Toscano speaking on this point:

> No politics of non-domination can be founded on the proposal of a new order with which to substitute the old. Not the figure of a new bond, but the invention – extracted from the singularity of an event and directed at the structure of representation – of an experiment

---

10 Ibid., 145.
11 Toscano 2004.
12 Badiou 2009, 6.

in political unbinding, is what, according to Badiou, the politics of non-domination requires.[13]

To use Toscano's framing, for Badiou, the politics of non-domination, as a truly emancipatory form of politics, calls for an 'unbinding' of the political from the state apparatus, since the state is itself inextricably linked to politics of domination. For Badiou, any emancipatory politics must happen outside of the state form itself. With this in mind, we can turn to Žižek's critique, cited at the outset of this chapter, as it is here that this can now come into its proper focus.

Žižek

Žižek claims that Badiou loses sight of the radical potential of the state that exists outside of the bourgeois capitalist state, which is based on class domination. Žižek's critique is based on a different conception of the 'outside'. He states:

> Where, then, does the flaw in Badiou's account reside? [...] The danger of this move is that by establishing a direct link between a particular historical form of social organization and a basic ontological feature of the universe, it (implicitly, at least) ontologizes or eternalizes the state as a form of political organization: the political state becomes something we should resist, subtract ourselves from, act at a distance from, but simultaneously something which can never be abolished (save in utopian dreams).[14]

This concern should come as no surprise given what has been said above. The state, for Badiou, is an ever-present tool of domination. Because of this, it can never be put in the service of a form of politics that is emancipatory, nor can the state be overcome. Žižek thus continues:

> As a consequence of this short-circuit, Badiou gets caught in the typical Kantian ambiguity apropos the question of whether abandoning the form of Party-State, subtracting oneself from the State, acting in the interstices of the State, is an a priori necessity of radical emancipatory politics as such, or just the expression of a certain (our) historical moment, that of the global defeat of radical politics.[15]

The problem, according to Žižek, is not simply that Badiou has taken a less historical perspective overall in favor of the building of his philosophical ontology in *Being and Event*, rather in this process, Badiou has mistaken the historical nature of the bourgeois capitalist state – which is indeed a state that is a tool for class domination – for an ever-present ontological state of the situation. In other words, for Badiou,

---

13   Toscano 2004, 212.
14   Žižek 2012, 842.
15   Ibid.

the state always works as a tool of domination over/against the inconsistent multiple in any and all 'situations'.

Žižek's claim is that Badiou has forgotten the lesson of Marx: that outside of the social relations of capital, we can – and, indeed, must – think of a state that is not a tool for domination:

> Instead of withdrawing into a distance from the State, the true task should be to make the State work in a non-statal mode. The alternative 'either struggle for State power (which makes us the same as the enemy we are fighting) or withdraw into a posture of resistance from a distance toward the State is a false one because both its terms share the same premise: the State form as we know it is here to stay so that all we can do is take over the State or remain at a distance to it. Here one should shamelessly repeat the lesson of Lenin's *The State and Revolution*: the goal of revolutionary violence is not the take over of State power, but to transform it, radically changing its functioning [...] The 'dictatorship of the proletariat' is a kind of (necessary) oxymoron, *not* a State form in which the proletariat is the ruling class. We effectively have the 'dictatorship of the proletariat only when the State itself is radically transformed, relying on new forms of popular participation.[16]

Rather than acting at a distance from the state, Žižek holds that a truly radical politics acts within the state in such a way as to open up a gap between the capitalist state (or the state of domination), and the state of emancipation. This should, furthermore, be done in such a way that the state of emancipation becomes a viable location from which to intervene in the situation as it exists.

One example of the kind emancipatory state that Žižek has in mind here is the 'dictatorship of the proletariat', as put forward by Marx. This is, in Žižek's view, a truly a radical state form since it seeks to challenge the seemingly static and eternal nature of the bourgeois state. The latter cannot be done by simply divorcing oneself from the state. The dictatorship of the proletariat is not a state power in the same vein as the state power that exists under the capitalist regime. It does not simply constitute a change in the hands of power from one class to another, while leaving intact the exact same power structure. Rather it embodies something entirely different, something that acts to challenge the notion of what a state is, was, and could be. I will return to this below, but I want to pause to note that there is an important and helpful link here back to Althusser's conception of the split between ideology and science.

---

16 Žižek 2010, 219-220.

In both *For Marx* and in his contribution to *Reading Capital,* Althusser argues that through his break with Hegel, Marx establishes the science of history known as 'historical materialism'. It is this science that enables him to comprehend the historical development of society through different social formations. Furthermore, it provides Marx with a philosophical method ('dialectical materialism') which, as Althusser describes it, allows us to mark the distinction between the ideological and the non-ideological (in Althusser terms: the scientific).[17] This distinction between the ideological and the scientific also signifies the difference between what Badiou himself, in an early review of Althusser's work, describes as the difference between 'repetition and transformation'.[18] While ideology simply repeats existing structures, Marxist science transforms these structures into something new and different by recognizing the existing (and repeated) structures themselves as ideological, and subsequently partitioning the ideological structures off from that which science deems non-ideological.[19]

It is only through the scientific practice of dialectical materialism that we come to see existing social forms as non-static, and also become able to recognize attempts to assert such stasis as ideological. The connection to Žižek's assertion that the Marxist state form of the dictatorship of the proletariat is a radically different state form is obvious: it is from this position that we can best come to view the capitalist state form as ideological and begin to work to erode its structure in practice. Whereas the capitalist state form – the form of domination in Badiou's parlance – is ideological, the state form of the dictatorship of the proletariat – as the state form of emancipation – is scientific: once opened up, it is the space from which we can best view the ideological nature of the bourgeois state and its attempted dominance.

Further, as Žižek points out here, the goal of this communist state form is the total transformation of the state. In Marxist terms, this is referred to as the 'withering of the state', but we should not be mistaken: the state that withers and dies is the capitalist state, not the state form as such:

> This is why then, in a properly Marxist perspective, the ill-famed 'withering of the state' does not aim at a de-politicization of society, but (in its first step at least) at its radical and thorough 'politicization': one does not 'abolish the state' by getting rid of its excess in a transparent harmonious self-organization of a society, but by abolishing the specter of apolitical spheres, by demonstrating how 'there is nothing which is not political,' up to and including people's most intimate dreams.[20]

---

17   For more specifics, see Althusser 2005 and chapters one and two of Geoff Pfeifer 2015.
18   Badiou 2012, 147.
19   See chapter 2 of Pfeifer 2015 and Pfeifer 2015a.
20   Pfeifer 2015a.

Where the capitalist state partitions society and the social structure into various forms of political and non-political (and, hence, non-historical) practices and institutions, the emancipatory state form seeks to show that this very division is itself ideological, that all practices are both political and historical. This is to say that all practices, regardless of their temporal location and grouping with other practices, are the result of particular historical social organizations and thus act to sustain those particular organizations. But this also means that these particular organizations are subject to the possibility of revision through a radical form of politics that seeks to reorient them in the ways that we have discussed above.

Again, there is a link to Althusser's work, this time to his notion of ideological interpellation. On Althusser's account, everything about us, down to our subjective (conscious) awareness is the result of the particular way(s) in which the social space is ordered at a given time (there is, here, broad agreement between Althusser, Žižek, and Badiou). For Althusser, it is through engaging in (and being engaged by) the particular sets of pre-existing social practices that we find in our world that we come to our self-understanding. These practices 'interpellate' us (or call to us) to act in certain ways – which are defined by the social structure – and to locate and understand ourselves as beings in that world. The example given above of different forms of work might again be helpful in this context. These different categories exist for us as various ways in which (portions of) one's life can be defined. They 'call' to us to insert ourselves into one or more of them so that we can achieve the identities that we would like or that we simply come to have. In this way, at least partially, they allow (or don't allow) the kinds of identities within which we recognize ourselves and others recognize us.[21] The key feature of these interpellative social practices (or 'ideological apparatuses', as Althusser calls them) is that they are ever-present. Though a given set of practices might come and go as differing forms of social organization might come and go (or shift and change), the overall structure of interpellation remains: our self-understanding is always subject to a given set of interpellative practices (or ideological apparatuses). Here is Althusser on this point:

> Ideology is as such an organic part of every social totality. It is as if human societies could not survive without these specific formations [...] Human societies secrete ideology as the very element and atmosphere indispensable to their historical respiration and life.[22]

---

21 For more on this, see: Althusser 1971.
22 Althusser 2005, 232.

Two Conclusions

There are two ways to understand the link between Althusser and the thought of both Badiou and Žižek in relation to notions of the state. On the one hand, one could say that if Badiou's conception of the state as the ideological enforcer of a situation's count is right, then we can see how Althusser's understanding of ideology is implicated in this. That is, if ideology is ever-present, then Badiou is right to think of the state of the situation as ever-present, always working to enforce a given count and working to subtract any inconsistencies so as to avoid any instability in the situation. From this perspective, one can certainly see why Badiou might claim that any way of overcoming this domination must find its origin outside of the coordinates of the state and ideology and thus must be a kind of politics that challenges the state as such.

On the other hand, we can also read Althusser differently. Although it may be true, given the structure of ideology, that there is no escaping its interpellative processes completely (as a mechanism that structures society), scientific practice can still make us aware of these ideological structures so that we can come to challenge them. The Althusserian notion of science provides us with a means to differentiate between the ideological and the non-ideological, but this is an ongoing process. For this, we need a state apparatus of our own, an outside *within* the state form itself. Such a communist state apparatus could act on, and in, the ideological plane in such a way as to offer a challenge to the existing state of affairs. This, then, is the goal of the dictatorship of the proletariat and how it works.

This latter position leads us back to the Žižekian emphasis on the importance of the state for revolutionary/emancipatory politics. If it is true that ideology and ideological practices are part of what make up our subjective awareness, then the self really is political all the way down. In this case, it is the job of the communist state form to bring that process to light and appropriate it for revolutionary and emancipatory goals.

This also brings to light another difference between Žižek and Badiou. While the latter ultimately searches for universal, non-historical truths, Žižek insists that there is no neutral, non-political/historical place from which to act. Such action always takes place from within a given historical present and a given set of social structures and social practices. In this respect it is a matter of finding those practices that allow for the opening of the revolutionary gap: the 'outside' inside the historical situation that opens up the space for change. Opening up this space will not end in the destruction of the state as such. Rather it will lead to the destruction of the bourgeois state form in favor of a renewed and emancipatory state form.

References

Althusser, Louis, 1971: Ideology and Ideological Apparatuses. Notes Toward an Investigation. In: Ibid.: *Lenin and Philosophy, and other Essays*. New York, 127-188.

Althusser, Louis, 2005: *For Marx*. New York and London.

Althusser, Louis, 2009: *Reading Capital*. New York and London.

Badiou, Alain, 2005: *Being and Event*. New York and London.

Badiou, Alain, 2005a: *Metapolitics*. London and New York.

Badiou, Alain, 2009: *Logics of Worlds*. New York and London.

Badiou, Alain, 2012: The (Re)commencement of Dialectical Materialism. In: Ibid.: *The Adventure of French Philosophy*. New York and London.

Pfeifer, Geoff, 2015: *The New Materialism. Althusser, Badiou, and Žižek*. New York.

Pfeifer, Geoff, 2015a: On Althusser on Science, Ideology and the New. Or: Why we should Continue Reading *Reading Capital*. In: *Crisis and Critique* 2:2 (2015), 125-141.

Toscano, Alberto, 2004: From the State to the World? Badiou and Anti-capitalism. In: *Communication and Cognition* 37:3-4 (2004), 199-224.

Žižek, Slavoj, 2010: How to Begin From the Beginning. In: Costas Douzinas and Slavoj Žižek (eds.), 2010: *The Idea of Communism*. London and New York, 219-220.

Žižek, Slavoj, 2012: *Less Than Nothing. Hegel and the Shadow of Dialectical Materialism*. London and New York.

Marc De Kesel

Authentic Rebellion, Terroristic Institutionalization.
On the Žižekian subject of the political

... the more 'authentic the rebellion, the more 'terroristic' is this institutionalization.
Slavoj Žižek[1]

A little rebellion now and then is a good thing.
Thomas Jefferson[2]

Not Without a State, Not Without a Party

The life of a society encompasses a lot more than only state power. It is first of all a 'system' that instils solidarity among people, manages an economy of production and trade, and shapes all forms of culture. If the state intervenes, it is basically in order to bring things under its own control, or, as is all too often the case, to manipulate these things under the pretext of protecting and enforcing the state as such in favor of those who are in power. The state can thus easily become the direct enemy of emancipatory and revolutionary politics. The history of the West's political Left illustrates this abundantly. Remember Karl Marx's thesis that the end of the fight against capitalism coincides with surpassing the state as such. In his view, society in the proper sense of the term – as a community of '*socii*', as associates in 'liberty, equality and brotherhood' – is irreconcilable with state power. For the same reason, many contemporary revolutionary activists consider it their main task to destabilize the state – or, as activists inspired by Deleuze and Guattari call it – to never stop de-territorializing its all too 'static' position. The real life of a society is too 'diverse', too 'differential', too 'rhizomatic' to be subsumed by the unifying stability principles of a state.

Although Slavoj Žižek is far from unsympathetic with this kind of de-territorializing revolutionary politics, he does not agree with its anti-state intentions.[3] In one of his more recent books, *In Defense of Lost Causes*, for instance, he agrees with Peter Hallward

---

1 Žižek 2008a, 419.
2 Jefferson in a letter to James Madison, January 30, 1787. Cited in Žižek 2010, 392.
3 The defense of the state has always been one of Žižek's topics. See for instance his contribution to a publication of the NSK (Neue Slowenische Kunst): RWIN 1993: np.

that the poetics of 'resistance', of de-territorialized nomadic mobility, of creating *lignes de fuite,* of never being where one is expected to dwell, is not enough; the time has come to start creating what one is tempted to call liberated territories, the well-defined and delineated social spaces in which the reign of the System is suspended: a religious or artistic community, a political organization, and other forms of 'a place of one's own'.[4]

The 'territories' or 'well-defined social places' Žižek is pleading for in this passage are the slums in the suburbs of so many capitalist metropolises. They possess the real potential for revolutionary resistance, and if that potential is to be turned into a reality, it is only because these 'proletarians' are not nomadic but stick to their territory. They constitute the 'part of no part' from where a revolutionary change is to be expected. This is what Hugo Chavez, the former revolutionary president of Venezuela, understood so well, as Žižek explains on the next page.

> Hugo Chavez's greatest achievement in the first years of his rule was precisely the politicization (inclusion into political life, social mobilization) of slum-dwellers; in other countries, they mostly persist in apolitical inertia. It was this political mobilization of the slum-dwellers which saved him from a US-sponsored coup: to the surprise of everyone, Chavez included, the slum-dwellers descended en masse to the affluent city center, tipping the balance of power to his advantage.[5]

And, Žižek continues, this move by Chavez went hand in hand, not with the de-territorialization of the state, but with the conquering of these territories by the state. More precisely, the slum-dwellers' revolutionary potential was integrated into the state and subsequently turned into the base of a new state power.

> The course on which Chavez embarked from 2006 is the exact opposite of the postmodern Left's mantra regarding de-territorialization, rejection of statist politics, and so on: far from 'resisting state power', he *grabbed* power (first by an attempted coup, then democratically), ruthlessly using the state apparatuses and interventions to promote his goals.[6]

Žižek concludes his reflection by stressing the necessity for any set of radical politics to aim at conquering and defending state power, since '[t]oday, it is the big capitalists, from Bill Gates to the ecological polluters, who "resist" the state'.[7]

In sum, revolutionary politics cannot do without something like a state. This is far from being in contradiction with the imperative requiring the 'impossible' that is at the base of every revolution. In *Demanding the Impossible*, a 2008 interview book, Žižek writes, referring to the anti-state criticism of May 1968:

> I think it's too easy to say that state power is corrupted, so let's withdraw into this role of ethical critic of power, etc. But here I'm almost a conservative Hegelian. How many things have to function in order for something to be done? Laws, manners, rules: these

---

4 Žižek 2008a, 426.
5 Žižek 2008a, 427. See also Žižek 2013, 103-107.
6 Žižek 2008a, 427.
7 Žižek 2008a, 427.

are what make us feel truly free. I don't think that people are aware of this fact. That was the hypocrisy of many leftists there [in the Paris of May '68]: their target was the whole structure of the state apparatus of power. But we still need to count on all the state apparatus functioning. So my vision is not some utopian community *without* a state. We can call it the state or whatever, but more than ever what we actually need are certain organisms of social power and its distribution. [...] What fascinates me, therefore, is the idea that we the left should now take over this ideology: 'We are the true law and order. We are the true morality.' I very much like this idea of the left taking this position.[8]

Revolution as the Basis of the State

Like no one else, Žižek is aware of the revolutionary basis and origin of the modern state. The American, the French and the Russian Revolutions have functioned as illuminating examples for the majority of the newly created states during the nineteenth and twentieth century. But while being the result of revolutions, these states, precisely by becoming states, have all been inclined to deny their revolutionary nature. They fought and destroyed state power, but once they had themselves grabbed power, many of them established state forms that were equally – or even more – rigid and oppressive than the ones they had overthrown. Their revolutions had fought the cruelties of the ancient regime, but often did not wait long to surpass them in cruelty, or even turn into regimes of terror. Fighting the *Ancien Régime*'s inequality and lack of freedom, Robespierre suspected all those who might have secretly preserved individual privileges and, at least in the eyes of Robespierre, allowed themselves more freedom than others. Soon, the leader of the *Commité du salut publique* (Commity of Public Safety) used both his party and the new state power to 'purify' the new revolutionary society from such enemies of the revolution. The guillotine became the face of freedom; state government turned into terror.

The modern state is thus the result of revolution, i.e. of an act of 'negating' the existing power, to put it in Hegelian terms (one of Žižek's main theoretical frameworks). The core problem of the new state is how to deal with that origin, since negation is inherently applicable to itself. What about negating the negation, i.e. revolutionizing the revolution itself? What would that mean? How can such a second negation be conceived? Must a revolution not simply stick to its revolutionary origins and strive for stabilization of the new regime? Is the latter not simply unavoidable and necessary to turn the 'negative' breaking of power into something positive, in a party taking power and creating a new state? How else could the negativity that the revolution is based upon create a positive foundation for the new society people fought for? In this case, the following question emerges: How can the party and the

---

8 Žižek 2013, 75-76. Žižek's italics.

(new) state deal with the negativity that is their origin, core and essence? Can the celebration and cultivation of its revolutionary origin be something else than a façade behind which the new power oppresses its opposition?

This question has grave implications. If 'terror' is an unavoidable and necessary part of modern politics – of breaking old and creating new states – how are new states to deal with this? Where does the boundary between liberating violence and repressive terror lie? This abysmal question forms one of the main threads in Žižek's political thought. How can we do justice to the radical negativity upon which all kinds of modern political order are based? How can we do justice to negativity without negating it? Is there a *right* way to negate negativity? These questions underlie Žižek's reflections on the past, present and future of revolutionary politics. It is here that Žižek aims to finds answers to the faults of global capitalism and the failure of today's democracy to solve them.

Democracy's Deficiency

Žižek is not afraid of phrasing the latter problem in the shape of the following suggestive question: What if today's political power is held by capitalism, and liberal democracy merely functions as its façade? Even though Žižek is not against democratic practices *per se*, he takes that question very seriously.

As is commonly known, Žižek endorses the Marxist thesis that globalized capital holds the real political power, and not national or international political bodies. How then are we to stop the inequality and injustice that inevitably result from a global capitalist world order? Žižek's answer is a classical Marxist one: only a radical negation of capitalism can change the existing unjust order of the world. He thus pleads for a revolution, in the strongest possible sense of the term: a radical denial, an act of negation without compromises, overthrowing the totality of the existing capitalist system.

One of Žižek's most controversial moves has been his counterposing of revolution and democracy. Why can democracy not be the agency of an anti-capitalist revolution? For is democracy itself not a game of negativity par excellence? In a democratic system, no one *really* possesses *the* power, since the one who has it has received it from others, more precisely from the 'general will', which is the only authority that *really* possesses the power. However, 'the people' can only speak when their supposed unity is 'denied' and split into the voices of every citizen separately. Only on Election Day do the people speak. Yet, every citizen's vote only expresses his or her own individual will, irrespective of what his or her fellow citizens vote. And the day after the elections, the people's 'general will' is immediately alienated by the voice of their representatives. Moreover, the whole procedure of democracy is organized in such a way that the voice – including the power – of the representatives is able to be contested and negated by parliamentary and other opposition: by trade unions, by the press and the media, and so on. In short, although democracy stands for the will of the people as the basis of all political power, that will performs in a principally *negative* way: negated by its representatives, negated by limited time of that representation, negated by the multitude of individuals unable to speak with 'one and indivisible' voice, et cetera.[9]

So why is it that this game of negativity that is democracy is not able to say 'no' to what, certainly on a global scale, causes disaster for the majority of the people: capitalism? Because democracy is not able to operationalize its own terror; thus one can summarize Žižek's provocative answer. Hence, 'the ultimate democratic illusion – and, simultaneously, the point at which the limitations of democracy become directly tangible – is that one can accomplish social revolution painlessly, through "peaceful means", by simply winning elections.'[10]

Žižek proposes a different definition of 'real' democracy, thus denouncing the 'procedural' form of democracy that is described above. For Žižek, the core of this 'true' democracy is harsh negativity. It is not the regime of the majority, but of those denied by that majority, of those who are not allowed to rise to platforms of political power. Society turns into democracy when the excluded are seen as its real representatives, those who are part of society but have no part in it. A society becomes democratic when it 'politicizes' those who up to that point were excluded from it, those who were considered to be insignificant outsiders of the political.

> This identification of the part of society with no properly defined place within it (or which rejects the allocated subordinated place within it) with the Whole is the elementary gesture of politicization, discernable in all great democratic events from the French Revolution (in which *le troisième état* proclaimed itself identical to the Nation as such, against the aristocracy and clergy) to the demise of East European socialism (in which dissident 'fora' proclaimed themselves representative of the entire society against the party *nomenklatura*). In this precise sense, politics and democracy are synonymous: the basic aim of anti-democratic politics always and by definition is and was depoliticization, the demand that 'things should turn to normal', with each individual sticking to his or her particular job. [11]

Žižek's point is that the historical forms of liberal democracy as they were put into practice in the nineteenth and twentieth centuries are in fact anti-democratic. These forms of democracy deny or neutralize the 'event' of the real '*demos*', the people as '*plebs*', negating that society. Liberal democracy *de*politicizes the (democratic and radically negative) core of politics, the very essence of democracy. That essence is

---

9   This paragraph briefly evokes the democracy theory of the French political philosopher Claude Lefort. See: Lefort 1986; Ibid 1989.
10   Žižek 2008b, lxxx.
11   Žižek 2008a, 415-416.

revolutionary, since it puts the excluded in the center of the society that excludes them. This radical kind of change is not possible within the boundaries of reformist liberal democratic procedures; it requires an 'explosion' of the existing society, a drastic rebellion which overthrows the social order, democratic procedures included. And, so Žižek concludes in the sentence following the ones just quoted:

> And this brings us to the inevitable paradoxical conclusion: *the 'dictatorship of the prole-tariat' is another name for the violence of the democratic explosion itself.* The 'dictatorship of the proletariat' is thus the zero-level at which the difference between legitimate and illegitimate state power is suspended, in other words, when state power as such is illegitimate.[12]

What seems to be the opposite of democracy is in fact its core: dictatorship[13], not dictatorship *as such* but dictatorship by those who, up to that moment, experienced the social order as a dictatorship: the excluded, the 'proletarians'. However, democracy is not able to keep itself at the level of its own core. A few lines further, we read:

> This strange coupling of democracy and dictatorship is grounded in the tension that pertains to the very notion of democracy. There are two elementary and irreducible sides to democracy: violent egalitarian imposition of those who are 'supernumerary'; and the regulated (more or less) universal procedure of choosing those who exert power. How do these two sides relate to each other? What if democracy in the second sense (the regulated procedure of registering the 'people's voice') is ultimately *a defense against itself,* against democracy in the sense of the violent intrusion of the egalitarian logic that disturbs the hierarchical functioning of the social system, an attempt to re-functionalize this excess, to make it a part of the normal running things.[14]

Democracy cannot but repress its very core, its explosive negativity. In its own eyes, this explosive negativity appears as mere terror. 'The "terroristic" aspect of democracy can only appear as its "totalitarian" distortion', we read a few lines further. Our democratic eyes are not able to see 'the line that separates the authentic democratic explosion of revolutionary terror from the "totalitarian" party state regime'.[15] Still, Žižek's political project is not simply about rehabilitating the democratic explosion. The question is how this democratic explosion can be 'inscribed' in a new social order. Referring to Jacques Rancière in deeming the social order as a 'police' order, Žižek states[16]:

> The true task lies not in momentary democratic explosions which undermine the established 'police' order, but in the dimension designated by Badiou as that of 'fidelity' to

---

12 Žižek 2008a, 416. Zizek's italics.
13 See also Žižek 2010, 393: 'Pure democracy *has* to appear as its opposite'. Zizek's italics.
14 Žižek 2008a, 417. Zizek's italics.
15 Žižek 2008a, 418.
16 See, for instance chapter 2 in Rancière 1999, 21-42.

the Event: translating/inscribing the democratic explosion into the positive 'police' order, imposing on social reality a *new* lasting order. *This* is the properly 'terroristic' dimension of every authentic democratic explosion: the brutal imposition of a new order. And this is why, while everybody loves democratic rebellions, the spectacular/carnivalesque explosions of the popular will, anxiety arises when this will wants to persist, to institutionalize itself – and the more "authentic" the rebellion, the more 'terroristic' is this institutionalization.[17]

Thus, Žižek claims that what is needed to combat capitalism is not procedural democracy but 'real' democracy. However, since the latter cannot but repress and betray its 'real' core, we do not need such things as democracy at all. Democracy is even our 'enemy', Žižek writes.[18] We need revolution, 'rebellion', '"authentic" rebellion'. Seen from our everyday liberal democratic perspective, we need 'terror', since the institutionalization of that rebellion – the 'negation of negation' that does not repress its original negativity – cannot but have a 'terroristic' appearance.

For Žižek, irrespective of its appearance, 'terror' is needed in order to make a rebellion 'authentic'. In this sense, Žižek pleads for 'good terror', although it remains unclear what he means by this and how it is different from terror sec.[19] Perhaps, our attachment to the liberal democratic order does not allow us to see the difference?

In sum, negativity, the negation of the present social order, forms the 'essence' of a just politics. This negativity may not be negated by the new order. And, yet, it cannot but be. The only way to deal with this conundrum is, according to Žižek, to 'translate' and 'inscribe' this negativity *as such* (as 'terror') into the new order. In the same move, the new order must establish new rules, take power and establish a state. For Žižek, the only actor capable of doing so in a conscious and reflective way – conscious and reflective of the problems discerned above – is the political party.

The Party/State as Subject of the Political

Žižek is never negative about the state *as such*. It is true that a revolution must overthrow the state, but an 'authentic' rebellion has to create a new state in the same move. To do so in a right way, to avoid the trap of the new regime evolving into a similarly repressive state, a platform is needed that remains conscious of the negative core and origin of the new regime. This is the only way in which mere negativity can be turned into 'good' negativity, the *right* way to negate negativity. The state

---

17 Žižek 2008a, 418-419. Zizek's italics.
18 In the 'Introduction' to a collection of Mao texts, Žižek includes a quote by Alain Badiou: 'Today the enemy is not called the Empire of Capital. It is called Democracy'. And, as Žižek explains: 'What today, prevents the radical questioning of capitalism itself is precisely *the belief in the democratic form of the struggle against capitalism*'. Žižek 2007, 7.
19 Žižek 2013, 835.

or party is capable of assuming such a role. Without the stable platform of a party or a state, the negativity at the origin of the new revolutionary society would give way to repressive terror. That party or state, however, will never be itself without some brutal negativity, some 'terror'.

Žižek thus stresses the necessity of a party or a state, emphasizes the inescapably terroristic side of its rule, and suggests that there is the possibility of 'good terror'. All this, however, conceals the theoretical problem at the heart of this issue. Who or what is the 'subject' of society and politics, i.e. its 'bearer', its 'base' or 'foundation'?[20] For Žižek, revolutionary politics must acknowledge that the real subject of politics is negativity, the negation of the present social order. The only way of doing so is by radically embracing that negativity. Thus, revolutionaries must take the plunge into it, must surrender themselves to that negativity without any reserve. As an example, Žižek refers to Lenin's decision to incite the Russian Revolution. This decision was not based upon the correct application of the Marxist theory, but rather upon the radical opposite. Marxism did not give Lenin the conviction that his Revolution would succeed. Rather, it was an all-or-nothing decision, an act that might work out in two ways, without guarantees. For Žižek, precisely the negative character of such an act requires an agency capable of turning that negativity into positivity.

In order to think in terms of that agency, Žižek refers to the philosophical theory of Alain Badiou. For Badiou, society is based on a radical contingency: the hidden possibility of any society reconnecting with its ontological 'ground'. This reconnection allows it to negate and revolutionize the existing order. Badiou's term for this is the 'event'. [21] Under the French *Ancien régime*, it was unheard of and unthinkable that all human beings were politically equal. Under that regime, men were divided into three 'estates', and the sum of these estates was supposed to be the state. For Badiou, those who were not represented in the state – the 'part of no part' as Žižek calls them – were the beholders of the 'event'. Not being represented, they were simply present: nameless, radical, contingent. The realization that Man 'is' and has a right to be heard, regardless of his belonging to any official representation, constituted an 'event' that reconnected society with its 'event-based' foundation. This real-

---

20 'Subject' is used here in the 'formal' sense of the term. Its origin is the Latin *subiectum*, in Aristotle's logic indicating the 'bearer' of an 'attribute'. For instance: a tree (*subiectum*) is green (attribute). In Late Antiquity, the word gains an ontological meaning. *Subiectum* becomes the 'bearer' of being as such. In medieval Christian philosophy, God is the subject. That divine subject 'dies' with the emerging of Modernity in the 17th century, when Man becomes his own bearer/subject. If the same goes for society or the state (society has 'itself' as subject/bearer), what, then, is that 'self'? This question about the core or essence of modern society continues to haunt modern political philosophy. Žižek follows Hegel and states that at the center of society there is 'nothing', that its 'self' is pure 'negativity'. Because of this, the core or essence of society is inherently revolutionary. For an introduction to the genealogy of the word 'subject', see for instance: Balibar, Cassin and Libera 2004.

21 Badiou 2006; Žižek 2014.

ization formed the basis of radical political action capable of radically reconstituting the basis of society. At the same time, there was 'truth' in that event: all men *are* equal simply because they exist; their political equality is based in the universality of their very being.

Although the possibility of an 'event' is always present in society, it can only happen when some recognize it, and on that basis start challenging the existing order. To be realized, the event needs a revolution and, thus, revolutionaries who perform that revolution – by forming a party and taking power to take over and transform the state. For Badiou, the event needs a 'subject', the revolution needs revolutionaries as 'bearers' of the event. Those who decide to be loyal to the truth acknowledged in the event – the idea that all human beings are politically equal – are its subject. The subject is the party fighting to turn the truth of the event into reality. For Badiou, the real basis of a society is the event, but the event itself is not the subject. In his theory, the word 'subject' is strictly preserved for the revolutionary agency, for those who turn the possibility of the event into reality.

It is important to note that Badiou's subject is not 'contaminated' – or: transformed – by the event (of, for example, the French Revolution). The event poses a radical negativity, haunting society as long as it is not realized. Its subject on the other hand, the revolutionary party, appears as mere positivity. At every moment, the party remains the self-assured party it considers itself to be, also when it starts ruling society in the shape of a 'dictatorship of the proletariat'. Even when the force that it uses turns out to be terroristic, it has to remain loyal to the truth-event, *despite* that terror.

With Žižek inspired by Hegel's philosophy, however, one would expect him to claim, against Badiou, that the event *does* contaminate its subject. Those who sustain and realize a revolution have to fight, not only against their opponents, but also against the negativity that is part of their very position as the bearer of the said revolution. In the end, the terror of Robespierre's government changed the revolutionary regime *itself*, including the revolutionaries who started the French Revolution. As a result, the new regime became its own negation. This example shows why the revolutionary subject – the party, for instance – can never hold any certainty about itself. At any time, it may discover it does *not* possess the truth it supposed it possessed.

Yet, Žižek does not pay much attention to the possibility of the subject being contaminated by the negativity of the event. This is remarkable, given that other main framework in which his thought operates: Lacanian theory. Lacan was a psychoanalyst and philosopher, who focused his work on theorizing the subject, both as personal identity and as political or social identities. In Lacanian theory, identity is marked by *desire*: one is never identical with oneself, rather one coincides with a desire to be so. However, that desire can never be fulfilled. That lack marks our existence, for the (individual, political or social) subject is a 'split subject'. To put it in typically Lacanian phrasing: the subject 'is' a 'lack of being'. This traumatic split defines the human condition. For Lacan, our condition is marked by a radical negativity, a negativity that contaminates us even on the level of the individual subject.

Žižek is familiar with and supportive of Lacan's theory. With Lacan, he stresses that, to overcome his 'split' state, the subject must confront itself and must face the traumatic negativity which is at its heart. Furthermore, he agrees with Lacan that this can only be done successfully in a way that is self-destructive for that very subject. That confrontation, the 'Act' in Lacanian terms, has become a central concept in Žižek's theory. In 'committing' an Act, the subject casts off the alienated identity it bears, and fully embraces the 'lack of being' upon which that identity rests. Thus, in deciding to try and seize power, Lenin jumped into the 'lack', embracing the groundlessness and uncertainty that were at the heart of his Act. In doing so, Žižek often repeats, he stopped being a 'Marxist' and instead became a 'Leninist'. The Act is by definition revolutionary. If successful, it incites a revolution that destroys the coordinates of the existing order and creates new coordinates for a new order. For Žižek, the Badiouian 'event' requires such an Act that destroys the subject and transforms it, so as to avoid the revolution giving way to bad terror. Robespierre remained committed to his original program and thus changed from a liberator into a tyrant. He was not able to build on the negativity that was at the heart of his revolutionary act.

For Žižek, the subject that decides to commit an Act has to give up its very position as a subject, whereas for Badiou the event requires a subject that firmly holds its position. Compared to Badiou's ideas about the relationship between the event and its subject, the Žižekian view on the relationship between the Act and its subject is thoroughly paradoxical. However negative and 'subjectless' a revolutionary Act may be, it still requires a subject, someone who commits to the revolutionary Act. In Žižek's writings on democracy, it is the excluded who Act, taking power of those who previously excluded them and, in taking power, constituting a power that is 'one and indivisible'. In countless reflections on the revolutionary Act, Žižek ends up claiming the necessity of a fully positive subject. Each time, however, when the question re-emerges of how this subject will subsequently have to deal with the negative core of the new society, Žižek refers to the transformative nature of the Act with regard to the subject. Is this one of the reasons why Žižek feels so close to the Badiouian system?

At this point, Žižek's thinking keeps revolving around questions. Who is to Act? Where does the boundary between liberating violence and revolutionary terror lie? Even if one agrees with the idea that, within the process of a revolution, a phase of dictatorship is unavoidable, one does not really find in Žižek's thinking indications of how that dictatorship will turn into a state that recognizes its inner negativity, its split condition (in the Lacanian sense of the term). Will this conclusion be countered by new reflections that will emerge within the flow of publications that will surely continue to appear?

References

Badiou, Alain, 2006: *Being and Event*. London and New York.

Balibar, Étienne, Barbara Cassin and Alain de Libera, 2004: Sujet. In: Barbara Cassin, *Vocabulaire européen des philosophies. Dictionnaire des intraduisibles*. Paris, 1233-1253.

Lefort, Claude, 1986: *The Political Forms of Modern Society. Bureaucracy, Democracy, Totalitarianism*. Cambridge (Mass).

Lefort, Claude, 1989: *Democracy and Political Theory*. Cambridge (UK).

Rancière, Jacques, 1999: *Disagreement. Politics and Philosophy*. Minneapolis and London.

RWIN, 1993: *Padiglione NSK. XLV Bienale de Venezia*. Ljubliana.

Žižek, Slavoj (ed.), Mao Tse-Tung, 2007: *On Practice and Contradiction*. London and New York.

Žižek, Slavoj, 2008a: *In Defence of Lost Causes*. London and New York.

Žižek, Slavoj, 2008b, *For They Do Not Know. Enjoyment as a Political Factor*. London and New York.

Žižek, Slavoj, 2010: *Living in the End Times*. London and New York.

Žižek, Slavoj, 2012, *Less than Nothing. Hegel and the Shadow of Dialectical Materialism*. London and New York.

Žižek, Slavoj, 2013, *Demanding the Impossible*. Cambridge (UK) and Malden (Mass).

Žižek, Slavoj, 2014, *Event. A Philosophical Journey Through a Concept*. London.

Geoff Boucher

Neo-communist Strategy and Revolutionary Warfare:
Reflections on the Distinction between the Politics of Antagonism and
the Logic of Hostility

Introduction

Alain Badiou has defined the twentieth century as characterised by the 'passion for the real', the longing to leap beyond superficial appearances into the authentic yet violent kernel of reality. He proposes that this was particularly true of revolutionary politics. The many variants of historical communism all aimed for the heart of social transformation, where it was believed that the construction of the Socialist New Man was coextensive with the destruction of actually existing human limitations.[1] But this desire for a ferocious purgation was not restricted to the communist movement. Badiou rightly defines the fascist mimicry of true communist revolution as a pseudo-event. Nonetheless, both revolutionary emancipation and radical authoritarianism have for a long time followed the same historical trajectory. That trajectory is the militarisation of politics – the tendency to substitute violence, as an index of revolution, for social transformation.

The militarisation of politics is a politically neutral, instrumental orientation to successfully overthrowing states. That makes it a technology that can be used by both poles on the political continuum. The strategy of revolutionary warfare, with its tactics of guerrilla insurgency, is well known. Guerrilla warfare involves the progressive spread of light infantry actions by designated irregulars, who aim to carve out revolutionary zones within the existing country. Making areas of the national territory ungovernable is followed by the creation of rural liberated zones as nuclei for a new state. Finally, the major cities are surrounded and overwhelmed by regular assault, generally supported by armed insurrection and irregular actions. The classical works on the topic are Lenin, Mao Zedong (a.k.a., 'Mao Tse-Tung') and Che Guevara, with a notable contribution by Vo Nguyen Giap.[2] Additionally, in a philosophical work, Carl Schmitt defines guerrilla warfare as the 'total war' arising from the 'absolute enmity' provoked by what he calls 'non-telluric' (i.e., internationalist)

---

1 Badiou 2007, 54-55 and 174-178.
2 Lenin 1965; Tse-Tung 1967, 79-194; Guevara 1998; Vo Nguyen 1970.

partisans. Schmitt's shorthand for this situation is the proper name of Mao, although he does not restrict the strategy to left-wing politics.[3]

As Slavoj Žižek points out, this is of more than historical interest. The militarisation of politics, characteristic of both left-wing and right-wing radicalism, remains an influential tendency despite the collapse of historical communism. The destiny of the democratic revolutions of the 'Arab Spring' illustrates the continued effects of this legacy:

> Reversing the well-known characterization of Marxism as 'the Islam of the twentieth century', a secularization of Islam's abstract fanaticism [...] Islam is turning out to be the 'Marxism of the twenty-first century', taking up, after Communism, its violent anti-capitalism.[4]

The militarisation of politics deeply influenced twentieth-century radicalism. Radical political thinking in the twenty-first century must come to terms with that legacy. That brings me to the question of Žižek's neo-communist politics and where he stands regarding revolutionary warfare. Žižek's striking provocations seem to advocate a prolongation of the militarisation of politics. His defense of the Jacobin politics of neo-communism connects its programmatic foundations in egalitarian justice to its aim of inaugurating a revolutionary state. Furthermore, Žižek links rehabilitating Robespierre's revolutionary Terror to repeating Leninist politics and stages a provocative retrieval of the nomenclature of the dictatorship of the proletariat.[5] 'The key premise of *State and Revolution*', Žižek writes, is that 'the State, in its very notion, is a dictatorship'. The conclusion: 'we are legitimately entitled to exercise full violent terror, since, within this domain, every democracy is a fake'.[6] The 'harsh consequence to be accepted' in the space of the eternal idea of revolutionary justice is the paradox of an anti-democratic institutionalisation of the egalitarian-democratic impulse, as 'revolutionary-democratic terror'.[7] That logic culminates in a rehabilitation of Mao's politics:

> In modern history, the politics of revolutionary terror casts its shadow over the epoch which spans from Robespierre to [...] its last instalment [which] was the Maoist Cultural Revolution.[8]

That statement might lead us to ask: is Žižek's neo-communism a variant of neo-Maoism? Certainly, at one point Žižek wrote an introduction to the work of the chairman of the (Maoist) Revolutionary Communist Party (USA), Bob Avakian.[9]

---

3 Schmitt 2007.
4 Žižek 2012c, 73.
5 Žižek 2008a, 160-163.
6 Žižek 2002c: 192. .
7 Žižek 2008a, 175.
8 Ibid.
9 Žižek 2005, vii-x.

Today, Žižek employs inflammatory slogans drawn from Mao and describes his global strategy as one of Cultural Revolution. The starting point for radical strategy today, he writes, is 'to fully endorse the displacement in Marxism concentrated in two great passages [...] from Marx to Lenin [and] from Lenin to Mao [...] from the most advanced country [...] to a relatively backward country [and then] from workers to peasants as the main revolutionary agent'.[10] Where, then, does Žižek stand on signature Maoist strategies, such as the militarisation of politics, guerrilla insurgency and revolutionary warfare?

The contention of this chapter deepens a reflection on the difference between political antagonism and military hostility that I have begun elsewhere, in relation to Žižek's effort to go beyond the militarisation of politics.[11] I maintain that Žižek encounters a persistent knot of theoretical problems that have their roots in an assumption that reduces politics to coercion. That assumption, in turn, results from a failure to fully consider the difference between democratic revolutions against semi-feudal absolutism and socialist revolutions under conditions of repressive tolerance and liberal democracy. The hypothesis of politics-as-coercion, defining the political as reducible to the repressive state apparatus, is linked to the Leninist conception of politics and to its right-wing inversion in Carl Schmitt's idea of political theology. In the ideological counter-position of liberal democracy to utopian politics, in which radical transformation only appears as terrorism or totalitarianism, the retrieval of Marx, Lenin and Mao seems to require a Jacobin strategy of political dictatorship. Consequently, Žižek seems to tremble on the threshold of a 'politics of the symbolic', as an alternative to the passion for the real, without successfully articulating it.

Rhetorical provocations and the 'War on Terror'

Before I discuss the main claims, however, I want to clarify the intention of this chapter with reference to its context of enunciation.

The critique of the militarisation of politics that I advance here is intended to expose the problems with the Leninist conceptualisation of politics-as-coercion, rather than to undermine the normative legitimacy of claims for social justice. The critical perspective on Žižek's positions that I adopt is an Althusserian Marxist one, influenced by Nicos Poulantzas' theory of politics and committed to a radically egalitarian social transformation of society, by democratic means wherever possible. Furthermore, my critique by no means brings into question the legitimacy of certain forms of political resistance that are sometimes forced on social agents who have a valid social justice agenda. Collective struggles against government-backed death

---

10   Žižek 2007, 1-2.
11   Boucher 2008, 165-228; Boucher 2017, 141-159.

squads, military dictatorships, imperialist invasions and fascist militias, for instance, may need to resort to armed struggle as legitimate self-defence. That is not what is in question in my critique of the militarisation of politics.

The fundamental theoretical coordinates for grasping contemporary socialist strategy are supplied by the final work of Poulantzas, which identifies the emergence of authoritarian statism as the consequence of the globalisation of deregulated capitalism.[12] The period following the publication of Poulantzas' *State, Power, Socialism* (1978), right through to the early 1990s, witnessed deliberate efforts by the governments of the imperialist heartlands to insulate economic maldistribution from mass protest. New Right governments in the mould of Thatcher and Reagan aimed to suppress the 'excess of democracy' that they held responsible for the 'crisis of governability' in the 1960s. That enabled the worldwide imposition of forms of economic deregulation that resulted in an extreme aggravation of economic inequality. At the same time, the centralisation characteristic of authoritarian statism, which included the transfer of power to the executive branch of government and the development of a national security state with emergency powers, advanced significantly. After 1990, this development became connected with the dominance of neo-liberal governance, which economically fragmented populations through the severe exacerbation of uneven development.

Against this background the 'victory of capitalism' after the collapse of historical communism was really the triumphant export of a plebiscitary form of authoritarian statism, together with neo-liberal economic deregulation. The question of violence, then, must be framed in light of the systemic violence of economic injustice and the military interventions supporting it, most recently in Afghanistan and Iraq. The draconian emergency legislation enabling the so-called 'War on Terror' is part of the landscape of transnational corporate capitalism and authoritarian statism. So too are the attempts by the US and its allies, including Australia, to normalize torture and assassination as valid means of intervention in crisis situations.

At the same time, it is crucial to recognize that the insurrectionary version of revolutionary strategy involves civil war. According to the Maoist vision, prolonged guerrilla warfare is a necessary component of a protracted social conflict leading to armed insurrection and culminating in international revolutionary war. The political struggle for state power necessarily entails military action and involves revolutionary warfare, something that is very likely to attract accusations of terrorism. That is a matter of the utmost gravity, in a context where rhetorical provocations and radical postures are completely out of place. In the superheated atmosphere of the current conjuncture, even the discussion of guerrilla strategy is liable to be misinterpreted in a hostile way. In the context of visa bans on radical thinkers, for instance, the associ-

---

12   Poulantzas 1978, 203-247.

ation between Žižek's name and lethality implied by the right-wing description of him as a 'deadly jester' is potentially serious.[13] Because of the repressive context of the discussion, the entire topic of revolutionary warfare necessitates restraint that is guided by philosophical wisdom.[14]

Žižek himself indicates the need for prudence when he critiques the underlying connection between the left-wing fool and the right-wing knave.[15] The right-wing knave is a supreme cynic, a neo-conservative 'political realist', who 'sees through' social relations to the lurking threat of coercion hidden in social forms. The left-wing fool is the court jester who believes that their duty is to 'speak the truth to power', rather than to address the dispossessed. The court jester also holds a cynical theory of reality, but does not really believe in it – which is why he or she is constantly involved in garrulous exposés that only attract violent retribution. By contrast with both the knave and the fool, Žižek is not speaking to power. Instead, his work is aimed at those left-wing thinkers who present themselves as advocates for the masses, but who secretly believe that resistance is futile. When Žižek describes himself as a Socratic 'imbecile', somebody who persists with troubling questions, but who has the wisdom to state that he 'knows only that he knows nothing', we should note the distance this implies from the fool and the knave.[16]

Nonetheless, Žižek routinely employs inflammatory rhetoric, such as the guillotine on the front cover of *In Defense of Lost Causes* (2008), which can seem like instances of foolish provocation. Although his positions successfully intervene in contemporary efforts to rethink the left-wing project, there is a danger of serious misinterpretation in the wider setting of restrictions on intellectual freedom imposed by anti-terrorist paranoia. The context for Žižek's interventions is what he describes as the contemporary *Denkverbot* on utopian projects. The problem, Žižek argues, is that the Left needs to work through its underlying acceptance of 'anti-totalitarian thought', introduced into intellectual life in the 1970s and 1980s by the French *Nouveaux Philosophes*.[17] Disastrously, the contemporary intellectual Left has accepted the idea that every utopian project of a new social foundation inevitably leads via terrorist excess to totalitarian catastrophe.

Žižek seeks to remind the Left that self-imposed restriction to the expansion and deepening of the Democratic Imaginary involves resignation to capitalism. The Left has become timid, locked into a protest position centred on the struggle for recognition and identity politics. But Žižek calls the politics of protest a 'hysterical demand for a new master', because it appeals to an established authority, accepting the

---

13 Kirsch 2008.
14 Strauss 1988, 42-48.
15 Žižek 1997, 45.
16 Žižek 2012a, 2.
17 Žižek 2001a, 4-7; 2008a, 4.

'recognition framework' of those in power.[18] What has been repressed here is the truth that the Left's prized 'Democratic Revolution of Modernity' was a *revolution*, not a mere change of government.[19] Political communities are always inaugurated 'from nothing' – that is, without reliance on pre-existing forms of authority for metaphysical guarantees.

Astutely, Žižek reads the Left's anxiety about totalitarian excess as *symptomatic*: the institutionalisation of the democratic egalitarian idea as revolutionary-democratic terror is a repressed *wish*; hence the energetic refusal of the terrorist potential of utopian ideals. Žižek confronts this with the 'analytic intervention' by interpreting anti-totalitarianism as a defence against this repressed desire. The aim here is not to bring the Left to embrace the wish, but to work through the repression surrounding it, so that the fantasy itself can be re-articulated as utopianism. Indeed, as Žižek says apropos his 'defense of lost causes', the 'true aim of the "defense of lost causes" is not to defend Stalinist terror, and so on, as such, but to render problematic the all-too-easy liberal-democratic alternative'.[20] Žižek does not endorse terrorism, or advocate totalitarianism. Rather, his thought is best described as anti-anti-totalitarianism – advocating the rejection of the *Denkverbot* on radical politics, through an extirpation of the legacy of the New Right in left-wing thinking. This is at the same time an effort to work through the repressed desire animating the 'passion for the real' on the radical Left.

The difference between democratic and socialist revolutions

Žižek, then, develops his position by critiquing the way that the Left's current exile in identity politics is the inverse of its former nostalgia for the lost cause. Both are defences against the anxiety that political inauguration without metaphysical guarantees might lead to totalitarian catastrophe, something connected with a repressed desire for revolutionary excess. Unfortunately, what Žižek does not do is to perform an equally searching analysis of the conceptual bases of the militarisation of radical politics that was so central to the destiny of historical communism.

The central problem for twentieth-century radical politics was pointed out by the Italian Marxist Antonio Gramsci in his *Prison Notebooks*. Lenin's Bolshevik Revolution happened against a feudal autocracy that turned toward military dictatorship, something characteristic of Eastern Europe and the colonial world.[21] By contrast, the socialist revolution in Western Europe was projected for conditions of parliamentary

---

18 Žižek 2000b.
19 Žižek 2000a.
20 Žižek 2008a, 12.
21 Gramsci 1971, 235-238 and 245-246.

democracy supported by civil society. Although Gramsci's formulations are sometimes equivocal, the key to this difference is not only in the characterisation of the state apparatus and its corresponding type of revolutionary transformation (that is, that the socialist revolution negates the capitalist state as the democratic revolution negates the feudal state). Gramsci also proposes that politics under the feudal state involves coercion alone, whereas under the capitalist state, politics involves a 'mobile equilibrium' between coercion and consent.[22] The history of communist politics in the twentieth century involves the repression of this difference, as a consequence of the worldwide adoption of Leninism within the Communist International. For the Leninist politics of the vanguard party, including the notion of fusing the democratic and socialist revolution, is a strategy that depends on the theory, elaborated in *State and Revolution*, that politics is coercion.[23] Lenin asserted the autonomy of the political, its independence from economics and ideology, by claiming that the state involves 'special bodies of armed men' with the result that politics is ultimately about domination.[24] Consequently, politics is about who will repress whom, about whether the state is the dictatorship of the aristocracy, the dictatorship of the bourgeoisie – or the dictatorship of the proletariat.[25]

Conceptually, it is Mao Zedong who completes Leninist politics. Mao's the vanguard party is explicitly a military institution representing the nucleus of a new state. The purpose of the party is to lead 'prolonged popular struggle' by conducting guerrilla warfare against the state apparatus and its imperialist supporters. Mao abandoned the metropolitan working class as the revolutionary class and instead turned to the recruitment of peasants into the vanguard apparatus. For Mao, the proletarian politics of the communist party flow from its Marxist program, something that can be adopted by every oppressed stratum. The implication is that the party represents all forces involved in political action against the state apparatus, which means every struggle that, by virtue of the conceptual connection between politics and coercion, latently contains political violence as its kernel. Accordingly, the strategy of the party is fundamentally military, involved with the liberation of territorial components of the nation through the conduct of widespread guerrilla operations.[26]

In light of the success of Maoist strategy, it is perhaps not surprising that fascist theory, especially as articulated by Nazi jurist Carl Schmitt, is deeply concerned with the problem of partisan warfare. The thing that makes the partisan so troubling to Schmitt is that these agents aim at civil war rather than at territorial defence against an invading army. For Schmitt, the political sovereign is not a legal entity,

---

22 Anderson 1976.
23 Lenin 1977, 94-214.
24 Lukács 1970, 72-96.
25 Lenin 1977, 132, 143.
26 Tse-Tung 1967, 79-112.

but that social force capable of deciding who the 'enemies of the state' are.[27] Partisans aim at this kernel of the real that founds the political, namely, the groundless decision, taken in an emergency situation, regarding the friend/enemy distinction. In other words, for Schmitt, Partisan struggle introduces a threatening new dimension into an essentially Hobbesian conception of politics, because it challenges the basis of popular allegiance to the state by undermining the state's ability to protect its citizens.[28] Accordingly, the partisan is creates what he describes as 'absolute enmity' and 'total war'.[29] For Schmitt, Mao's version of Leninist politics is the ultimate threat to social order.[30]

The theoretical fortunes of Carl Schmitt – sometimes described as 'the right-wing Lenin' – have recently reversed, from reactionary pariah to radical political thinker. Both Schmitt and Lenin dismiss parliamentary democracy and liberal politics as an illusion that prevents individuals from grasping the antagonistic constitution of the political, its foundation in repression. What Schmitt and Lenin have in common is a vision of the autonomy of the political based on violence, according to which the distinction between politics and warfare is one of intensity, not an opposition between consent and coercion.[31] On this conception, a politics of radical transformation of the social formation must inevitably involve an armed confrontation with state power, with dictatorship at the heart of every regime. It must, in other words, reveal the latent civil war that structures the political, and therefore leads directly to guerrilla insurgency, armed insurrection and revolutionary warfare.

The Jacobin Imaginary

The core assumption determining the underlying agreement between Lenin and Schmitt is their conviction that politics is exclusively coercive. Indeed, as Eckhard Bolsinger accurately – if uncritically – identifies, for both thinkers, politics and war belong to a continuum of the intensity of violence, ranging from class struggle to civil war.[32] This implies that the dictum that politics is an extension of politics is reversible: politics is a prolongation of war, another modality of force. Against this background, one can grasp why Žižek's development of a theoretical alternative to the Left's 'hysterical' protest politics led straight to Schmitt, the moment that Žižek decided to rehabilitate Lenin.

---

27 Schmitt 2005, 8-12, 35-39.
28 Schmitt 2007, 85.
29 Schmitt 2007, 51-52.
30 Bolsinger 2001, 167 note 18.
31 Ibid., 1-19.
32 Bolsinger 2001, 18-19.

The key intermediate step here is Ernesto Laclau and Chantal Mouffe's theoretical manifesto, *Hegemony and Socialist Strategy: Towards a Radical Democratic Politics* (1985). For Laclau and Mouffe, Marxism involved a teleological philosophy of history, according to which the communist utopia is the culmination of an ascending sequence of stages. These unfold with historical necessity by virtue of inevitable economic progress, consequent upon the maturation of humanity's productive forces.[33] For them, classical Marxist theory defines the state as the centre of society, with the result that revolutionary transformation by the proletariat depends upon the conversion of the locus of power into the dictatorship of the proletariat. With the construction of a socialist state, the social contradiction at the heart of political conflict – the contradiction between the productive forces and social relations, expressed as class struggle – is eradicated, resulting in a harmonious society free from class divisions.

Laclau and Mouffe characterise Leninist political strategy as a 'Jacobin imaginary', opposing it to Claude Lefort's interpretation of modern politics as the 'democratic revolution of modernity'.[34] Lefort proposes that the democratic revolutions that unfolded around the paradigm of the French Revolution have evacuated the locus of sovereignty. Popular sovereignty represented through political parties has replaced the sacred body of the sovereign, with the result that democratic government revolves around an 'empty place of power'.[35] Laclau and Mouffe extend Lefort's position along Gramscian lines by explaining how parties and movements occupy the empty place of power by manipulating ideological symbols. From their theoretical perspective, ideological symbols such as 'socialism', or 'the nation', are 'floating signifiers', empty signs, capable of taking on a variety of political meanings depending on their articulation to concrete political struggles and particular social groups.[36] The implication is that political struggle actually consists in striving to set up a floating signifier in the empty place of power. This is achieved by articulating an ideological symbol across a wide variety of causes and groups, a process resulting in the tendential universalisation of the symbol in question.

Hence, hegemony is achieved when the articulation of every new struggle or group interest to the dominant political symbol, or 'reigning universal', seems the natural thing to do.[37] Social alliances construction ideological and political forms of hegemony with the capacity to accommodate diverse demands, but, because all signs work contrastively or 'differentially', this is done at the cost of the construction of out-groups, illegitimate interests and 'impossible' demands.[38] Describing

---

33 Laclau and Mouffe 1985, 3, 7-46.
34 Ibid., 152-159.
35 Lefort 1988, 16-18.
36 Laclau and Mouffe 1985, 132.
37 Ibid., 136.
38 Ibid., 137.

these as 'social antagonisms', Laclau and Mouffe propose that the main task of post-Marxist strategy is to accept the permanence of social antagonism, through a principled renunciation of the utopian desire for social harmony.[39] From this perspective, the 'Jacobin temptation' represented by Leninist politics involves the idea that a party or class might seek to permanently fill the place of power. For Laclau and Mouffe, the 'Jacobin temptation' leads to totalitarianism. Radicals must renounce the 'Jacobin Imaginary' and instead embrace forms of democratic equality that maintain a space for political difference. That involves a strategy that regards the aim of the socialist movement as the preservation of the role of contestation in politics, rather than the 'eradication of contradictions'.

What is ideological about this opposition between Jacobin totalitarianism and the democratic Imaginary is its elision of history, its erasure of the difference between the two revolutions. The French Revolution happened against repressive Absolutism, *where there was no Democratic Imaginary*, but rather the military repression of the popular classes. Lenin's revolution, too, was an insurrection against a semi-feudal police state. The problem that Gramsci confronted was, by contrast, socialist revolution under conditions of capitalist democracy. This is something that Laclau and Mouffe's mystifying conflation of socialism with Jacobinism occludes. 'What is now in crisis', they propose, in a sweeping dismissal of all socialist revolutions:

> is a whole conception of socialism which rests upon the ontological centrality of the working class, upon the role of Revolution, with a capital 'R', as the founding moment in the transition from one type of society to another, and upon the illusory prospect of a perfectly unitary and homogeneous collective will that will render pointless the moment of politics. The plural and multifarious character of contemporary social struggles has finally dissolved the last foundation for that political imaginary. Peopled with 'universal' subjects and built around History in the singular, it has postulated 'society' as an intelligible structure that could be intellectually mastered on the basis of certain class positions and reconstituted as a rational, transparent order, through a founding act of a political character. Today, the Left is witnessing the final act of the dissolution of that Jacobin imaginary.[40]

Although Žižek correctly critiques the resignation to capitalism that Laclau's position presupposes, his own alternative remains within the anti-totalitarian oppositions that frame *Hegemony and Socialist Strategy*.[41] Indeed, Žižek's response has often been to rhetorically invert radical democracy into a provocative advocacy for the 'Jacobin imaginary'.

I have elsewhere critiqued Žižek's inversion of the radical democratic imaginary into a Jacobin politics.[42] Nonetheless, some aspects of his rhetoric are worth review-

---

39   Ibid., 142.
40   Laclau and Mouffe 1985, 2.
41   Žižek 2000a.
42   Boucher 2010.

ing because they make it extremely difficult for him to theorise the specificity of modern politics. First, where Laclau rejects the universal status of the proletariat and its role as the subject of history, Žižek maintains that any agent of revolution is, by definition, the proletariat, by virtue of its absolutely empty and formally-specified universality. Second, against the proposition that social complexity militates against revolutionary transformation directed from a central institution, Žižek advocates the social inauguration of a new order in a revolutionary Act that involves seizing power. Rejecting the idea of an empty place of power at the heart of democracy, Žižek announced that the concept of the dictatorship of the proletariat was back on the agenda (although he explained that every state-form involved dictatorship). Third, in agreement with Laclau's suggestion that the basis for Jacobinism is radical populism combined with the substitution of the egalitarian party for the actual masses, Žižek advocates the articulation of the unified people as a political sovereign through a vanguard party whose role is to represent egalitarian ideals to the recalcitrant populace. Fourth, with Laclau, Žižek links Jacobin politics to the vanguard party and Leninist strategy, merely reversing Laclau's critique of the mutation of Leninism into Stalinism into an affirmation of a 'repetition of Lenin'. If Laclau sought to avoid the totalitarian problems of historical communism, Žižek maintains that the notion of totalitarianism is merely an ideological scarecrow and that, moreover, Stalin and Mao should be critically rehabilitated. Finally, in response to the rejoinder that Leninist politics today is a religious conviction regarding the 'proletarian chiliasm',Žižek avers that his position is that of 'messianic Marxism' supported by a radical political theology grounded in belief in the imminence of revolution. Defiantly placing a bloodied guillotine on the front cover of his 'defense of lost (revolutionary) causes', Žižek completed this series of Jacobin gestures with a rehabilitation of Robespierre.[43]

The theoretical context for Žižek's Jacobin rhetoric, however, is a politics that aims to achieve egalitarian goals while embracing historical openness. Central to Žižek's political theory is the proposition that history consists in a contingent series of socio-cultural totalities whose sequence is defined by political struggle.[44] According to Žižek, the imaginary closure of a social totality depends on the 'existence of the Other', the unconscious assumption of a metaphysical guarantee for the success of the inauguration of a political community. Žižek's analysis indicates that the totalitarian politics of Stalinism and fascism, as well as fundamentalist terrorism, are animated by unconscious belief in the existence of the Other.[45] Communist belief in Historical Necessity and fundamentalist belief in Divine Will both involve a perverse subject-position, which is the root of the fanatic's transformation of himself-

---

43 Žižek 2007, 2008a.
44 Žižek 2002a, 214-219.
45 Ibid., 234-235; 2001a, 74-75 and 119-120.

or herself into an 'instrument for the enjoyment of the Other'.[46] In his critique of perverse self-instrumentalisation, Žižek insists that belief in the existence of the Other is supported by an ideological fantasy that conceals the moment of uncertainty in which a new beginning happens without metaphysical guarantees.

Between politicisation and militarisation

Žižek's critique of the *Nouveaux Philosophes'* rejection of the utopian vision of the end of politics does not return him to classical Marxism's fantasy of social harmony. Instead, Žižek's main theoretical efforts have been dedicated to constructing the ideological coordinates of a new form of political subjectivity that is capable of engaging in radical politics without reliance on historical teleology. Importantly, his insistence on the 'non-existence of the Other' is equivalent to an affirmation of the persistence of social antagonism. This affirmation is why Žižek insists that there is a 'kernel of the Real' in politics. In general, Žižek maintains that the 'zero matrix' of a political community is the contradiction between the reigning universal signifier and its repressed social symptom, i.e. between the 'included' and the 'excluded'.[47] In the current conjuncture, Žižek is especially interested in the role of the global slums and the immigrant proletariat as agents of the antagonism between liberal democracy and its excluded others.[48]

Aside from rhetorical provocations that sometimes misleadingly suggest that his neo-communism is a return to classical Marxism, however, the difficulty that readers of Žižek encounter is that it is not clear what his strategic aims actually are. Part of that difficulty is caused by the fact that Žižek does not directly advance a political theory, but instead proposes a meta-theory of politics. For Žižek, left-wing thinkers such as Laclau and Mouffe, Alain Badiou, Jacques Rancière and Étienne Balibar propose political theories. Political theories are value-laden evaluations of an object domain leading to strategic prescriptions for social agents. By contrast, Žižek's analysis is a theory about how all existing political theories 'evade the political' by avoiding the 'kernel of the real' of social antagonism.[49] Like any meta-theoretical position, Žižek's theory of the 'zero matrix' of social antagonism and the 'kernel of the real' in political conflict is a descriptive apparatus intended to reveal the mechanism behind an entire array of theoretical claims about the political domain.[50] Indeed, as a meta-theory which claims that political theories avoid the kernel of destructiveness inherent in social antagonism, Žižek is excellently placed to explain a

---

46 Žižek 2002a, 234-237.
47 Žižek 2008a, 438.
48 Žižek 2002b, 74, 2006b, 125, 2008a, 427, 2014, 19.
49 Žižek 1999b, 171-244.
50 Ibid., 171-244; Žižek 2008a, 428.

whole series of manifestations of political violence, from riots through uprisings to insurrections, insurgencies and civil wars.

Although Žižek's analysis of political theory is incisive, a question remains about how he proposes to convert meta-theoretical description into the partisan commitment presupposed by neo-communist politics. On the one hand, his meta-theoretical perspective facilitates a neutral description of political strategies that result from various theoretical recommendations, in terms of their avoidance of the real of antagonism. Žižek's theory of the 'kernel of the real' in social antagonism explains the persistence of political conflict within every effort to reconcile all groups within a harmonious society. On the other hand, he attempts specific programmatic recommendations about strategic directions, something necessarily involving a value-laden set of evaluations of politics. As we have seen, Žižek advocates a neo-communist policy of strict egalitarian justice, supports the divine violence inherent in revolutionary experiments,[51] proposes the construction of the dictatorship of the proletariat and even envisions a stateless post-revolutionary society.[52] But where can these partisan commitments come from and how can Žižek elude the problems he detects in other theories?

Probably the most straightforward way for Žižek to do this is to claim that his meta-theory enables the construction of a true political theory, one that embraces the political because it accepts, indeed, aggravates, social antagonism. Indeed, at the rhetorical level, Žižek's position sometimes resembles a lethal plunge into violence typical of the 'passion for the real' diagnosed by Badiou. Žižek proposes to embrace the revolutionary Act by entering the 'psychotic passage to the act',[53] to assent to a 'religious suspension of the ethico-political' that amounts to a 'moment of madness', to open the void of an inaugural declaration that is without precedents or guarantees.[54] At the same time, it is evident from Žižek's critique of perverse self-instrumentalisation that the 'repetition of Lenin'[55] that he proposes will be significantly different from Robespierre, Stalin, or Mao. But how? What role does political violence have in this conception?

There is a real nucleus uncertainty in Žižek's thinking here, as he has zigzagged back and forth, from abstention to activism. Žižek's hesitation between politicisation and militarisation is mainly conditioned by the legacy of the assumption that politics is fundamentally coercive. His encounter with this problem passes through Lenin and Schmitt, whose thinking influences the idea that the revolutionary Act derives its authenticity from political violence.[56] Yet simultaneously, Žižek's meta-theory

---

51 Žižek 2008b, 169.
52 Žižek 2008a, 401, 461.
53 Žižek 2002a, 101, 139.
54 Žižek 1999b, 223, 2008a, 478.
55 Žižek 2001b.
56 Žižek 2008a, 418-419.

accurately diagnoses the perversely instrumental entailments of the notion that politics and warfare are merely intensities on a continuum. At these moments, his stance becomes therapeutic, according to which the role of the meta-theory is reconstructive. It facilitates a rectification of the ideological fantasies that promote violence as an end, across the entire field of political theories. It is only once Žižek directly confronts the 'Left Schmittianism' of contemporary theory that he begins to articulate a position on the specificity of the political that differentiates between politics and war.

A Left Schmittianism?

In chapter four of *Ticklish Subject*, 'Political Subjectivization and its Vicissitudes', Žižek undertakes his most sustained theoretical synthesis, seeking to combine Laclau's notion of hegemony with ideas from radical French theory (Badiou, Balibar and Rancière).[57] From Badiou, Žižek takes the concept of the irruption of the social symptom into the space of a social totality as an 'Event', an anomalous disturbance of societal routines that can either be dismissed as a meaningless intrusion of political violence, or embraced as the emergence of a new universal – and thus: the nucleus of a different order. From Balibar, Žižek adopts the idea that the emergence of the social symptom logically involves an empty demand for '*égaliberté*' (or: 'equaliberty'), for the absolute equality of all speaking beings and their freedom to speak politically – a demand that logically precedes any actual demands. From Rancière, Žižek accepts the thesis that the Event – the demand for *égaliberté* – signifies the entry of the excluded onto the political stage. Their emergence announces a moment of irreconcilable 'disagreement' – in other words: the confrontation between incommensurable totalities.[58] Finally, for Žižek, this confrontation involves a 'substanceless subjectivity', a subject position in which the individual or the collective has no political identity within the existing order.[59] Instead, for Žižek, it must 'impossibly' (from the standpoint of the reigning ideology) forge a new universality and inaugurate a new political community, through the 'psychotic' passage to the revolutionary Act.[60]

The chain of equivalences that Žižek sets up between psychological repression and social oppression, and between political marginalisation and violent suppression, belongs to politics-as-coercion. Consequently, Žižek fails to explicitly differentiate between revolt against absolute exclusion and political struggle against other forms of oppression. As Rancière points out, there is only warfare between slaves

---

57 Žižek 1999b, 171-244.
58 Žižek 1999b, 188.
59 Ibid., 232.
60 Ibid., 236.

and their masters, but no politics.[61] Rancière distinguishes the revolt of the slaves from the uprising of the plebeian citizens, for amongst citizens there can be disagreement, that is, politics. Following this line of reasoning, politics exist when a political community is constituted by an equality that the social hierarchy refuses or subverts. Politics involves what Rancière calls a 'wrong', an inequality, whose model is the legal trial by jury, not the military test of battle.[62] Rancière provides examples of such struggles drawn from what we might call the Marxist canon – plebeians, workers, women – who are wronged by the contradiction between social hierarchy and political community. Although recognised as equal citizens, they are confronted with an array of inequalities.

Žižek does not explicitly distinguish between the two types of struggle. Significantly, Žižek's paradigmatic instances of contemporary 'proletarian subjectivity' – immigrant workers and slum dwellers[63] – fall on either side of this distinction between politics and warfare. Immigrant workers have rightly been described as the 'new helots'.[64] Their protest, necessarily violent as Žižek himself acknowledges, is 'phatic'. It constitutes a demand for recognition, for inclusion in the political community as something other than 'illegal', based on their position in the distribution of social functions.[65] But the slum dwellers are citizens whose neglect by the governing classes is criminal in a more than rhetorical sense.[66] As with plebeians, workers and women, they are legally citizens, yet denied political representation, social and civil rights, and so forth. The result is that their irruption of speech (and not just the animal voice of their suffering, or the extra-legal violence of their spontaneous uprising) suddenly transforms the 'political theatre', by introducing a new actor. Yet Žižek appears not to notice this. He often introduces these two different kinds of social agents in lists of the 'excluded', as if the political/military distinction were irrelevant.

Žižek's failure to highlight this point makes it difficult for him to explicitly theorise the distinction between the 'two revolutions', between the domination exercised by most premodern states – the maintenance of a regime by force – and oppression by modern states. Struck by the political violence involved in the revolutionary inauguration of democratic regimes – for instance, the American War of Independence, or the Jacobin Terror in the French Revolution – Žižek sometimes speaks almost as if the radical transformation of democratic polities might involve the same methods, but with a different flag.

---

61 Rancière 1999, 12-14.
62 Ibid., 35-39.
63 Žižek 1999b, 224.
64 Cohen 1987.
65 Žižek 2008b, 63-64.
66 Davis 2006.

Once again, however, appearances can be deceptive. For it is Žižek who astutely notes that Laclau and Mouffe's position is in fact a form of 'Left Schmittianism'. Indeed, Žižek's critique of Schmitt is based on the insight that the transmutation of politics into warfare is a key form of what he describes as the 'neutralisation' or 'denial' of the antagonistic logic of the political. In Schmittian 'ultra-politics', antagonism is acknowledged in the form of the friend (included) versus enemy (excluded) distinction, but it is then exiled from the political sphere through its prolongation into warfare. In their contributions to Mouffe's collection, *The Challenge of Carl Schmitt*, both Žižek and Mouffe point out the proximity of the notion of the 'constitutive outside' to the Schmittian friend/enemy distinction. Significantly, Mouffe's contribution grasps this proximity as equivalence, for she seeks to mitigate the implications of the theoretical identity between the Laclavian theory of hegemony and the Schmittian notion of the sovereign decision. To do this, she seeks to institutionalise political conflict while restricting its scope to democratic means, proposing that the ideal of democratic citizenship might act as a social cement preventing violence, 'transforming (hostile) adversaries into (political) antagonists'.[67] Žižek is correct to describe this as 'Left Schmittianism', an effort to retain the friend/enemy logic of a certain conception of the antagonist while mitigating the problem of hostility with a dose of democratic ideology.[68]

Žižek's strategy for escaping from the logic of Left-Schmittianism is dialectical: he proposes to 'intro-reflect' an external opposition as an internal contradiction. Specifically, Žižek suggests a distinction between Schmitt's 'projection' outwards of social antagonism onto the external enemy and Žižek's own 'intro-reflection' of adversarial hostility as 'class struggle' with an internal antagonist. Schmitt, Žižek alleges, attempts 'to depoliticize the [political] conflict by bringing it to an extreme, via the direct militarization of politics... – it is deeply symptomatic that, rather than class struggle, the radical Right speaks of class (or sexual) warfare'.[69] The crucial point here is that Žižek is not just inverting 'external enmity' into 'internal antagonism' through a change in nomenclature. As Žižek notes:

[P]olitical conflict designates the tension between the structured social body in which each part has its place, and the 'part of no part', which unsettles this order on account of the empty principle of universality – of what Balibar calls *égaliberté*, the principled equality of all persons qua speaking beings. Politics proper thus always involves a short circuit between the Universal and the Particular, the paradox of a 'singular universal'. [...] This identification of the non-part with the whole, the part of society with no properly defined place [...] with the universal, is the elementary gesture of politicization, dis-

---

67 Mouffe 1999.
68 Žižek 1999a.
69 Žižek 1999b, 190.

cernible in all great democratic events from the French Revolution [...] to the demise of ex-European Socialism.[70]

The concept of *égaliberté* indicates a description of the politics of antagonism rather than the logic of hostility. Žižek then continues, apropos Rancière's distinction between war and politics:

> Let us return to Rancière's basic emphasis on the radical ambiguity of the Marxist notion of the 'gap' between formal democracy (human rights, political freedom, etc.) and the economic reality of exploitation. One can read this gap between the appearance of equality-freedom and the social reality of [cultural oppression and economic exploitation] in the standard 'symptomatic' way [...] or in the much more subversive sense of a fundamental tension in which the appearance of *égaliberté* is not a 'mere appearance', but evinces an effectivity of its own, which allows it to set in motion the process of the rearticulation of socio-economic relations by way of their progressive politicization. [...] [T]he appearance of *égaliberté* is a symbolic fiction, which, as such, possesses an actual efficiency.[71]

The difference, then, between Žižek's Lacanian dialectics and the 'Left-Schmittianism' of some forms of contemporary radical theory is that Žižek preserves the claim, crucial to both Balibar and Rancière, that politics originates in a historically specific gap between social reality and political community. *Politics is the opposite of the police*, of 'special bodies of armed men', of dictatorship and repression – which is not to deny that political struggle often triggers the foreclosure of the space of disagreement, a militarisation of politics, by the dominant social alliance.

Although Žižek hits the target here, what is missing is a theoretical apparatus capable of registering the distinction explicitly through a contrast between politics and force. What Žižek needs is a strong conception of the specificity of the political in terms of contestation, rather than conflict. Because that is exactly what he lacks, as he hesitates between a set of theoretical intuitions that coincide with those of Rancière, and a rhetorical commitment to the Leninist-Schmittian conception of politics. This explains why Žižek for a long time espoused only a politics of abstention, before swinging over into the idea that political violence is an unmistakeable index of the authenticity of the revolution. His theory provides no clear alternative to the reading of antagonism as aggression, so he can defend himself against this conclusion by avoiding conflict altogether ('Bartleby' politics), or enthusiastically embracing it.

70   Žižek 1999b, 188.
71   Ibid., 195.

According to the Gramscian interpretation of the state developed by Althusser's co-thinker, Nicos Poulantzas, politics functions to maintain the unity of the social formation. The implication is that the political is a function in social arrangements rather than an intensity of conflict or the result of a hypothetical social contract. The modern nation state is a 'centaur', a hybrid combination of force and fraud with negotiation, because it involves political functions alongside the repression necessary for the maintenance of oppressive social relations. The paradoxical dialectics of inclusion and exclusion, representation and domination, characteristic of the nation state, happen because the unity of capitalist formations depends on maintaining exploitation.[72] The entailment is that politics involves the contestation (or affirmation) of social relations. Contestation ranges across a spectrum, from improvisation, modification and negotiation, through to disagreement, refusal and withdrawal. Neither force nor fraud are modalities of contestation, for force is the *breakdown* of contestation into conflict, while fraud is manipulated consent that *blocks* contestation. Furthermore, there is politics even in the absence of the state, for politics involves the direction of collective actions, the negotiation of different interests and the reconciliation of disagreements. Politics is a set of social practices that execute a function, rather than a specific institutional locus. The state (where it exists) condenses political contestation onto a centralised apparatus, in the effort to protect a form of domination from the potential of contestation to slide into conflict. Finally, the historical emergence of the state is linked to the need for supplementary protection of social relations from excessive contestation, through the employment of force in asymmetrical conflict as soon as dissent turns into resistance.

The key distinction employed by Marx between 'economic compulsion' and 'extra-economic coercion' in forms of exploitation has consequences for the role of politics in the state. By contrast with slavery and serfdom, capitalist production involves social relations that rely on economic compulsion rather than extra-economic coercion. Nonetheless, the concentration of ownership of the means of production and the property rights of the possessors of capital entails the existence of distinct classes of labourers and capitalists. The distinctively capitalist state form, the modern democratic nation state, reflects this historical peculiarity, because citizenship rights include the people as a whole despite the exclusive implications of the institution of private property. Representative government in the form of parliamentary democracy aggravates the potential contradiction between inclusion and exclusion into a situation that makes possible a historically unique variant of emancipatory strategy. Where for the slaves and the serfs, there is only revolt in the form of war-

---

72   Poulantzas 1973, 62-65; 2008, 82-86.

fare, the paradoxical combination of inclusion (of citizens) and exclusion (of workers), creates a novel space for politics in terms of contestation rather than confrontation.

The idea of politics as coercion, although valid for premodern class societies and modern dictatorial regimes, is everywhere opposed to the conception of politics-as-contestation. Mao's notion of politics as represented in guerrilla insurgency and Schmitt's theory of partisan warfare are both instances of the reduction of modern politics to premodern coercion. For Mao, guerrilla warfare is a necessary part of the civil war that is class struggle. For Schmitt, revolutionary partisans unleash a total war dynamic involving 'absolute enmity'. Because politics and warfare are distributions of the intensity of coercion, poles on a continuum of violence, the logic of hostility played out on the confrontation between insurgents and regulars marks it out not only as the apotheosis of war, but also as the completion of politics. Revolutionary warfare, as the confrontation between two peoples in arms, represents two potential sovereignties in collision. In this clash, popular sovereignty is reconstituted through the arbitrary decision for or against the movement, with no possible middle ground. Politics-as-coercion leads to the basic Hobbesian problem: men and women yield their natural rights and give allegiance to the state on prudential grounds of its protection of their lives. Should the reigning power divide, in civil war, then each individual loses the prudential basis of their allegiance to the existing arrangements. They must choose between rival sovereigns based on a rationally self-interested calculation of who is likely to win, plus any residual superstitious anxieties regarding breaking their oaths of loyalty. This is the fundamental reason that Hobbes introduces religion into his conception of politics, because men and women can only be relied upon to keep their oaths of loyalty in the context of supernatural enforcement of such promises.

Although framed as a form of Marxism, neo-Maoism is a radical application of the Hobbesian conception of politics-as-coercion common to Schmitt and Mao. Of course, endless sectarian debates on the exact point in history at which the Chinese Revolution is supposed to have gone down the 'capitalist road' are peculiar to neo-Maoism alone. Neo-Maoism takes from Maoism a characteristically reductionist focus on the role of force in state power. What it adds to Maoism, however, is a distinctive interest in a potent blend of peasant folklore and religious mythology. For instance, the Peruvian Revolutionary Communist Party, led by Abimael Guzman (aka Chairman Gonzalo), promulgated the mythology of a 'shining path' to revolution based on Incan myth combined with Christian theologies of redemption. The movement's manifesto, 'Develop Guerrilla Warfare', explicitly bases its neo-Maoist strategy on a military demonstration of the regime's inability to govern effectively.

This is combined with the synthetic cult of the 'Shining Path', as devised by the Communist Party.[73]

Perhaps as a consequence of the incompleteness of Žižek's critique of the militarisation of politics, his theoretical attention has also been drawn to supplementing political struggle with a new theology. Žižek is extremely interested in the idea of a radical transformation of communist ideology whose model is an unprecedented reformation of Christian theology. The strategy of a new Cultural Revolution that he frequently invokes as the way forward today involves retaining the utopianism of communism but discarding its belief in the historical inevitability of socialist revolution. Significantly, that line of thinking is linked to the idea that the replacement of the state institution with a religious commune embracing the entire people is as a way of reformulating the classical Marxist idea of the 'withering away of the state'. That is the context for Žižek's episodic engagement with neo-Maoist parties.[74]

Unlike neo-Maoism, however, Žižek is not proposing a synthetic religious ideology as supplement to guerrilla warfare. Instead, he is developing the potential for a communism without metaphysical guarantees, through an exploration of cognate developments in theology. The idea is that a theology without God is structurally equivalent to a communism without History. So the claim here is not that Žižek's neo-communism is crypto-Maoist. Instead, I am proposing that Žižek's sympathy towards neo-Maoism is grounded in his insufficient foregrounding of the difference between his position and that of the Leninist and Schmittian conception of the autonomy of the political. Žižek needs to further develop his definition of the state, and distinguish between feudal and modern state dynamics if he is to develop a convincing theoretical alternative to neo-Maoism. Just such an alternative conception of the political exists in the very Marxist tradition that Žižek claims to originate from, that of Althusserian Marxism.

In conclusion, Žižek aims to shift from the 'passion for the real', with its militarisation of politics, to a fully contemporary Marxist politics of the revolutionary transformation of socio-symbolic structures. For Žižek, the failure of historical Communism (including the restoration of capitalism in China) is grounded in Marxism's economic reductionism, and its consequent neglect of the ideological and political superstructures.[75] He interprets Stalinist cultural humanism as ideological compensation for economic militarisation and political authoritarianism, and Mao's Cultural Revolution as a destructive negation that failed to dislodge economic stagnation and political bureaucratisation. By contrast, Žižek aims at the transformation of everyday life needed to sustain popular revolutionary energy in the transition period.[76] At the

---

73 Partido Communist del Peru 1987.
74 Žižek 2005.
75 Žižek 2007, 7; Žižek 2008a, 174.
76 Žižek 2008a, 157-263.

same time, Žižek proposes to renew the relevance of Marx, along the lines of the shifts that have already happened in the history of Marxism. Renewal happened in the movement from Marx to Lenin and then Mao, in the displacement of the location of revolutionary action from the imperialist heartlands to the semi-colonial periphery, and in the shift in social agent from the industrial proletariat to the poor peasants. Pointing to the social antagonisms generated by the structural unevenness of global capitalism, Žižek argues that 'the new proletarian position is that of the inhabitants of the slums in the new megalopolises [...]the slum-dwellers are literally a collection of those who are the part of no part, the supernumerary element of society'.[77]

Žižek's is a promising argument with the potential to renew Marxism. The contention of this chapter, however, is that to succeed, Žižek needs to fully think through the *political* implications of the claim that proletarian subjectivity is substanceless because it is supernumerary.[78] The excluded masses of the global system are the result of a degenerate form of democratic invention, one that refuses their inclusion within an apparatus of representation and instead focuses repression on them, because their social exclusion is structurally necessary to the world economy. Maintaining that contradiction, with all that it implies for cheap consumer goods and corporate super-profits, is central to the repressive tolerance of liberal democratic imperialism and to the authoritarian 'guided democracies' of the semi-colonial world. To theorise this historically new relation to the two revolutions requires that we abandon the imaginary terrain of 'Jacobinism versus liberalism' and 'Schmitt as the right-wing Lenin', and begin to think instead of the strategic implications of a 'mobile equilibrium' of force and fraud, coercion and consent, violence and politics.

References

Anderson, Perry, 1976: The Antinomies of Antonio Gramsci. In: *New Left Review*100, 5-78.

Badiou, Alain, 2007: *The Century*. Cambridge.

Bolsinger, Eckard, 2001: *The Autonomy of the Political. Carl Schmitt's and Lenin's political realism*. London.

Boucher, Geoff, 2004: The Antinomies of Slavoj Žižek. In: *Telos. A Quarterly Journal of Critical Thought* 129 (2004), 150-172.

Boucher, Geoff, 2008: *The Charmed Circle of Ideology. A Critical Analysis of Butler and Zizek, Laclau and Mouffe*. Melbourne.

Boucher, Geoff, 2010: An Inversion of Radical Democracy. The Republic of Virtue in Žižek's Revolutionary Politics. In: *International Journal of Žižek Studies* 4:2 (2010), np.

---

77   Ibid., 424-425.
78   Ibid., 412-415.

Boucher, Geoff, 2017: The Long Shadow of Leninism. In: Matthew Sharpe (ed.), *100 Years of European Philosophy since the Great War*. Berlin, 141-159.

Cohen, Robin, 1987: *The New Helots. Migrants in the International Division of Labour*. Aldershot.

Davis, Mike, 2006: *Planet of Slums*. London.

Gramsci, Antonio, 1971: *Selections from the Prison Notebooks*. London.

Guevara, Ernesto 'Che', 1998: *Guerilla Warfare*. Lincoln.

Kirsch, Adam, 2008: The Deadly Jester. In: *The New Republic*, 3 December 2008.

Laclau, Ernesto, and Chantal Mouffe, 1985: *Hegemony and Socialist Strategy. Toward a Radical Democratic Politics*. London.

Lefort, Claude, 1988: *Democracy and Political Theory*. Cambridge.

Lenin, Vladimir Ilych, 1965: Guerrilla Warfare. In: Ibid., *Lenin: Collected Works*, 213-223. Moscow.

Lenin, Vladimir Ilych, 1977: *Selected Works in Three Volumes*. Moscow.

Lukács, György, 1970: *Lenin. A study on the Unity of his Thought*. London.

Meier, Heinrich, 2011: *The Lesson of Carl Schmitt. Four chapters on the Distinction between Political Theology and Political Philosophy*. Chicago.

Mouffe, Chantal, 1999: Carl Schmitt and the Paradox of Liberal Democracy. In: Ibid. (ed.), *The Challenge of Carl Schmitt*. London, 39-55.

Partido Communist del Peru (ed.), Comite Central, 1987: *Desarrollar la Guerra Popular Sirviendo a la Revolución Mundial*. Berkeley.

Poulantzas, Nicos, 1973: *Political Power and Social Classes*. London.

Poulantzas, Nicos, 1978: *State, Power, Socialism*. London.

Poulantzas, Nicos, 2008: Preliminaries to the Study of Hegemony in the State. In: James Martin (ed.), *The Poulantzas Reader*. London, 74-119.

Rancière, Jacques, 1999: *Disagreement. Politics and Philosophy*. Minneapolis.

Schmitt, Carl, 2005: *Political Theology. Four Chapters on the Concept of Sovereignty*. Chicago.

Schmitt, Carl, 2007: *Theory of the Partisan. Intermediate Reflections on the Concept of the Political*. New York.

Strauss, Leo, 1988: *Persecution and the Art of Writing*. Chicago.

Tse-Tung, Mao, 1967: *Selected Works of Mao Tse-Tung in Four Volumes*. Peking.

Vo Nguyen, Giap, 1970: *The Military Art of People's War. Selected Writings of Vo Nguyen Giap*. New York.

Žižek, Slavoj, 1993: *Tarrying with the Negative. Kant, Hegel and the Critique of Ideology*. London and New York.

Žižek, Slavoj, 1997: *The Plague of Fantasies*. London and New York.

Žižek, Slavoj, 1999a: Carl Schmitt in the Age of Post-Politics. In: Chantal Mouffe (ed.), *The Challenge of Carl Schmitt*. London and New York, 18-37.

Žižek, Slavoj, 1999b: *The Ticklish Subject. The Absent Centre of Political Ontology*. London and New York.

Žižek, Slavoj, 2000a: Class Struggle or Postmodernism? Yes, Please! In: Judith Butler, Ernesto Laclau and Slavoj Žižek, *Contingency, Hegemony, Universality. Contemporary Dialogues on the Left*. London and New York, 90-135.

Žižek, Slavoj, 2000b: Holding the Place. In: Judith Butler, Ernesto Laclau, and Slavoj Žižek, *Contingency, Hegemony, Universality. Contemporary Dialogues on the Left*. London and New York, 308-329.

Žižek, Slavoj, 2001a: *Did Somebody Say Totalitarianism? Five Interventions on the (Mis)Use of a Notion*. London and New York.

Žižek, Slavoj, 2001b: Repeating Lenin. http://lacan.com/replenin.htm.

Žižek, Slavoj, 2002a: *For They Know Not What They Do. Enjoyment as a Political Factor*. London and New York.

Žižek, Slavoj, 2002b: The Real of Sexual Difference. In: Suzanne Barnard and Bruce Fink (eds.), *Reading Seminar XX. Lacan's Major Work on Love, Knowledge, and Feminine Sexuality*, New York, 57-75.

Žižek, Slavoj, 2002c: Afterword: Lenin's Choice. In: Ibid (ed.), V.I. Lenin, *Revolution at the Gates: A Selection of Writings from February to October 1917*. London and New York, 167-336.

Žižek, Slavoj, 2005: Foreword: On Eggs and Omelettes. In: Bob Avakian and Bill Martin (eds.), *Marxism and the Call of the Future. Conversations on Ethics, History and Politics*. Chicago, vii-x.

Žižek, Slavoj, 2006a: *How to Read Lacan*. London.

Žižek, Slavoj, 2006b: *The Parallax View*. London and Cambridge.

Žižek, Slavoj, 2007: Mao Tse-Tung, the Marxist Lord of Misrule. In: Slavoj Žižek (ed.), Mao Tse-Tung, *On Practice and Contradiction*. London and New York, 1-28.

Žižek, Slavoj, 2008a: *In Defense of Lost Causes*. London and New York.

Žižek, Slavoj, 2008b: *Violence. Six Sideways Reflections*. London.

Žižek, Slavoj, 2012a: *Less than Nothing. Hegel and the Shadow of Dialectical Materialism*. London and New York.

Žižek, Slavoj, 2012b: The Occupy movement, a Renascent Left, and Marxism today. An Interview with Slavoj Zizek. In: *Platypus Review* 42 (2011-2012), np.

Žižek, Slavoj, 2012c: *The Year of Dreaming Dangerously*. London and New York.

Žižek, Slavoj, 2014: Answers to Today's Crisis. A Leninist View. *Crisis & Critique* 1:3 (2014), 13-39.

The Two Žižeks: The Performer and the Leninist

Alex Del Duca

Marxism After Marxism: Žižek Playing the Field

Introduction: Reclaiming Marxism Proper

Slavoj Žižek's relationship to so-called practical political theory has mostly been an ambiguous and obfuscated one. Žižek's passionate remarks on revolution sweeping down from the *favelas* and other variants of divine violence, including his infamous plea for a return to Jacobin style terror, did seem at first to foreshadow a different approach to progressive politics in the 21st century. Indeed, there were many Žižek readers who waited with baited breath for him to deliver us unto the promised land of revolutionary politics. As time passed, however, the disappointment and frustration with his vague and bombastic allusions to a violent purge of the existing order, *sans* positive proposals or any patronage of organized political associations on the ground, grew. The enigmatic master has refused time and again to provide us all the answers. Still, frankly, this is his most endearing feature as a political philosopher.

The seemingly hollow rallying cries and slogans found in Žižek's books and on-line appearances perhaps reached their zenith in his empty speech to the Occupy Wall Street movement on October 9, 2011. Here, Žižek failed to provide any positive political insight to the protesters, which was made all the more painful by his later admonitions of the movement as a protest without any content or demands (and the irony should not be missed here).

Žižek's relationship to state theory and his track record of analyses of the state fall into a woefully similar pattern. For even the casual reader, it is clear that there is nothing remotely resembling the systematic analyses of, say, a Bob Jessop or Nicos Poulantzas, renowned Marxist state theorists who tackle the state as the core object of analysis in their works. Truthfully, what best characterizes Žižek's approach to the state is the glaring absence of any *explicit* approach at all. Anything resembling 'state theory' in Žižek's works is determined more by the absence of any systematic treatment of the subject and via detours through 'old-fashioned' Marxist problematics like the dictatorship of the proletariat and Žižek's insistence on a return to Lenin.

In defense of Žižek, it should be noted that it was never his goal to develop and popularize a new revolutionary politics. Žižek has no intention of providing the ultimate answers to the 'total catastrophe' of 20th century communism, nor does he care to provide the long-awaited solution to capitalism or the alternative to postmodern practices of resistance. Far from producing something legitimately novel in terms of content, Žižek is engaging in a polemical practice to reclaim Marxism as a political practice.

The issue that Žižek concerns himself with is the ongoing (and seemingly perennial) crisis of Marxism, which is above all defined by its 'taming' or depoliticization. Žižek thus remarks:

> On the one hand, in the English-speaking world, we get the cultural-studies Marx, the Marx of the postmodern sophists, of the messianic promise; in continental Europe, where the 'traditional' division of intellectual labor remains stronger, we get a sanitized Marx, the 'classical' author to whom a (marginal) place can be accorded in the academy. On the other hand, we get the Marx who foretold the dynamic of today's globalization and is as such evoked even on Wall Street. What all these Marxes have in common is the denial of politics proper [...] it is essentially post-Marxist.[1]

Marx is quite literally used 'everywhere' and by 'everyone,' appropriated and re-appropriated as just another form of theoretical validation for particular schools of thought. Schools of thought which, at least to Žižek's chagrin, have nothing to do with Marxism proper (and his use of the prefix 'post' accentuates this; the 'post-Marxist' Marx literally signals an age 'after Marx').

What is left for the surviving and would-be defenders of the faith is thus the difficult task of re-appropriating lapsed authority and re-establishing the parameters of Marxism proper. Žižek's aim is to re-inaugurate *authority* or, in other words, to modify the current politico-theoretical coordinates of Marxism. According to Žižek, Marxism currently exists as something fluid, and only an authority that monitors the transmission of concepts and themes and defends its borders can salvage Marxism's emancipatory potential. Such an attempt requires sustained textual *violence*; and this is done by Žižek by deploying particular concepts to displace, disturb, and effectively demotivate those others that have, in Žižek's eyes, parasitically latched onto the Marxist imaginary and polluted the field. This struggle thus involves (re)creating a field with its own particular interlocutors; authority must ultimately monitor who is allowed to participate in the dialogue, in addition to what is at stake and what is up for debate.

These interventions within the field of Marxism point towards an activism that is primarily concerned with first re-determining the contours of Marxism and radical leftism as such. Only then do questions of more practical political bearing follow. In line with much of Marxism's political history, Žižek holds that right theory will determine right practice. As a result, Žižek never well and truly treats the concept of the state in any systematic manner. Throughout his texts and interventions, only

---

1 Žižek 2007a, 2. It is, however, worth considering how traditions such as analytical and political Marxism à la Brenner, for example, continue to fall outside the purview of 'post-Marxism'. Žižek's 'reconstitution' of Marxism's borders thus implicitly depends on its shifting emphasis on the prefix 'post'.

hints of Žižek's thoughts on the state can be traced. Nevertheless, these hints are telling. If existing positions of post-Marxist and postmodern thought are insufficiently able to resist global capitalism (because they reject classical political narratives of seizing state power), then by default Žižek oscillates between a Bartlebyesque shrug of contemplative disdain and, perhaps more productively, a position that implicitly treats the state as the site of political struggle.

This chapter will focus on Žižek's engagement with particular concepts and icons of Marxism. It concentrates on Žižek's consistent reiteration of a need for renewed 'critique of political economy' alongside his assault on classical Marxism and 'nostalgic' communists. Within this practice, Žižek assigns a central role to Lenin as an instructive case for both theory and practice today. Thus, he advocates the redeployment of the notion of the 'dictatorship of the proletariat' and stresses the value it *could have* for leftist political projects and horizons. Beginning with Žižek's understanding of the current political conjuncture and Marxism's relationship to it, this chapter will take a closer look at Žižek's positions on orthodox Marxism and 'classical revolution' before engaging with his resuscitation of Lenin, whom Žižek reads as both a useful cache of political knowledge relevant to our modern times and as a subversive figure that potentially may reinvigorate Marxism today. This engagement with Lenin is, in my view, necessarily accompanied by other of Žižek's constant, 'controversial' positions, such as his self-professed obsession with Stalinism, the lack of solid and tangible political prescriptions (including the absence of a state theory proper), and the rhetorical value behind the concept of a dictatorship of the proletariat and what this means for Žižek today. Finally, this chapter will tie together these discordant pieces to produce a notion of Žižek as a midwife for a new political position that transcends 20th century revolution and old politics.

The Quest for Intellectual Authority

Žižek has pointed out that Marx is utilized in a number of fields for a number of purposes, many of which he does not share. To 'simply' talk about Marx would be to reproduce the same rituals and acknowledge Marx as an author who can be assimilated anywhere, as one who belongs to a field where authority has broken down into borderless wilderness, open to anyone with the will to access it. Žižek's goal, however, is to reclaim what he defines as Marxism proper.

To do so, he must first establish himself as an authority in the field. This is done by accruing knowledge capital: Through texts, interviews, and public engagements he artfully deploys and cultivates his expertise and authority (and is, ultimately, recognized as one). Indeed, Žižek regularly calls on the pantheon of great Marxists, skillfully displaying an in-depth knowledge of each and setting them forth to buttress his arguments when necessary.[2] Knowledge capital is thus developed and maintained as a *practice*. Authority needs to be constantly founded and re-founded through practices which act to set the perimeters of the field in question. The source of authority of any actor in a certain intellectual or political field is the knowledge that he or she reiterates and recites, and the authority figures that he or she invokes (in order to ground him or her in the traditions of the field).

Intellectual authority thus derives from the practices which *reiterate* knowledge rather than from those golden souls who stand alone as the sole beneficiaries of it. Far from a rationalist notion that there resides inherent truth within each work, and that the ability to reproduce this truth is to establish oneself as an authority, philosophical authorities rather establish themselves by *material* means; i.e. through positions held, works published, their social capital within the field of lecturers and writers, etc. While this authority is still determined, in the last instance, by their expertise on a subject matter (itself a practice which depends in part on the validation of others), the books, pun intended, are never closed.

In this light, 'misreadings' or 'misunderstandings' of philosophers and concepts become relative. Rather, a locutionary act is required to establish any production as erroneous. There is no reading that is wrong 'in itself'. Even the great authorities in a specific field have always had to stand up for their own readings of texts against other creative spirits.

Žižek follows this logic when he produces a demarcation within the amorphous field of Marxism (amorphous precisely because authority has broken down, and Marx exists 'everywhere' for 'everyone'). He does so by stating that, indeed, *there are* those who misuse Marx. It is this nomination (a practice) that assists him in the development of his own authority in the field of Marxism.

'Orthodox Marxism' as a Foil...

Žižek viciously attacks 'economistic' leftists who, 'fascinated by the functioning of today's global economy [...] preclude any possibility of a political intervention proper'.[3] Žižek retorts that 'today, more than ever, we should return to Lenin: Yes, the economy is the key domain, the battle will be decided there, we have to break the spell of global capitalism – but the intervention should be properly *political*, not economic.'[4] Who exactly these practitioners of economism are is left to the reader's imagination, and this is exactly the point in such a polemic.

---

2 Žižek calls on Marxists as disparate as G.A. Cohen and Walter Benjamin with ease, even if at times superficially. When the dust settles, however, it is Stalin who tends to be the winner in this bibliometric war.
3 Žižek 2006, 320.
4 Ibid., see also 327.

Žižek produces a foil to his model of political struggle, a foil which can be assumed by any position that is not his own. After all, if the renewed myth of Lenin teaches us anything, it is that politics is a question of will and heroism. Our failures thus become failures of will and courage.[5] The *violence* behind the anonymity of Žižek's foils is twofold. It not only raises the question of self-doubt, that is, whether we (the readers) are condemned as part of such a group. It also enjoins us, as sympathizers of Žižek, to root out such economism on behalf of Marxism proper. Žižek thus deploys an argument that hinges not so much on the strength of its validity (by citing who these leftists are, for example), but rather on the authority that his assertions must carry (or, at least, the authority he and sympathizers believe they must carry).

Žižek's dismissal of economism is not his first and last word on the contemporary left and contemporary Marxists. In *First As Tragedy, Then As Farce*, Žižek contrasts 'new Kravchenkos' (those disenchanted with both communism and postmodernism) with orthodox Marxists. He writes: 'They, not those nostalgics for twentieth-century "Really Existing Socialism", are our only hope.'[6] In *The Parallax View*, he criticizes 'the few remaining "orthodox" Marxists' for continuing to 'act as if nothing has really changed'.[7] What is so interesting in these critiques is the way in which Žižek effectively uses catch-all terms such as 'orthodox Marxists' and 'nostalgics' as a foil. Through them, he can distance himself from caricatures of Marxism and communism that float around academia and the public sphere; caricatures which are rarely if ever embodied in specific academics. This powerful gesture draws a dividing line between Žižek's own seriousness and the ridiculous, clownish nature of 'nostalgics'.

… and 'Orthodox Marxism' in Practice

In his address at the Marxism 2009 conference in London, under the headline of 'What does it mean to be a revolutionary today?', Žižek delivers the following joke:

> In the good old days of Really Existing Socialism, a joke popular among dissidents was used to illustrate the futility of their protests. In the fifteenth century, when Russia was occupied by Mongols, a peasant and his wife were walking along a dusty country road; a Mongol warrior on a horse stopped at their side and told the peasant he would now proceed to rape his wife; he then added: 'But since there is a lot of dust on the ground, you must hold my testicles while I rape your wife, so that they will not get dirty!' Once the

---

5   On p. 409 of Žižek 2008a, for example, even Hezbollah's 'ambiguous relation to state power' is described as paralleling 'something like the old Leninist notion of "dual power" – which was for Lenin also a temporary tactic, laying the groundwork for the later full takeover.'.
6   Žižek 2009, 156.
7   Žižek 2006, 297.

Mongol had done the deed and ridden away, the peasant started laughing and jumping with joy. His surprised wife asked: 'How can you be jumping with joy when I was just brutally raped in your presence?' The farmer answered: 'But I got him! His balls are covered with dust!'

The joke is intended to illustrate how leftists today are content with merely 'getting dirt on the balls of those in power', reading their own impotent conduct as something truly subversive. Žižek ends his address to wild applause by claiming that, contrary to this approach, the point is to cut off the balls of those in power.

What makes disparaging remarks like these all the more interesting is the fact that it is utterly unclear what it means to cut off the balls of those in power, while Žižek himself relies heavily on 'old-fashioned' concepts. He unsurprisingly says nothing in the way of strategy or tactics.

The case of charity is instructive here. In the animated version of his *First As Tragedy, Then As Farce* talk, Žižek calls for a return to the lessons of Oscar Wilde against charity and compassion. However, such a plea recalls the classic Marxist formula that philanthropy treats the symptoms, not the cause, of poverty.[8] He decries the rise of philanthropy (and its increasing collapse into consumerism) as 'global capitalism with a human face'. Again, this is not exactly an original characterization. When one considers what is 'new' in Žižek, at least on this point specifically, the answer is 'nothing'. It is difficult to distinguish where, conceptually, Žižek would fundamentally differ from orthodox Marxists on the question of charity, or even on the essential declaration behind his rape joke, that revolutions change societies, not revolts or unseen, self-validating practices.

Similar to this is, of course, one of the central claims in *Violence* that localized, 'criminal' violence (subjective violence) needs to be understood as enabled and made possible precisely on account of the everyday workings of capitalism (objective violence). Akin to Žižek's declaration that charity does not resolve the real causes of poverty, this thesis reiterates in different words a basic Marxist position vis-a-vis crime and capitalism, simultaneously stressing the need to focus our attention on the much more demanding task of resolving the contradictions of capitalism in order to do away with subjective violence.

Reloading Lenin…

Although Žižek's opposition to 'orthodox Marxists' may be riddled with contradictions, it is the practice of asserting authority that is central in his effort to re-establish the authority of Marxism proper. Yet, for this, citing Marx and criticizing nostalgic

---

8   Žižek 2010.

Marxists alone are not sufficient. Rather, it is necessary to resuscitate other names, other thinkers, and thus establish a natural link between these others and Marx (or, more precisely, what it means to be Marxist). This is exactly what Žižek intends to do when he advocates a return to Lenin.

Every field has its pantheon, sacred names that are called upon to safeguard theses as much as they are to intimidate detractors. Žižek's favorite Marxist has long been Lenin, whom he nominates as the 'St.Paul' of Marxism.[9] His glorification of and fascination with Lenin ranges from the academic to the banal. In *Violence*, for example, Lenin is lightheartedly deployed as part of the central joke (and, simultaneously, the central thesis) of the opening chapter. In *In Defense of Lost Causes*, on the other hand, Žižek's engagement with the icon is much more pronounced and in depth. And while Žižek has effectively sponsored the re-publishing of certain of Lenin's works, collected under the title *Revolution at the Gates*, Lenin trivia – and sometimes nothing more than a passing nod like 'as Lenin would put it' or 'as Lenin said in 1914...' – are a popular trademark of many of Žižek's own works.

Nonetheless, what defines Žižek's project to resuscitate Lenin is not so much a sustained, scholarly spirit of investigation. Rather, it is part of his efforts to recalibrate the lacking authority within the field of Marxism. Reciting Lenin is especially helpful in displacing the 'faint of heart' and thus reconfiguring the field's parameters. As has been recognized before, Marx belongs to 'everyone and no one', to the liberal disciplines and business schools alike. By drawing on a figure like Lenin, however, a Marxist who continues to conjure feelings of distaste, Žižek disturbs the existing usage of Marx. This becomes especially clear in Žižek's foreword to *Revolution At The Gates*. There, he states:

> The first public reaction to the idea of reactualizing Lenin is, of course, an outburst of sarcastic laughter: Marx is OK, even on Wall Street, there are people who love him today — Marx the poet of commodities, who provided perfect descriptions of the capitalist dynamics, Marx of the Cultural Studies, who portrayed the alienation and reification of our daily lives -, but Lenin, no, you can't be serious![10]

Žižek subsequently continues to discredit those interpreters of Marx whom he sees as 'liberal communists'. In *Violence*, he defines the latter as philanthropists and philanthropically-minded individuals. They seek to ameliorate the mayhem caused by capitalism by recourse to charity; that is, by treating the symptoms of the illness

9   'In the same way that St. Paul and Lacan reinscribed original teachings into different contexts (St. Paul reinterpreting Christ's crucifixion as his triumph; Lacan reading Freud through mirror-stage Saussure), Lenin violently displaces Marx, tearing his theory out of its original context, placing it in another historical moment, and thus effectively universalizing it.' Žižek 2007a, 2.

10   Žižek 2002, 3.

rather than the cause itself. Likewise, he mocks post-Marxists and faux-Marxists for their 'all-too-slick accommodation to "new circumstances"'.[11]

It is this context which sets the stage for Lenin's 'shocking' reintroduction. Reciting Lenin, however, will not simply horrify schools of Marxist thought into submission. Furthermore, Leninist would-be 'vanguard parties' and old-school Trotskyists already roam freely over many campuses, and are hardly a disturbance to all but the most resentful free-marketeers and conservative fanboys. Rather, the horror must be artfully deployed and something new must be added to truly upset the parameters of the field. Therefore, Žižek emphasizes that the goal should not be to simply reread Lenin, but to *reload* him. In the introduction to *Lenin Reloaded*, a collection of papers from a 2001 conference on Lenin organized by Žižek and several other like-minded academics, Lenin is presented in the following terms:

> Why Lenin, why not simply Marx? Is the proper return not the return to origins proper? [...] For us, 'Lenin' is not the nostalgic name for old dogmatic certainty; quite the contrary, the Lenin that we want to retrieve is the Lenin-in-becoming, the Lenin whose fundamental experience was that of being thrown into a catastrophic new constellation in which old reference points proved useless, and who was thus compelled to *reinvent* Marxism. The idea is that it is not enough simply to return to Lenin [...] for we must *repeat* or *reload* him; that is, we must retrieve the same impulse in today's constellation.[12]

For Žižek, Lenin thus takes on a dual purpose: not only as an icon that elicits a predetermined response, but also as a model of emulation and, perhaps most importantly, a fertile source for creativity. With respect to Lenin's first purpose, consider only the quoted section from *Lenin Reloaded*: the authors literally detail how distasteful it is for them to reload Lenin.[13] This is an explicit register of Lenin's subversive use, and serves again to highlight how the authors' understanding of a field shapes the way they seek to interact with and transform it.

More importantly, Lenin is utilized, for better or worse, as a role model. The only way that Žižek is successful in doing so is by subverting the traditional two understandings of Lenin by traditional Marxists. He claims that the obsession of many Marxists with discovering the 'wrong turn' in Marxism that accounts for its downward spiral as both a theory and a practice once and for all is irrelevant. As a result, he is able to suggest an original position claiming:

> One of the most devious traps which lurk for Marxist theorists is the search for the moment of the Fall, when things took the wrong turning in the history of Marxism [...] This entire trope [was it Engels? Lenin? Stalin?] has to be rejected: there is no opposition here, the Fall is to be inscribed in the very origins. (To put it even more pointedly, such a

---

11 Žižek 2008a, 3.
12 Žižek 2007a, 2-3.
13 This sentiment is echoed elsewhere; for example, Žižek 2007b, 217.

search for the intruder who infected the original model and set in motion its degeneration cannot but reproduce the logic of anti-Semitism.).[14]

Further:

> The proper task is thus to think the *tragedy* of the October Revolution: to perceive its greatness, its unique emancipatory potential, and, simultaneously, the *historical necessity* of its Stalinist outcome. One should oppose both temptations: the Trotskyist notion that Stalinism was ultimately a contingent deviation, as well as the notion that the Communist project is, in its very core, totalitarian.[15]

In the same stroke, Žižek sweeps aside both the worst kind of vulgar Marxism and the classical trope of Marxism as a totalitarian master-narrative, even through the co-optation of both positions. The Revolution and its Marxist legacy are praised *and* decried, effectively, as a project that was doomed to failure from the beginning. The *why* behind this claim is not examined by Žižek in any historical or sociological detail, nor are these details what are at stake; the statement serves to remove the 20th century project as an object of discussion and relevance by owning our failed past (not making excuses for it, simply owning it as a failure) and allowing for the beginning of a new discussion on revolutionary potential *today*.

Thus, while Žižek displays an in-depth knowledge of the history of communist movements, leaders, revolutionary moments, and ideas, he recognizes that they *are dead*. According to him, the way in which Marx, Lenin, Mao et al. attempted to reject the existing order and realize a new one must be read as objective failures, yet failures which were (and here is the tragedy) nonetheless the best possible efforts put forth. A central thesis of Žižek's *In Defense of Lost Causes* thus reads: 'Better a disaster of fidelity to the Event than a non-being of indifference towards the Event. To paraphrase Beckett's memorable phrase [...] after one fails, one can go on and fail better.'[16]

... and The Absence of State Theory

Žižek's argument for a return to Lenin hinges on his willingness to take risks and keep revolution (and the revolutionary imaginary) on the agenda, even in the face of hopelessness. As if in response to pleas for answers and convincing political alternatives to global capitalism, he remarks: 'The situation is "completely hopeless", with no clear "realistic" revolutionary perspective; but does this not give us a kind of

---

14 Žižek 2008a, 175; this claim is literally echoed in: Ibid. 2006, 292.
15 Žižek 2007a, 74.
16 Žižek 2008a, 7; see also 2009, 125.

strange freedom, a *freedom to experiment?*'[17] Recalling Mao and Beckett, Žižek notes that Lenin was

> a Beckettian *avant la lettre*; what he basically proposed that the Bolsheviks should do in the desperate situation at the end of the Civil War was not to directly 'construct social-ism', but to *fail better* than a 'normal' bourgeois state [...] the point of Lenin's famous notion of the 'weakest link in the chain' is, again, that one should use the 'anomaly' as a lever to exacerbate the antagonism so that they render possible a revolutionary explosion.[18]

What recurs most amongst Žižek's references to Lenin is the claim that, put simply, leftists must be proactive, rather than reactive. Yet in spite of this, there is not a single instance throughout Žižek's resuscitation of Lenin where he pleads with readers to leave their sofas and laptops and enlist in a revolutionary vanguard party, or start their own. Leftists must instead first learn how to dream again, to 'do the impossible'.

As a result, throughout his experimentation with Lenin, there is hardly a sustained and ongoing conversation on Lenin's most infamous tract, *The State and Revolution*. Indeed, the state sits silently in the background, relatively untouched and undiagnosed, but precisely because nothing more needs to be said about it. If Žižek's interventions in the field of Marxism aim to provocatively restore validity to unfashionable notions, if re-grounding Marxism as a political theory and movement proper fills the bulk of the space Žižek takes up, it's because some of the tasks on the revolutionary agenda remain the same, and we need now only bring ourselves to discuss them again. Lenin is a Beckettian *avant la letter*, Žižek reminds us, and we should be too: better to fail again (seizing state power) than do nothing at all.

Stalinism...

Žižek perhaps reaches a peak on this general point in his 'obsessive' fascination with Stalinism. Provocatively claiming that '[o]ne should be careful not to throw out the baby with the dirty water',[19] Žižek occasionally attempts to defend 'Soviet Communism which, despite the catastrophe it stands for, *did* possess true inner greatness'.[20] Confronting the fashionable postmodern claim that all totalitarianisms share a common logic, Žižek suggests instead that '[i]n the Stalinist ideological imaginary, universal Reason is objectivized in the guise of the inexorable laws of historical

---

17   Žižek 2008a, 361.
18   Ibid. See also Žižek 2009, 86.
19   Žižek 2008a, 7.
20   Žižek 2006, 285; see also Chapter 5, 'Stalin Revisited: Or, How Stalin Saved the Humanity of Man' of Žižek 2008a.

progress, and we are all its servants, the leader included'.[21] Part of the support for this argument is simply in the way the leader participates in formal events: 'After a Nazi leader delivers a speech and the crowd applauds, he just stands and silently accepts the applause, positing himself as its addressee; while in Stalinism, when the obligatory applause explodes at the end of the leader's speech, the leader stands up and joins the others in applauding.'[22]

The point in defending Stalinism has a double significance. Firstly, it needs to be contextualized as neither the first nor the last attempt to defend the heritage of October 1917. Žižek here is simply participating in an apology for the Russian Revolution, and not the excesses of Stalinism *per se*. Nowhere does Žižek glorify the breakneck speed at which Stalin subjected the people of the Soviet Union to during the years of collectivization, though he does describe it as in sync with the Enlightenment goals of Soviet Communism, contra the irrational, Romantic excesses of the Nazis' Holocaust.[23] Generations of Marxists have participated in a similar denunciation of Stalin's excesses without writing off the Revolution's emancipatory potential.

Secondly, there is a significance in the use of deploying the figure of Stalin himself. Like Žižek's use of Lenin, utilizing the figure of Stalin to make a point (that communism, as catastrophic a system as it was, should never be considered synonymous with fascism) is a move which re-appropriates the history of Marxism. As Žižek writes, '[o]ur side no longer has to go on apologizing'.[24] Part of this new, 'no regrets' direction that Žižek would like to take 'our side' in involves being able to speak freely about 'our' historical lapses of judgment. Why? Precisely so that once the debris is shoveled aside and a space for new thought is cleared, we can speak lucidly on how political struggle for real emancipation will take place in the 21st century.

Žižek's frenetic activity masks an absence of solutions for the left. However, providing these answers was never part of his project. Rather, his actions and utterances must be interpreted as part of his attempt to re-orient the field of Marxism, to rework the questions that the Left deals with, and ultimately to re-ground the strategies that found political action. This is the reason why Žižek has never published a tactical manifesto. There is no existing socialist party that well and truly meets with his

---

21 Žižek 2006, 291; see also Žižek 2009b.
22 Ibid. Žižek continues to draw out this point, ultimately claiming that as '[c]razy and tasteless as this may sound, this last distinction illustrates the fact that the opposition between Stalinism and Nazism was the opposition between civilization and barbarism: Stalinism did not sever the last thread that linked it to civilization. The lowest Gulag inmate still participated in the universal Reason: he had access to the Truth of History.' See also 2007a, 83.
23 Ibid., 285.
24 Žižek 2009a, 8.

approval. Despite his allusions to an intervention that must be properly political, rather than economic, he has no solid stratagem yet.

What is left unsaid through these diagnoses is the central importance of the state. According to Žižek, our activism must above all be political. Furthermore, we should address the failure of the Russian Revolution, rather than apologizing for the attempt. What remains, then, is a political theory that very classically implies that change hinges on who controls the state apparatus, in a matter akin to 'old-fashioned' Marxist theory. This is the reason why Žižek wrestles so frequently with the legacy of the Russian Revolution and attempts to resuscitate political figures like Lenin. His goal is to de-suture classic themes of radical political action from the reigning narrative. The result of this is, however, that to even think of a better world (let alone one that still borrows heavily from Marxism) is to participate in the logic of totalitarianism.

… and the Dictatorship of the Proletariat

Žižek asserts that it is the task of leftist thinkers to re-deploy Marx's notion of the proletariat, but 'well beyond Marx's imagination'.[25] He takes up Marx's distinction between the working class and the proletariat, and states: '[T]he "working class" effectively is a particular social group, while the 'proletariat' designates a subjective position.'[26] While the working class is a pre-existing social group, any particular group can function as the proletariat. He goes further: 'What if we take the risk of resuscitating the good old "dictatorship of the proletariat" as the only way to break with biopolitics?'[27]

Žižek claims that the particularity of the proletariat lies in the fact that they are 'part of no part'. They are those whose particular demands cannot be met without transforming the very logic of the system that produces them. Their particular demands stand for something universal. The beauty of Žižek's deployment of the term proletariat goes beyond the fact that Marx himself tended to use the terms working class and proletariat synonymously. There is more at stake here than Žižek's (in)fidelity to Marx's *oeuvre*. Even if Marx most likely did not have this distinction in mind, Žižek's argument is fascinating. While remaining within Marxism at the level of *words*, Žižek de-sutures the emancipatory potential from the working class (the privileged revolutionary agent). And he thus states: 'What we should be looking for

---

25 Žižek 2009b.
26 Žižek 2007a, 89. This claim is echoed virtually verbatim on p. 285 of 2008a, and much of the remaining chapter is given over to a defense of this idea (albeit in a roundabout way) while refuting Laclau. See also 2008a, 238 and 239; see also 2006, 30 and 269.
27 Žižek 2008a, 412.

are the signs of the new forms of social awareness that will emerge from the slum collectives: they will be the seeds of the future.'[28]

Žižek draws broadly on his reinterpretation of the proletariat. He cites Cohen's 'four features of the classical Marxist notion of the working class' in order to claim that 'none [...] applies to the contemporary working class.'[29] Elsewhere, along similar lines, he claims that

> [i]t is in fact surprising how many features of the slum-dwellers fit the good old Marxist description of the proletarian revolutionary subject: they are 'free' in the double meaning of the word even more than the classic proletariat ('freed' from all substantial ties; dwelling in a free space, outside state police regulation); they are a large collective, forcibly thrown together, 'thrown' into a situation where they have to invent some mode of being-together, and simultaneously deprived of any support in traditional ways of life, in inherited religious or ethnic life-forms.[30]

Of course, in this passage there is a kind of slip when Žižek alludes to the 'classic proletariat', running counter to his claim a year later in *Lenin Reloaded* that, in fact, Marx himself made no such distinction between the proletariat and the working class.

Just as significant as Žižek's re-envisioning of the proletariat is his emphasis on dictatorship. In classical fashion, Žižek derides democracy itself as a kind of totalizing 'dictatorship' under capitalism, an institutionalized deadlock that is never able to address the fundamental questions of its economic base. Calling on the authority of Lenin in this regard Žižek writes: 'When Lenin designated liberal democracy as a form of bourgeois dictatorship [...] he meant that the very *form* of the bourgeois-democratic state, the sovereignty of its power in its ideologico-political presuppositions, embodies a "bourgeois" logic. One should thus use the term "dictatorship" in the precise sense in which democracy is also a form of dictatorship, that is, as a purely *formal* determination.'[31]

This anti-democratic rhetoric is called on time and again. For example, Žižek claims that '[d]emocracy, it may seem, thus not only can include antagonism, it is the only political form that solicits and presupposes it, that *institutionalizes* it.'[32] This institutionalized antagonism is *never* truly radical according to Žižek, since time and time again liberal democracy seems able to happily co-opt all but the most 'extreme' demands of its dissidents, thereby marginalizing positions which seek more fundamental transformations. And while, in typical fashion, Žižek never describes what he wishes would replace this less than perfect system, his anti-demo-

---

28 Žižek 2006, 269.
29 Žižek 2008a, 420.
30 Žižek 2006, 268.
31 Žižek 2008a, 412.
32 Žižek 2007a, 85.

cratic rhetoric serves two purposes. Primarily, it serves to create a distance between Žižek and other (post-)Marxists (such as Badiou, Hardt and Negri, Laclau, etc.), especially when it allows him to draw on iconic figures such as Lenin to do so. In a more secondary capacity, it provides Žižek with a set of provocative fireworks, alarming the reader (at least initially) and producing a sense of intrigue. Typically, of course, Žižek elaborates to the point where it becomes relatively clear that claims such as 'we need the dictatorship of the proletariat' or that 'liberal democracy should be our enemy first and foremost' are used to negate competing claims, and ultimately wind up discarded once they have served their polemical purpose.

Putting Revolution back on the Menu

The picture I have so far painted of Žižek's engagements with Marxist history and its postmodern turn is full of contradictions. Indeed, Žižek is a contradiction. How can it be that, on the one hand, he can claim that the class struggle effectively continues in subterranean form, disguised by misdirected working-class resentment towards minorities or populist mistrust of wealthy elites, while, on the other hand, he tells us that the proletariat is really an empty word, one which can be occupied by any particular group? How can it be that, on the one hand, Lenin is presented as a model of political struggle, while orthodox Marxists are simultaneously disparaged and harangued as an archaic and endangered species? Is the point of Žižek to confuse us? The title of Žižek's first contribution to *Contingency, Hegemony, Universality* is telling: 'Class Struggle or Postmodernism? Yes, please!'. In the text, Žižek elaborates: 'In a well-known Marx Brothers joke Groucho answers the standard question "Tea or coffee?" with "Yes, please!" – a refusal of choice.'[33] Confronting and overcoming this false antinomy of choice among the left is precisely what Žižek's interventions aim to do. This antinomy is *false* because both 'radical' routes offer no truly creative, anti-capitalist, and emancipatory alternatives.

Throughout all the texts that stand as testament to this twin refusal, Žižek is 'doing' something: through his 'terrorist acts', he pushes those who describe themselves as radicals to question the limitations they have placed on what is possible. Žižek describes leftists as, for the most part, holding to 'the idea that we have to live with our imperfect world, since any radical alternative sooner or later would lead to the Gulag.'[34] This goes for most political theorists, but that it applies to leftists today is, to Žižek, tragic.

Despite all the contradictions, there is a political ontology that underwrites Žižek's philosophical interventions. The most telling proof of this is the fact that on

---

33 Žižek 2000, 90.
34 Žižek 2005, 59.

this issue he *does not* contradict himself. The consistency with which Žižek rails against the popular consensus that capitalism is here to stay is matched only by the frequency with which he claims that it is not. This is precisely what makes his expositions relevant. Class struggle, the dictatorship of the proletariat, Lenin; all of these themes and concepts are venues for Žižek to reiterate what is at stake here. To understand Žižek's interventions, we must acknowledge this most elementary political ontology, and consequently recognize whom Žižek is addressing with his theses. They are not directed against leftists *tout court*. They are not directed against leftists just for being leftists. Rather, they address 'post'-Marxists who have come to terms with capitalism and are determined only to limit its damaging effects as much as possible.

Still, 'solving' the problems of the left poses a difficult problem, at least partially owing to the limited role of the philosopher. In Žižek's eponymous documentary, he describes the role of philosophy along very minimalist lines: 'Philosophy does not solve problems. The duty of philosophy is not to solve problems, but to redefine problems, to show how what we experience as a problem is a false problem.'[35] At stake here is the age old Marxist dilemma of the relationship between theory and practice. Understanding the conjuncture is the first step towards hypothesizing the political direction that partisans of communism need to take. Žižek's diagnoses of his fellow (non-)radical leftists may help to establish and reiterate the stakes of the present theoretical conjuncture. Simultaneously, they foreclose the possibility of any serious dialogue.

In terms of content, Lenin can *only* stand for the position of unmediated will and heroic overcoming. The message of Lenin in the way Žižek quotes him is that revolution is never off the table. That is, ultimately, Žižek's message to his contemporaries: Put revolution back on the menu! Lenin does *not* stand as a role model in a literal sense. Žižek does not, for example, use Lenin as a segue to defending democratic centralism or authoritarianism. Rather Lenin stands as a model of political shrewdness coupled with revolutionary imagination. This model acts in the abstract: Žižek enjoins us to be *like* Lenin, not *be* him. Here it is worth recounting Žižek's explicit recognition of the Russian Revolution as an objective failure from the very start. There is no room in his analysis for Trotskyist pipe dreams.

Žižek's thesis in *Violence* functions similarly. It is a clear demand for radicals today *not* to behave like 'liberal communists', *not* to frantically hope to solve each pressing issue as it arises without first carefully diagnosing the real cause (and, in a reductionist fashion, for Žižek the 'real cause' is always 'capitalism'). Žižek's claim that these 'liberal communists' betray themselves in their inability to really 'violently' change the situation is a challenge to post-Marxists to reconsider what the real

---

35   Taylor 2005.

end goal of change must be. Of course, when violence is understood as something that fundamentally transforms or disturbs the existing order (and the existing order is totalizing), anything less necessarily constitutes a form of surrender or 'renunciation'.

Conclusion

The negative, impossible gesture in Žižek's interventions simultaneously embodies the insistent quality of his work. This insistence necessarily accompanies the negative. Since philosophy advances by theses (with all their conceptual baggage) and is not a question of Truth, everything depends on practice. As Žižek 'practices' his philosophy, he insists and repeats himself *ad nauseam*. His jokes and analogies reach dizzying heights, precisely because the philosopher can do nothing else but insist when he or she exists on the margins of a field he or she wishes to transform. He or she must learn the art of the pen before the art of the sword. Indeed, if philosophy is 'merely' the nomination of a false problem, then insistence and repetition necessarily become a valuable strategy, for there is little else the philosopher can do once he or she has staked out these problems. To be clear: Žižek may see himself as a firm defender of a politics of Truth (though we should not be in the habit of trusting authors). But this is ultimately a moot point when it comes to analyzing his oeuvre: after all, the Truth alone, sans practice, has never broken any chains, won any wars, or effected any change.

Regardless of what he may claim from time to time, there is in practice no either/or to Žižek's intellectual coordinates. Unlike analyses which remain closed to the many positions he takes up as a foil against post-Marxism's 'surrender' to global capitalism, I read Žižek as both occupying these many positions, while simultaneously transcending them. It is clear in his insistence that the current conjuncture remains defined by the left's submission to the status quo, and its inability and unwillingness to formulate new alternatives. If Žižek's role as a philosopher is to nominate a false problem, then Žižek could be seen as the midwife of the new coordinates necessary to 'save us'. This position does not yet exist, and cannot exist amongst the current positions, which are too heavily constrained by the imaginaries of the past.

Žižek's project thus takes on a kind of double impossibility. There is the impossibility of the empty space which he occupies or, rather, the fleeting quality of his occupations. Žižek is sometimes required to play the part of the classic Marxist, and at other times the critical postmodern thinker, in order to negate one or the other position. The second impossibility is the impossibility of a real break from the past. If the current politico-theoretical constellation is found as possessing none of the qualities necessary to deal with what Žižek understands to be the single most pressing issue of our time (global capitalism's excesses), then we need a new position that can. Part of his struggle depends on convincing existing positions that they are inadequate, thus reorganizing the problematic that drives them. Žižek's first task is to continue to insist that post-Marxist positions ultimately remain trapped within capitalism's horizons.

Žižek's project to redefine Marxism proper thus remains impossibly entangled in the trappings of old coordinates and traditions, and it seems most likely that Žižek will create new traditions by mutating old ones. All Žižek's many prefaces to his theses, such as 'to put it in Leninist terms', or 'as an old-fashioned Marxist', etc., function to produce the contours of this new tradition.[36] What Žižek accomplishes in his invocations of Lenin, Leninism, and Marxism is a redefinition of the very words. If Žižek prefaces a claim with a nod to Lenin or Leninism, it is because there is no pre-existing, authentic 'vernacular' for the things he is about to say. It is not self-evident to his audience what 'Lenin's terms' are; the coordinates that Lenin occupies are in such disuse (there is no 'serious' school of 'Leninists') that Žižek is free to mold them as he wishes. They are, rather, traditions that are in the process of being renewed or recreated; he must 'remind' us that he is speaking a particular vernacular so that we can learn the language too.

The force Žižek applies to produce the transformations he seeks can be discerned in the form which his interventions take. These include taking up the impossible position which allows him to parry every position's counter-thrust, his insistence and repetition, the frequency with which the same themes crop up in his works, and the rhetorical devices nestled in his theses which enjoin readers to re-think emancipation. What counts in Žižek far more than the question of the state is the form of his writings themselves and how his interventions transform the field of Marxism. At a certain point, Žižek invokes a Keyser Söze analogy, thus referring to the main protagonist of the movie *The Usual Suspects*. The radical left's only way out of its current impasse is to *first* 'murder its family', that which constrains and delimits it, *and as a result* acquire the freedom to ruthlessly pursue its enemies.

---

36 Žižek 2006, 341; see also Žižek 2008b, 102, 150, 154; see also Žižek 2009a, 19, 67, 76, 99, 100.

References

Badiou, Alain, 2010a: *The Communist Hypothesis*. London.

Badiou, Alain and Slavoj Žižek, 2010b: Audio: Badiou and Žižek at Jack Tilton Gallery. http://www.imposemagazine.com/bytes/audio-badiou-.

Taylor, Astra (dir.), 2005: *Žižek!*

Žižek, Slavoj, 2000: Class Struggle or Postmodernism? Yes, Please!. In: Judith Butler, Ernesto Laclau and Slavoj Žižek: *Contingency, Hegemony, Universality. Contemporary Dialogues on the Left*. London, 90-135.

Žižek, Slavoj, 2002: Introduction. Between the Two Revolutions. In: Ibid. (ed.), V.I. Lenin: *Revolution at the Gates. A Selection of Writings from February to October 1917*. London, 3-12.

Žižek, Slavoj, 2005: Philosophy is Not a Dialogue. In: Peter Engelmann (ed.), Alain Badiou and Slavoj Žižek 2009: *Philosophy in the Present*. Cambridge, 49-72.

Žižek, Slavoj, 2006: *The Parallax View*. Cambridge.

Žižek, Slavoj, 2007: A Leninist Gesture Today. Against the Populist Temptation. In: Sebastian Budgen et al (eds.), 2007: *Lenin Reloaded. Toward a Politics of Truth*. Durham, 74-100.

Žižek, Slavoj, 2008a: *In Defense of Lost Causes*. London.

Žižek, Slavoj, 2008b: *Violence. Six Sideways Reflections*. New York.

Žižek, Slavoj, 2009a: *First as Tragedy, Then as Farce*. London.

Žižek, Slavoj, 2009b: What Does it Mean to Be a Revolutionary Today? http://www.youtube.com/watch?v=_GD69Cc20rw.

Žižek, Slavoj, 2010: RSA Animate – First as Tragedy, Then as Farce. http://www.youtube.com/watch?v=hpAMbpQ8J7g.

Agon Hamza

The distance between Party and State.
An outline of a Žižekian theory of the State

A report from the ideological-political fronts

At the very beginning of *The State and Revolution*, Lenin diagnoses the status of Marx's theory:

> What is now happening to Marx's theory has, in the course of history, happened repeat-edly to the theories of revolutionary thinkers and leaders of oppressed classes fighting for emancipation. During the lifetime of great revolutionaries, the oppressing classes con-stantly hounded them, received their theories with the most savage malice, the most furi-ous hatred and the most unscrupulous campaigns of lies and slander. After their death, attempts are made to convert them into harmless icons, to canonize them, so to say, and to hallow their *names* to a certain extent for the 'consolation' of the oppressed classes and with the object of duping the latter, while at the same time robbing the revolutionary theory of its *substance*, blunting its revolutionary edge and vulgarizing it. Today, the bourgeoisie and the opportunists within the labor movement concur in this doctoring of Marxism. They omit, obscure, or distort the revolutionary side of this theory, its revolu-tionary soul. They push to the foreground and extol what is or seems acceptable to the bourgeoisie. All the social-chauvinists are now 'Marxists' (don't laugh!).[1]

One cannot fail to notice a similar phenomenon occurring in the present. Marx is present everywhere, in debates about the economic crisis and the future of the left, precisely because he has been neutralized. Everyone on the Left speaks of 'Marx', but they do so in a distorted way. Whenever socialists refer to him, they render Marx as a poet of a revolutionary past or an archaic messiah and thus transform him into a harmless icon. Communists elevate Marx to a sacred position, which is another way of not engaging with what is at the core of Marx's work, that is, his *Capital*. It is at this point that one should locate the contemporary Left. Or, to go a step further, we can say that at every conjuncture, we have a 'distorted' Marx – this was the case in Lenin's time and it certainly is the case now. But the difference lies in the form of this distortion, for today it is through over-exposure that we ultimately leave Marx alone.

The majority of the Left today, including socialist governments and parties, silently accept that capitalism is the ultimate form of social organization. They are

---

1 Lenin 1987, 272.

'Marxist' at the level of analysis, and non-Marxist when it comes to practice. Their discourse takes this kind of form: Yes, we know capitalism is bad, but Marxism does not provide a solution or vision for politics; therefore, the struggle against capitalism has to be fought on a cultural level, etc. As a consequence, Leftist politics and theory exist only as a reaction to the actions of the ruling class. Precisely because Marxism is merely accepted as an analytical tool, it only allows for reactive politics.

The Left is being confronted with one of the darkest and weakest moments in its history. While accepting Marx's fundamental thesis that capitalism is a global system, the Left is struggling for moderate changes and reforms within the socio-political system, without ever even contemplating a transformation of that system.

Being a Marxist without being a communist ultimately means that even when one does speak of systematic change (from a Marxist point of view), one still ends up lacking a practical point of departure from which to bring about such change. This lack of a communist practice is the result of the previously discussed postmodern turn of the Left. For while postmodernism accepts Marxism as a deconstructionist tool, it is at the same time dismissive of 'grand narratives' of class struggle and revolution, choosing to highlight the oppressive sides of collective politics. Thus, for the postmodern Left, class struggle is replaced with a cultural politics of recognition (gay rights, anti-racist struggles, multiculturalism, and so on). While it ignores class analysis and struggle, it aims at improving the position of specific groups within the coordinates of capitalist social organization.

In a similar way, the contemporary left is haunted by the specter of post-colonial theory.[2] Although this topic requires longer deliberation, I will limit myself to putting forward the following thesis: The problem of post-colonial theory is well encapsulated in the distinction proposed by Badiou between the ethics of difference and the ethics of truth. The former is mostly oriented towards the past, and focuses on reparations paid to formerly repressed groups, governmental support in the reconstruction of their cultural heritage, and an official endorsement of a politics that aims at avoiding past mistakes in the future. The latter paradigm, on the other hand, acknowledges the historical basis of any action, but maintains a perspective of future systemic transformation and emphasizes what people have in common (politics of truth, i.e. universality). Post-colonial theory reconstructs the history of colonial struggles and focuses on culture as a receptacle of lost heritage, equating power invariably with repression so as to ultimately dismiss universality as a dangerous return towards euro-centric ideology.

The Left has abandoned the Marxist critique of political economy and ideology, and is content with analyzing and criticizing the symptoms of capitalism: austerity, neoliberalism, authoritarianism and so forth. As a result, the Left is either engaged in

---

2 Žižek 2001, 13-19; Chibber 2013.

false struggles (reformist critiques of neoliberalism, austerity) or in struggles that in no way challenge the ruling ideology (cultural politics).

Finally, the Left has abandoned the party form of politics in favor of horizontal ways of organizing itself (for example, in the Occupy movement). Self-organization has become the predominant form of political organization, as all strands of the Left denounce Leninism, that is, class struggle, communism and party organization. This, then, is the true nature of the defeat of the Left. In the face of the terrible defeats suffered by twentieth century socialism, anti-Leninism is a conservative choice that throws out the baby with the bathwater.[3]

However, there is a way in between the blind repetition of previous failed solutions and the abdication of the problem altogether; a way to rethink the party form of political organization in a new relation to the state and society. The true task of the revolutionary left today is exactly this: to rethink the party form and the transformation of the state. Fighting state power and seizing state power is what the contemporary Left abhors the most. The problem of the Left thus lies in its theory of power.

During the 1970s, French philosophers produced a theory of power that only leaves space for emancipatory politics from a position of resistance to power, never in exercising it. The links between this philosophical strand, postmodernism and postcolonial studies thus become clear. The revolutionary left currently lacks a theory of power which is active and prepositive rather than reactive and merely critical. It is precisely in this field that we should return to Lenin. One of the most polemic aspects of Slavoj Žižek's 'return to Lenin' is his simultaneous attempt to revitalize the Hegelian theory of the State. At the crossing point of these two lines of reasoning – Leninism and Hegelianism – it becomes necessary to recuperate the 'analytic' dimension of the Leninist party form and to rethink Lenin's critique of the state. Such a practice will allow us to conceive a 'non-statal state', a form of the state that goes beyond the traditional form, which is inherently fused with the capitalist mode of production. This, then, is the goal of this contribution: a modest attempt to lay the foundations of the Žižekian theory of the state.

Before we do so, however, it is important to note that up to now Žižek has never put forward a theory of the state. In his entire work, from *The Sublime Object of Ideology* up to his last major philosophical books, *Less Than Nothing* and *Absolute Recoil* and *Disparities,* one cannot find a fully developed critique of the capitalist form of the state or a basic outline of the structure or workings of the post-capitalist state. It is true that Žižek engages with other thinkers, such as Hegel, Marx and Lenin, developing a systematic critique of both theories and practices of the twentieth century socialist experiments and Marxist theories. In what can be referred to as his 'communist series', Žižek develops some elementary positions (theses) on the critique

---

3 For a more detailed elaboration on this topic, see: Hamza and Tupinambá 2016.

and theory of the state, as well as some very general outlines of his understanding of post-revolutionary situations. The aim of my argument is, however, not to offer an exegesis or hermeneutics of Žižek's work, but rather to work through Žižek's system to arrive at a Žižekian theory of the state.

In this endeavor, specific challenges lie ahead of us. The first issue is that when we talk about a Žižekian theory of the state and search for it in his works, are we not caught in the transference investment? Are we not expecting *too much* from a philosopher, expecting a ready-made program of how to proceed from capitalism to twenty-first century forms of communist organization? The first obstacle thus lies in the relationship between philosophy and politics. Philosophy does not *think* politics, nor does it provide a specific political program for revolution. The position occupied by Žižek is that of decentered subjectivity, stripping himself of the false philosophical and political hopes of the many. In this sense, the true question is not what Žižek's ideal state would be. In all probability, this is not clear to Žižek himself. Exactly herein lies the greatness of a philosopher: he provides us with a general framework and concepts through which one can think further.

The notion of the state as such remains highly under theorized, both by Žižek and his critics and followers. However, this is not exclusively a problem of Žižek's work as such. The entire Marxist tradition has largely neglected the theorization of the state. Thus, the aim of this chapter is to address this issue by presenting the elementary and basic contours of a Žižekian theory of the state. For any reader of Žižek, this presents an impossible task, for none other than the simple fact that Žižek himself never claimed to be constructing such a theory, nor does he aim to provide a systematic critique or analysis of the state. Additionally, at many levels his work resists and opposes such a formalization. But although Žižek himself never claimed that the goal of his writing was to construct a theory of the state, his writings nonetheless seem to 'betray' his conviction. There are elements in his work that can serve this purpose. The crucial sources for such an endeavor are Hegelian philosophy, Žižek's return to Lenin and his theorization of the contemporary mode of capitalist production. However, in order to do so, a crucial philosophical detour is needed. Such a detour is important in order to set straight Žižek's status as a philosopher, against the predominant reactionary appropriations of him in contemporary academia.

Culture, that sickness

Slavoj Žižek holds a singular position in contemporary academia. His philosophical project can be defined as a 'Lacanian return to Hegel' and the reversal of the standard Marxist formula of 'from Hegel to Marx' into 'from Marx to Hegel'. This is a profound philosophical and political position, the implications of which, as we shall see, are far-reaching. In the terms of our present conjuncture, we are closer to the Hegelian rather than the Marxian universe. While Marx was writing on a revolutionary situation (that is, 1848), identifying and theorizing revolution, forms of political organization and revolutionary agents, Hegel was mostly concerned with the effects of a revolution on a post-revolutionary situation (that is, the post-Napoleonic era). Hegel was concerned with the failure of the French revolution and with the problems of creating a unified state in nineteenth century Prussia. We are presently living in a similar historical and political conjuncture: the period of socialist revolutions is over and capitalism has become a global system. The socialist era has come to a close, and we need to radically rethink the idea of communism. In this context, Žižek aims to repeat Hegel in order to rethink dialectical materialism. Žižek maintains that every kind of materialism that is worthy of the name must return to (and repeat) Hegel, for by returning to the Hegelian dialectic we are able to rethink about class struggle, political radicalism and emancipation, and so on.[4] This return is all the more important because for Hegel, philosophy and (political) crisis are interconnected. In a sense, the latter always conditions the former.

Yet, Žižek does not simply base himself on the work of Hegel. Rather, he triangulates Hegel's work with that of Lacan and Marx. At the end of the introduction to *The Sublime Object of Ideology*, Žižek thus writes that

> The only way to 'save Hegel' is through Lacan, and this Lacanian reading of Hegel and the Hegelian heritage opens up a new approach to ideology, allowing us to grasp contemporary ideological phenomena [...] without falling prey to any kind of 'post-modernist' traps (such as the illusion that we live in a 'post-ideological' condition).[5]

In the introduction to *For They Know What They Do* (published two years later), he continues to state that:

> As with *The Sublime Object of Ideology*, the theoretical space of the present book is molded by three centers of gravity: Hegelian dialectics, Lacanian psychoanalytic theory, and contemporary criticism of ideology. These three circles form a Borromean knot: each of them connects the other two; the place that they all encircle, the 'symptom' in their midst, is of course the author's (and, as the author hopes, also the reader's) enjoyment of what one depreciatingly calls 'popular culture' [...] The three theoretical circles are not, however, of the same weight: it is their middle term, the theory of Jacques Lacan, which is - as Marx would say - 'the general illumination which bathes all the other colors and modifies their particularity'.[6]

Although in his recent writings, Hegel occupies the privileged position in this triad, the three thinkers of Žižek's Borromean knot are of equal importance.

---

4 Hamza 2015..
5 Žižek 2008, xxxi.
6 Žižek 2008a, 2.

Strangely enough, many scholars dismiss the references to Hegel and Marx in Žižek's work so as to turn Žižek into a commentator on Lacan, someone who can explain Lacan to them in culturalist terms. This elaborate but ultimately selective reading of Žižek leads to what I call a culturalist appropriation of Žižek's philosophical system. As Lacan becomes their tool and horizon of understanding, it subsequently informs their interpretation of Žižek. In his usual dismissive tone, Jacques-Alain Miller has thus asked the Freudian question 'what do Americans want?', only to answer his question with 'They want the Lacan of Slavoj Žižek.'[7] In his 'partial answer', Miller is partially correct: this version of Lacan is truly not Lacanian, but then again neither is the Žižekian Lacan. The Lacan that Miller refers to is the Lacan as read by Žižek's fans, or those Žižek scholars who work in cultural studies, and subsequently cleansed of any political notions.

But Žižek's Borromean knot cannot be unraveled like this. His project does not exist if one excludes one of the thinkers from this totality. This is why the culturalist Žižek is an incompetent theoretical creation. Furthermore, the culturalist interpretations of Lacan result in a diluted reading of Lacan, which merely provides an 'impression on and of Lacan', which is extracted from a decaffeinated reading of Žižek's work.

The culturalist dimension in contemporary academia focuses on Žižekian cultural analysis. Like Marx, Žižek becomes yet another poet of commodities, of cultural phenomena, cultural antagonisms, and so on. Against this reactionary and monstrous theoretical enterprise, we should propose the real Žižekian thesis: he calls for a break with the standard cultural critique of Marxism. Marx's *Capital* is not a work of cultural critique, nor is capitalism a product of culture. The aim of cultural critics or critical theorists is to theorize ethical capitalism, ecology, human rights, et cetera. What such politically correct protagonists are missing, however, is that even in culture, as such, class struggle is the determining instance. Given this, a problematic question arises: how can we move beyond the journalistic catchwords of so-called critical theory in our approach to Žižek? We should reaffirm that there is only one way to read Žižek: *as a philosopher.* Žižek is only comprehensible if read philosophically.

Thus, my first thesis is that we need to separate the culturalist Žižek from the actual Žižek. In order to fully grasp his conceptualization of the state, we need to radically break away from the cultural theorist horizon that Žižek has been squeezed into. Against that, we need to evoke Žižek himself, who, in defining communism, writes that

> In contrast to socialism, communism refers to singular universality, to the direct link between the singular and the universal, bypassing particular determinations. When Paul

---

7 Miller 2008.

says that, from a Christian standpoint, 'there are no men or women, no Jews or Greeks'; he thereby claims that ethnic roots, national identities, etc., are not a category of truth. To put it in precise Kantian terms: when we reflect upon our ethnic roots, we engage in a private use of reason, constrained by contingent dogmatic presuppositions; that is, we act as 'immature' individuals, not as free humans who dwell in the dimension of the universality of reason.[8]

The only way to engage in the *private use of reason* is by bypassing the particular mediation and not engaging in the universal. The whole lesson of Žižek is that there is no singular universality through the position of culture.

But, why this rather long detour? My thesis is that one can only construct a Žižekian theory of the state from his philosophical positions. The Žižekian solution to the classic problem of the 'philosopher king', who thinks philosophy but practices politics – and thus does both badly –, is to claim that the only theses a philosopher can formulate concerning the state are theses that separate the state from its mystification. Hegel himself did this by distinguishing the state from civil society.[9] Žižek now repeats Hegel by further dividing the sphere of the state more precisely by insisting that the party is not a part of the state. In this sense, he can be regarded as a Leninist, that is, influenced by politics, while remaining a philosopher.

Symptoms in communism

Psychoanalysis, Marxism and philosophy are characterized by an immanent tension, an unsurpassable impasse. The fundamental difference between psychoanalysis and Marxism resides on two fundamental structural and constitutive differences. On one level, psychoanalysis begins where Marxism ends. For Marxism, as well as for psychoanalysis, the suffering of the people (or, individuals respectively) is the starting point. Psychoanalysis aims at reducing the pain and the suffering of individual subjects through analytic sessions and by means of providing interpretative intervention through speech. Marxism is concerned with the suffering of the proletariat as an oppressed class. Todd McGowan has pointed out that 'there is no revolt of the patients that would correspond to the revolt of the proletariat'.[10] Interestingly, both Freud and Lacan were not politically progressive. Their political comments were very skeptical of any emancipatory project, or, to paraphrase Mladen Dolar, neither Freud nor Lacan were men of politics. Neither could envisage the consequences of psychoanalysis in politics. McGowan nicely defines a distinctive second difference, which goes as follows: 'Marxism is able to theorize sacrifice as necessary for future plea-

---

8   Žižek 2009, 104.
9   Incidentally, Marx slightly confused the two, by way of reducing the logic of the former to that of the latter.
10 McGowan 2013, 1.

sure, but it is unable to conceive sacrifice as an end in itself, as a source of enjoyment.'[11]

But what if we take a further step and argue that, strictly speaking, there is no individual in psychoanalysis. The individual in psychoanalysis is always already a part of social products and relations. As such, an individual is conceivable only insofar as she/he is placed in relationships with others. It suffices to recall the title of Freud's *Group Psychology and the Analysis of the Ego* to show that he was not talking about isolated individuals. One of the dreams of Left Liberals and Socialists is a society in which individual pathologies, suffering and misery will be eradicated. For many, socialism equals an ideal society in which exploitation and oppression as well as psychosis, neuroses and other obstacles to an individual's wellbeing and happiness belong to the past.

In his *Studies on Hysteria*, Freud states 'You will be able to convince yourself that much will be gained if we succeed in transforming your hysterical misery into common unhappiness. With a mental life that has been restored to health you will be better armed against that unhappiness.' If we were to replace three words from Freud's passage about the purpose of analysis with the purposes of communism, we would get the following result: You will be able to convince yourself that much will be gained if we succeed in transforming *expropriation of labor* into common unhappiness. With a *social life* that has been restored to *justice* you will be better armed against that unhappiness.[12]

The whole point of communism should be to include discontent as an integral element of society. Discontent as such will never disappear, but we can utilize it for more creative and progressive purposes. In other words, I want to propose the following thesis: Communism transforms capitalist exploitation into common unhappiness. This is exactly the difference between Lacan and other psychoanalytic currents. The goal of Lacan's psychoanalytic practice is not 'healing wounds', but rather transforming the coordinates of one's desire. Based on this, I argue that in the Žižekian theory of the state we need to find a proper place to deliberate social discontent. Individuals always have to constitute themselves as individuals and find their place in the world. As such, they are confronted with the questions and problems of belonging, inclusion, identity, et cetera. Our suffering is thus an effect of our alienation within and by the social order. The question beckons of what sorts of institutions are necessary to give proper form to social suffering. My thesis is that the Žižekian theory of the state gives a form to discontent that makes it unnecessary to identify with an emblem of it. As a result, it makes discontent useful as such. Thus,

---

11   Ibid., 2.
12   Breuer and Freud 1955, 305.

the party can serve also as a tool for rendering suffering productive for the benefit of collective social life.[13]

The Party, the Military and the Left

For Žižek, the party is the site of politics. For politics to exist, it has not only to exist in an organized form, but in order for activities to be qualified as politics, they have to be organized in the party form. Why does Žižek hold that we need to go back to party form politics, given the catastrophic failure of socialism in the experiments of the previous century? According to him, the communist party form (in contrast to the bourgeois party) is the only political form of organization which is organized around indifference, rather than differentiation. This manifests itself both in its 'unreal' claim to aim at the abolition of capitalism – which makes it detached from the world – and in the sense that it produces an identification of 'comrades' that is not grounded on any concrete or particular aspect of the militants other than their militancy. Therefore, the communist party form is the only appropriate form of politics with which to deal with problems that are not reducible to local or 'moral' issues (the environment, refugees, gay rights, minority rights, etc.).

In this sense, communist politics differs fundamentally from the rest of the Left. This can be illustrated by the Left's response to the refugee crisis in Europe. During this crisis, the majority of the Left practiced politics of moral authority, aimed at humanizing refugees and their plight. Such politics, however, does not only emphasize difference, but also leads to gratuitous gestures, such as publicly welcoming refugees. What is, however, equally important is the 'systematization' of refugees; their access to social provisions, on-going, timely and appropriate medical care, enrolment and participation in the education process, and so on. The point is not that one should not feel sympathy with refugees, but rather that truly radical politics is based on the understanding that the causes of their suffering are the results of the deadlock in the global system of late capitalism. Consequently, it is not enough to explain the problems of refugees only as a result of imperialist or colonial struggle; they must be analyzed within the framework of global capitalism (as well as the problem of ecological catastrophes, for example – which will precipitate the next influx of massive population displacement). Merely sympathizing with refugees depoliticizes the very cause of their predicament and reduces the refugee crisis to a moral issue. The refugee crisis is not a moral crisis, but a crisis precipitated and exacerbated by the dynamics of global capitalism. The slogan 'they are also like us' ultimately serves to replace class struggle with politics of empathy.

---

13   For an analysis of the relationship between Marxism and psychoanalysis, see: Hamza 2016.

Crises like the refugee crisis furthermore illustrate the organizational limits of grassroots democratic movements. This issue, too, can be illustrated with reference to the plight of refugees. During the Kosovo war of 1998-1999, most of the refugees were settled in neighboring Albania and Macedonia, where military and humanitarian organizations where in charge of running the camps. Not only was the 'systematization' of the refugees completely carried out by these organizations, but so was their transport to these camps. This is what Žižek referred to when he drew from Jameson's thesis on global militarization,[14] and opposed sympathizing with refugees to unconditionally supporting the organizations transporting and systematizing the refugees. This point illustrates the distinction between organizing around indifference and difference (identity). The army is one of the few instances where this indifference is still maintained to some extent. The military support for refugees cuts across particular identification by focusing on the logistics and organization of life. This was, in fact, what interested Lenin and the Bolsheviks about the military form of life: the militarization of life during the civil war following the Russian Revolution was not only part of an attempt to survive in a very difficult and rough situation, but also an experiment with some level of productive indifferentiation.

I want to move a step further and propose my next thesis, which holds that we must break with the taboos of the Left, so that we can re-envision socialist struggle for and with organizational tools that today are monopolized by the ruling class. While right-wing politics currently occupies the monopoly of forms of organization that do not depend on consensus or on identity – such as the commodity form, the state form, global logistics, informational networks, et cetera – the Left seems content merely with resisting these bodies of power in the name of diversity. Against this attitude, Žižek evokes Lenin's dictum, that one must make a 'concrete analysis of a concrete situation'. The real difficulty, however, is not *analyzing* a 'concrete situation' (i.e. stating what is going on), but rather providing a 'concrete analysis'. Such an analysis is not committed to reinforcing the identity of the analyst, but gives priority to the concrete situation. It takes the side of the people over the 'correct line' of the Left, and does not wait for the effects of the subsequently proposed analysis/ intervention in order to find out where one stands. This makes it such a traumatic and risky endeavor. One cannot but argue that refugees would rather endorse Žižek's proposal of a military organization of their lives than choose to be surrounded by a thousand 'Marxists' claiming that their ties should be further loosened, the fragile organization of their lives being further dissolved in the name of an abstract notion of freedom.

---

14   Jameson 2016.

The Party and the State

The standard critique of twentieth century socialism holds that, as a state form, it was predicated on the unification of the party and the state. Yet, in the USSR everything belonged to the state, with one exception: the Communist Party, which was organizationally separate from the state. In Soviet Russia, the status of the Communist Party was that of a public organization. This fact causes Žižek to conclude that the failure of twentieth century communism was not so much due to its proximity, but rather to its deliberate distance from power. He thus states that

> [t]he failure of the Communist State-Party politics is above all and primarily the failure of anti-statist politics, of the endeavor to break out of the constraints of the State, to replace statal forms of organization with 'direct' non-representative forms of self-organization ('councils').[15]

The present neoliberal state form provides no answer to the growing contradictions of global capitalism. Given this situation, we need to re-envision the Leninist party state, and rethink its original anti-statist politics. Such politics does not entail subtraction from the state, nor simply taking over government – as the latter would mean accepting a state form and a political agenda set by the enemy. Instead, Žižek claims, 'the true task should be to make the State itself work in a non-statal mode'. And on the Left's taboo on discussing state and (taking over) state power he states 'If you do not have an idea of what you want to replace the State with, you have no right to subtract/withdraw from the State.'[16]

This, then, brings the state to the fore in contemporary communist politics. Its *sine qua non* is the rehabilitation and reappropriation of the necessity of having a strong body capable of radically transforming and reorganizing the whole of social life. Rather than fearing a new totalitarian project, revolutionary politics must focus on breaking with global capitalism and imagining new forms of social organization that are not based on private interests and profit. To bring this about, a strong political body is a necessary condition. As a new form of organization thus emerges, it takes the form of people-movement-party-leader, which is the 'civic' form of Jameson's universal military form of organization.[17]

Given this, what is to be done? One of the first issues that the contemporary Left has to come to terms with is that of representation versus participation. Domenico Losurdo has suggested that the Left should reappropriate the Hegelian idea of the ethical state, a state which is founded on shared ethical norms.[18] Hegel stated that 'the ethical order has been represented by mankind as eternal justice, as gods abso-

---

15 Žižek 2010a, 219.
16 Ibid.
17 Žižek 2013, 188.
18 Losurdo 2004.

lutely existent, in contrast with which the empty business of individuals is only a game of see-saw.'[19] According to him, this ethical order is 'an absolute authority and power infinitely more firmly established than the being of nature'.[20] For Žižek, the present ethical order is the Party. The Party, in Žižek's conceptualization, is not an electoral organization, but a cohesive body which does not only represent the people, but includes everyone in it.

The Hegelian state, if it were to be rethought today, would have to take a different form. It needs to be rethought in more radically global terms and frameworks than global capitalism itself. This difference can be thought of in terms of multinational-ism (capital) versus internationalism. During the time of the Second International, before the First World War, Marxists debated the issue of international political as-sociation. The debate was centered on the question of whether the Second Interna-tional should take the form of a uniform party or an association of parties. At that time, Lenin preferred the latter, which brought him closer to Hegel than to many Marxists. According to Lenin, the Second International should be an international state, that is, an association of emancipatory forces from each local fight against global capitalism. The former shows that, when Žižek discusses the state and Hegel, he does so under Marxist conditions, that is to say, he talks about it from the per-spective of internationalism and associationism.

The current crisis of capitalism, with all its 'excesses' (refugee crisis, et cetera) has, if nothing else, rendered visible one fact: the nation-state is *not* an answer to the antagonisms produced by the dynamics of global capitalism. Rather, the 'enclosure' of a set of commons offers ways to think about the contradictions within late capital-ism and transformative strategies towards socialism, and compels us towards a radi-cal reinterpretation of Marx's notion of proletariat. Žižek identifies four such 'enclo-sures', which he also refers to as the 'four horse riders of the apocalypse'. They are conflicts over intellectual property, which can be shared globally via the internet to the benefit of the many, but are enclosed behind paywalls to the profit of the few; the biogenetic revolution, which has the potential to open up immense possibilities for human progress, but under capitalism only profits a small minority; environmen-tal development and the steady increase in ecological disasters, both of which under-line the unsustainability of global capitalism; and the steep rise in conflicts over so-cial divisions, which again highlights the inability of capitalism to fulfill people's needs. Thinking of solutions to these problems helps us to think beyond global capi-talism.

Such an endeavor automatically leads us to conceptualize the actor who is capa-ble of bringing about such change. Employing the notion of the proletariat is crucial for remaining within the field of revolutionary politics. The proletarian position to-

---

19   Hegel 1942, 152.
20   Ibid.

day is the position which relates to the deprived substance of our subjectivity. It is the position of the 'worker whose product is taken away from him, reducing him to a subjectivity without substance'.[21]

In the struggle against global capitalism, rethinking the party form and working for a party-state form is the only way to move beyond the bourgeois state form. The party's task is to take over the state and state power, and transform it in such a way that the party does not simply remain a party – but effectively *becomes* the state. The party form enables us to face the challenges that lie ahead of us precisely because it is essentially tied to politics of indifference. It practices universality through indifferentiation, instead of embracing identity paradigms or moral universalism. Thus, the party should be our starting point. However, unlike previous incarnations, which upheld the separation between the logic of indifference and the logic of the state, our task is to create a version of the party form that, by taking over the state, can also guarantee people's right to 'live' in the same way as anyone else. This requires a strong organization that does not focus on individual particularities, but rather acknowledges the latter from the standpoint of cold logistics and other 'technicalities'. Only such an organization can produce an internationalist subjectivity that is politically potent today. One of the main challenges of twenty-first century communism is to think a radically new form of social organization, which is neither reminiscent of the previous century state-controlled economy, nor of the contemporary market economy. This cannot be done by local, libertarian communities, nor can it be done within the confines of the nation state. In this sense, the new party form has to be envisioned as an alternative to the state and market-based organization of society. Therefore, my hypothesis is that one way of thinking of the new form of social organization, both beyond the (nation) state and the market is through envisioning a universal party.

This new party form, no matter how utopian it might sound, is the only organization capable of combatting global capitalism, and it seems increasingly clear that in desperate situations, such as those we are currently facing, utopias provide the only viable solutions.

---

21 Žižek 2010, 313.

References

Breuer, Joseph and Sigmund Freud, 1955: Studies on Hysteria. In: Sigmund Freud, *The Standard Edition of the Complete Psychological Works of Sigmund Freud*. London.

Chibber, Vivek, 2013: *Postcolonial Theory and the Specter of Capital*. London.

Hamza, Agon, 2015: Going to One's Ground. Žižek's Dialectical Materialism. In: Agon Hamza and Frank Ruda (eds.) *Slavoj Žižek and Dialectical Materialism*. Basingstoke, 162-195

Hamza, Agon, 2016: Lacan contra Althusser. Dialectical Materialism versus Nominalism. In: *Continental Thought & Theory* 1:1 (2016), 137-155.

Hamza, Agon and Gabriel Tupinambá, 2016: On the Organisation of Defeats. In: *Crisis and Critique* 3:1 (2016), 427-441.

Hegel, G.W.F., 1942: *Philosophy of Right*. Oxford.

Jameson, Fredric, Slavoj Žižek (ed.), 2016: *An American Utopia. Dual Power and the Universal Army*. London.

Lenin, V.I., 1987: *The State and Revolution*. In: Ibid., *Essential Works of Lenin*. New York.

Losurdo, Domenico, 2004: *Hegel and the Freedom of the Moderns*. Durham.

McGowan, Todd, 2013: *Enjoying What We Don't Have. The Political Project of Psychoanalysis*. Nebraska.

Miller, Jacques-Alain, 2008: *Ordinary Psychosis Revisited.* http://www.nlscongress.org/wp-content/archivos/Miller-Ordinary-Psychosis-Revisted-PN26.pdf

Slavoj Žižek, 2001: *Repeating Lenin*. Zagreb.

Žižek, Slavoj, 2008: *The Sublime Object of Ideology*. London and New York.

Žižek, Slavoj, 2008a: *For They Know Not What They Do. Enjoyment as a Political Factor*. London.

Žižek, Slavoj, 2009: *First as Tragedy, Then as Farce*. London.

Žižek, Slavoj, 2010: *Living in the End Times*. London and New York.

Žižek, Slavoj, 2010a: How to Begin from the Beginning. In: Costas Douzinas and Slavoj Žižek (eds.), *The Idea of Communism*. London and New York, 209-226.

Žižek, Slavoj, 2013: Answers without Questions. In: Slavoj Žižek (ed.): *The Idea of Communism*, vol.2. London and New York.

On the authors

Geoff Boucher is Associate Professor in the Faculty of Arts and Education at Deakin University. He is the author of a number of books on politics, culture and psycho-analysis, including *Žižek and Politics* (2010) and *The Charmed Circle of Ideology* (2008). His most recent books are *Understanding Marxism* (2012) and *Adorno Reframed* (2012). He is currently working on the development of a post-Althusserian general theory of social antagonism.

Alex Del Duca is a Graduate of the University of Ottawa Masters in Political Science Program. His research previously focused on the history of Marxist thought in continental Europe and critical materialist reading methodologies – combining textual analysis with the economics and sociology of textual production. Today, he is on a permanent sabbatical and works as a bartender and general manager for a small Irish pub in Toronto whilst performing burlesque under the alias of Jack Sabbath. He has never been happier.

Agon Hamza is a PhD candidate in philosophy at the Postgraduate School ZRC SAZU in Ljubljana, Slovenia. He serves as the co-editor-in-chief of the international philosophical journal *Crisis and Critique*. His latest publications include *Repeating Žižek* (2015) and *Slavoj Žižek and Dialectical Materialism* (2016, edited with F. Ruda). Together with Žižek, he authored *From Myth to Symptom: The Case of Kosovo* (2013) and *Althusser and Pasolini: Philosophy, Marxism and Film* (2016). Currently, he is working on a book entitled *Reading Marx*, together with Slavoj Žižek and Frank Ruda (2018).

Geoff Pfeifer is Associate Teaching Professor of Philosophy at Worcester Polytechnic Institute. His research focuses on Contemporary Continental Philosophy, Social and Political Philosophy, and Global Justice. In addition to a number of chapters and journal articles, he is the author of *The New Materialism: Althusser, Badiou and Žižek* (2015) and co-editor of *Phenomenology and the Political* (2016, with S. West Gurley).

Santiago M. Roggerone holds a postdoc position at the Gino Germani Institute and the University of Buenos Aires. His research focuses on Marxism and new critical theories. He co-authored ¿Colapso de la ideología? Un recorrido clásico y contemporáneo por el concepto (2016) and among other published: 'Slavoj Žižek: "Nuestra tarea es complicar las cosas, no simplificarlas"', Metapolítica (2016) and 'Nombres de Lacan, o Slavoj Žižek y la actualidad del psicoanálisis', Diferencia(s) (2015).

Sina Talachian is a Research Master's Graduate in Philosophy (University of Amsterdam) and History (Leiden University) and a PhD candidate at Cambridge University. His research interests include contemporary European intellectual history, the philosophy of history and political and social philosophy. Recent publications include 'Transcending the Realism/Anti-Realism Divide in the Philosophy of History', Philosophy 92:2 (2017), 'Between Universalism and Particularism: The Later Marx's Conception of Reformism', Krisis: Journal for Contemporary philosophy (2016), and 'The Late Wittgenstein and Marxian Thought', Erasmus Student Journal of Philosophy (2015).

Erik Vogt is Gwendolyn Miles Smith Professor for Philosophy at Trinity College, USA. His research focuses on Twentieth Century and Contemporary Continental Philosophy, especially political theory and aesthetics. He is authored and (co-)edited twenty books, the most recent of which are: Aesthetisch-Politische Lektueren zum 'Fall Wagner' (2015); Bruchlinien Europas (2016, edited with G. Unterthurner) and Adorno and the Concept of Genocide (2016, edited with R. Crawford). He is currently completing a book on contemporary Italian and French aesthetic thought.

On the editors

Bart van der Steen is University Lecturer in Modern History at Leiden University, the Netherlands. His research focuses on interwar labour movements and New Social Movements from 1968 to the present. His published works include: A European Youth Revolt: European Perspectives on Youth Protest and Social Movements in the 1980s (2016, edited with K. Andresen), Een Banier waar geen Smet op Rust: De Geschiedenis van de Trotskistische Beweging in Nederland (2015, with R. Blom) and The City is Ours: Squatting and Autonomous Movements in Europe, 1980-2014 (2014, edited with L. van Hoogenhuijze and A. Katzeff).

Marc De Kesel is Academic Secretary and Senior Researcher at the Titus Brandsma Institute of the Radboud University Nijmegen, the Netherlands. His research focuses on philosophical inquiries on the Theory of Religion and Mysticism, Holocaust Reception, and Freudo-Lacanian Theory. Recent publications include: *Eros and Ethics: Reading Jacques Lacan's Seminar VII* (2009), *Auschwitz mon amour* (2012) and *Žižek* (2012). He is currently preparing a monograph titled: *Down with Idols: Monotheism as Religion Critique*.

Bereits erschienen in der Reihe STAATSVERSTÄNDNISSE

Vom Ethos der Freiheit zur Ordnung der Freiheit
Staatlichkeit bei Karl Jaspers
hrsg. von Prof. Dr. Karl-Heinz Breier und Dr. Alexander Gantschow, *2017, Band 99*

Der sterbliche Gott
Thomas Hobbes' Lehre von der Allmacht des Leviathan im Spiegel der Zeit
hrsg. von Dr. Thomas Lau, Prof. Dr. Volker Reinhardt und Prof. Dr. Rüdiger Voigt, *2017, Band 98*

Symbolische Gewalt
Politik, Macht und Staat bei Pierre Bourdieu
hrsg. von PD Dr. Michael Hirsch und Prof. Dr. Rüdiger Voigt, *2017, Band 97*

Das Staatsverständnis von Norbert Elias
hrsg. von Dr. Erik Jentges, *2017, Band 96*

Staaten und Ordnungen
Die politische und Staatstheorie von Eric Voegelin
hrsg. von AkadOR PD Dr. Hans-Jörg Sigwart, *2016, Band 95*

Demokratie und Öffentlichkeit
Geschichte – Wandel – Bedeutung
hrsg. von Prof. Dr. Henning Ottmann und Prof. Dr. Pavo Barišić, *2016, Band 94*

Walter Benjamin. Politisches Denken
hrsg. von Prof. Dr. Christine Blättler und Christian Voller, *2016, Band 93*

Der Staat des Neoliberalismus
hrsg. von Dr. Thomas Biebricher, *2016, Band 92*

Staat und Politik bei Ernst Bloch
hrsg. von Prof. Dr. Hans-Ernst Schiller, *2016, Band 91*

Staatsverständnis in Japan
Ideen und Wirklichkeiten des japanischen Staates in der Moderne
hrsg. von Prof. Dr. Kazuhiro Takii und Dr. Michael Wachutka, *2016, Band 90*

Die Aktualität des Republikanismus
hrsg. von Dr. Thorsten Thiel und Jun.-Prof. Dr. Christian Volk, *2016, Band 89*

Der Staat im Empire
Zur Staatstheorie des Postoperaismus
hrsg. von Dr. Thore Prien, *2016, Band 88*

Staat und Gesellschaft in der Geschichte Chinas
Theorie und Wirklichkeit
hrsg. von Apl. Prof. Dr. Gregor Paul, *2016, Band 87*

Verfassungs-Kultur
Staat, Europa und pluralistische Gesellschaft bei Peter Häberle
hrsg. von ORR Dr. Robert Chr. van Ooyen und Prof. Dr. Martin H. W. Möllers, *2016, Band 86*

weitere Bände unter: www.nomos-shop.de